THE FOURTH EXPEDITION

DJC

The Storm Seekers

Gwen Moffat

The Storm Seekers

SECKER & WARBURG
London

First published in Great Britain 1989
by Martin Secker & Warburg Limited
Michelin House, 81 Fulham Road, London SW3 6RB

British Library Cataloguing in Publication Data

Moffat, Gwen
    The storm seekers.
    1. Colorado. Rocky Mountains, Exploration, history
    I. Title
    917.88′3042

    ISBN 0-436-28431-6

Printed and bound in Great Britain by
Butler & Tanner Ltd, Frome and London

For Gwen Williams,
who taught me English
at Hove County Grammar School
from 1935 to 1941.

Contents

List of Illustrations

The author and the publishers would like to thank the following for permission to reproduce illustrations: the Bancroft Library for 1, 7 and 8; the Henry E. Huntington Library for 3, 4, 6 and 9; the Southwest Museum for 2 and the Arizona Historical Society Library for 10. The contemporary photographs are by the author with the exception of 25, which is by Malcolm McWhorter. The maps are by David Charles of The Kirkham Studios.

Acknowledgments

Mark Hamilton, my agent, had the idea for the book. At Secker & Warburg Jane Wood and Max Eilenberg fostered it initially, while Lesley Bryce nursed the book through its final stages.

Credit for the photographs goes to Malcolm McWhorter, who did all the dark-room work. Elizabeth Dixon ran the British clearing house for mail and other business; Janet McWhorter handled the American side. Charles Martin of Omaha saw to it that shopping for a Jeep was painless, and coped with all the associated logistics. I had invaluable assistance from the staff of the American Library at London University, and from librarians in Caernarfon, Wales; at Alamosa in Colorado, and at Parker, Arizona.

Finally there were all those people along the way who informed and entertained me, and provided hospitality. It is a pleasant thought that, as I followed a company, another kept pace at a distance. This book is the product of a team.

Introduction

AT TWELVE THOUSAND feet I was on my own in Colorado. The view was a full circle, probably a radius of a hundred miles, but nowhere was there a mountain which I could identify. I knew the way I had come up, I also knew that if I turned round once on this whale-back of a ridge, only the sun could guide me down.

Clouds were easing across the sky. In perfect visibility I didn't know where I was except that I was nine miles from my camp. If I couldn't find some point on which to take a bearing before the cloud dropped, I would be lost.

I refused to get the compass out, and I didn't retreat, although I could now see pale showers hanging motionless above the continental divide. Conditions were building up for the afternoon storms. I wasn't being perverse in staying high and I was alone only in the conventional sense. Somewhere close by, give or take a few miles, thirty-four men and over one hundred mules floundered and starved, and some of them died, on their way from the Missouri to the Pacific Ocean in 1848. I was trailing a company of ghosts and although there was no way I, in summer, could share their experiences, I could catch a glimpse of the hazards.

The glimpses were faint, sensed rather than seen, but I came close to both the dangers and the men that day on Mesa Mountain above Wannamaker Creek. If I was intimidated by threatening weather in June, how must they have felt crossing the Rockies in December, in a winter that was the worst in living memory?

They were looking for a route for the first transcontinental railway and their leader was John Charles Frémont, a veteran of three great exploring expeditions through the West. They embarked on this journey at a season when animals were in hibernation or had moved down to lower altitudes, when even the trappers – those hardiest of men – were holed up in Pueblo or Taos or Santa Fé.

The motivation fascinated me. Why would anyone join such an expedition? Why did some die, others survive? What made Alexis

1

Godey, the guide, go back for stragglers who would have frozen to death but for his magnificent rescue? Over a year before I trailed that spectral party to the high whale-back in Colorado I had lunched with my agent, Mark Hamilton, in London. We were discussing American pioneers and I mentioned Frémont and his five journeys through the West. I dwelt on the fourth expedition because the others were successful, because this one involved a leader's relationship with his guides; it concerned people lost in winter in high mountains – and it involved rescue.

Mark suggested that I write a synopsis for a book dealing with a personal journey as I followed the fourth expedition. The suggestion was apposite. I had been a mountain guide, I am a novelist, and I love the West. The proposed book was my province in every sense of the term. In the sixties I wrote *Two Star Red*, the story of the RAF Mountain Rescue Service. I had been closely involved with search and rescue for twenty years, and not only with the technical side. After *Two Star Red* I wrote *Hard Option*, a novel dealing with a rescuer past his prime and obsessed with his image. Then, in the seventies, I made the transition from rescue to crime and began to produce mysteries. I was intrigued by the way people's minds worked under stress and I had discovered that there were strong similarities in their reactions to elemental violence and to the violence of man. For me the art of detection lay as much in the observation of behaviour as in following the track of a lost person through the wilderness. Everything in my work – as guide, rescuer, crime writer – was integrated. I loved that. The milestones in my life have been when the pieces clicked into place, and that London luncheon was one such milestone.

Tracing the route of Frémont's fourth expedition would involve meticulous field-work, detection and empathy. It would be dangerous; although I had guided in the Alps I had never worked alone at high altitudes, but that was a stimulus, an additional incentive.

I wrote a synopsis and it sold, but it couldn't fail. The story had everything: flawed heroes, wild country, wilder weather. It had cannibalism, Apaches, mysterious disappearances – and that was their story. As for mine, I am a prudent mountaineer and my risks are carefully calculated but if one proposes to follow a previous party, the route can't be chosen, and there are going to be deadlines. The margin of safety narrows accordingly. I would have my own adventures and the prospect was daunting.

The difficulties of navigation, violent storms, the possibility of breaking a hip out there, alone; these didn't bother me so much as the likelihood of becoming so involved with the men I was following that I would catch their despair. When I write a novel I live inside my characters: vicious with delinquents, serene with pregnant women, wise with the old, lascivious with whores. Such waking nightmares and delights continue in my dreams. With my first novels I would wonder if the job were too nerve-racking to be worth the money, and I didn't like to climb because the risks on rock are too great to allow of anything but complete concentration. So what was going to happen in America at twelve thousand feet when I looked at the land and the elements through the eyes of men I knew would shortly die?

But my unruly emotions were no excuse to give up the job; like my body they would have to be subjugated. So I worked on Frémont at London University, had a brief spell of intense discipline when I wrote a new mystery, Snare, and completing it, returned to the fourth expedition.

A year went by, a year of research, of crime, of Welsh mists when I walked the mountains of Snowdonia above my cottage and dreamed of a dry wild country where you could see for a hundred miles. During a damp and dismal spring I sold my little miner's house above Llanberis and caught a plane to Omaha, Nebraska; the airline ticket and the purchase of a Jeep costing considerably more than what I got for the house. In Wales I lived frugally; travelling I have the best.

The Jeep was a Cherokee Laredo, a magnificent beast: fully automatic, all-electric (even the wing mirrors were adjusted by controls in the cab). He was adorable. Within a few days of any big journey a relationship is evolving with my vehicle. This is a defence mechanism. I may not be alone but a supreme supernatural force and a company of ghosts are not tangible. My Jeep is tactile, audible, visual: humming down the shining roads; creeping into dark corners where we will spend the night; wading through rivers or deep sand; grinding uphill, tilting down; dropping from rock to rock – he is more lovable at four miles an hour than wafting along at fifty with Beethoven's Choral blasting from all his open windows and the sunshine roof.

I made a special trip to London's West End for the music to accompany this expedition but even then I was to have my favourites, my regrets, and the sad moments which I had to rise above. I thought my love affairs with Schubert's Great Symphony and Paganini's first Violin Concerto were over. They weren't, and I never found them because I was never in a city with a music shop large enough to have a comprehensive classical department.

For me music is association: with people, places, animals, writing. The association may end with the close of a book; it can continue long after the death of a relationship. 'The Battle Hymn of the Republic' had no meaning for me after I finished *The Buckskin Girl*, an uproarious Western about the California Trail, but after thirteen years my heart still turns over at the opening bars of one movement of a Mozart piano concerto because that was my favourite piece when my last cat died.

La Traviata is associated with my lovely 1983–4 journey – deserts and Rocky Mountains and Sierras – that produced wildly evocative mysteries, *Last Chance Country* and *Grizzly Trail*, the latter researched in an attempt to come to terms with my terror of grizzlies. (Aberrant bears have been known to eat people: one kind of death that I cannot face with equanimity.) But mainly *La Traviata* is the deserts of New Mexico and Texas. One morning, with the early sun climbing above the Mexican border, I was forced to pull out on the sand and stop, so overcome with grief when Violetta died that I couldn't see to drive.

That *La Traviata* had been worn out and I bought another in London. Five months later I would exchange it with a Californian friend for a superbly taped *Rigoletto*: a magnificent rendering, a better opera, but it doesn't make me cry as *Traviata* did.

I took Beethoven's Seventh and Ninth, and then regretted I hadn't taken more of his symphonies and some piano concerti, but tapes I carried on my back as I crossed the Atlantic, they were too valuable to be sent ahead. I had *Cosi Fan Tutti* (which I found too light for the West), and presents arrived: more Mozart concerti, Bach, Vivaldi. One of my most exquisite experiences was when the Jeep crested a nine-thousand-foot ridge in the Rockies at the moment that 'Spring' from *The Four Seasons* started, and we surprised a group of pronghorn antelope which took off over the vast and sun-drenched grasslands. We rolled gently after them as they trotted to the music. I didn't get out the binoculars, I didn't stop: we drifted through space; the antelope, Vivaldi and me, fused in a unity that was more than human, and only afterwards would I realise that life could hold nothing more than that, and I would never want more.

I left Britain in a dull cool spring and flew west to the land of rioting extremes. Within a few days I was sweltering in a heat wave and the snakes were out of hibernation. A few days more and I camped on

4

snow. By June the snow was melting and on June 24th I reached Frémont's highest point.

The wind was powerful on top of Mesa Mountain, lashing the dead grass. I descended a ridge and worked myself into a position from which I could study the high tongues of forest across Wannamaker Canyon. All the documents of the fourth expedition stated that they camped in trees at twelve thousand feet, and the upper limit of those trees was at the correct altitude, but the steepness of the ground bothered me. It was at an angle where trees may just cling but a person, going down, would have to slide from trunk to trunk. No one could sleep there for one night, let alone camp for a week as they had done.

On December 17th, 1848, they came along the ridge from Difficult Creek past a high bald mountain, and they were exhausted. The temperature was twenty degrees below zero*, and cold combined with altitude resulted in bleeding from the nose and ears. Progress was arduous in the extreme. One diarist said that the snow on top was between four and twenty feet deep; below the ridge it was drifted to a hundred feet: 'reaching within a few feet of the top of the tall pines.'

The mules were giving out and the light was failing. It was late afternoon for me too but there were a few hours left before sunset. I had spent much of the day on the skyline of Wannamaker Canyon and now, on Palmer Mesa, at last I knew where I was. I should know. I had been exploring this area for ten days and if I couldn't recognise one of the mountains I had climbed, even from a new angle, I should give up because I had lost my touch.

I dropped down Palmer then, making for the place where Alexis Godey must have stopped and surveyed the ground, looking for a camp site. I thought he would have had a hard job, but long before I reached the spot I saw the tops of trees below on my left. A few more paces and a shelf appeared: a hanging terrace above the canyon, scattered with firs. Here was shelter, fuel, level ground – and here were tall tree stumps marking the depth of the snow in 1848. I had found the high camp, the one from which they retreated, the camp where the trouble started, as if they hadn't had trouble enough up to that point.

They had been warned. As far back as the plains, at Bent's Fort, the old trappers told them that they should expect a winter of

---

* Readings throughout are on the Fahrenheit scale.

5

unprecedented ferocity. Ice was forming on the Arkansas River and already there were heavy snowfalls, on the low ground as well as in the mountains. And this was only the third week in November.

It was a terrible winter but not a cruel one. Weather, like mountains, is inanimate, and there was no danger for the trappers at Pueblo and Bent's Fort, warm in the shelter of adobe houses, living well on salt beef and beans. But outside the walls the blizzards raged, blizzards into which Frémont rode with thirty-three men. And emerged with twenty-three. The golden hero of the forties, leader of three successful expeditions, had treated the Fourth like a battle with the elements, and lost.

One

His mother was a southern belle who left her middle-aged husband to run away with a dashing French *émigré*: Charles Frémon. John Charles was born to them in 1813 at Savannah, Georgia. He grew up handsome and intelligent, with the ability to charm men as well as women. He courted Jessie, the beautiful daughter of Senator Benton from Missouri. The father opposed the match so they married secretly and then charmed Benton into a forgiveness that was to deepen rapidly to wholehearted support of Frémont's projects.

I came across his name as I was researching *Hard Road West*, a book about my journey along the California Trail following early settlers from the Missouri River to the Pacific. No one interested in the great western trails can remain ignorant of Frémont's contribution to the overland migrations of the 1840s. The ordinary people – mainly farming folk – were astounding in their fortitude, travelling west in their ox-drawn wagons, following ruts across two thousand miles of wilderness – but they did not blaze the trail. Someone was there before them, crossing the passes and the dangerous rivers, marking and mapping, recording the springs of good water and the distance between them, noting the quality of grass and timber, which land was good for settlement, which Indians were hostile. The Indians came first of course, then the trappers, finally John Charles Frémont, a lieutenant in the Army Topographical Engineers, and a professional explorer.

He mapped the Oregon and California trails and vast regions between them. He crossed the Great Basin: formidable desert country that extends from the Colorado River north to Idaho: over four hundred miles where, say the Indians, no man should go in summer unless he can sleep in the shade of an arrow, and where, in winter, the land is starved with the cold.

His first journey was with a seasoned traveller, J. N. Nicollet, and they explored the upper Mississippi and Missouri basins. It is amazing to realise that as late as the mid-nineteenth century, very little was known of the country between St Louis and the Canadian border.

Frémont's first big adventure as leader was to the Rocky Mountains, specifically to South Pass, which was to become a crucial feature on the overland trails to Oregon and California. From there his party, guided by the legendary Kit Carson, continued into the Wind River Range. It was here that, idling away a summery weekend in 1979 while waiting for my truck to be fettled, I first crossed his trail.

I had slept by a lake cupped in granite under a high pass and, in the morning, looking back at my bivouac site and a string of blue tarns set in rock among black pines, I wondered at the stamina of men who came through here before the days of trails. Last night I had lost the path and been forced to fight my way through timber – half a mile of mosquito-ridden discomfort – and they had that kind of travel for much of the time, leading horses into the bargain.

Over the years my admiration increased. Snug in a double-skin tent and goosedown sleeping bag, with the thermometer a few degrees above zero, I would lie and contemplate the minds and bodies of men without tents or sleeping bags, with one blanket apiece under the stars on a night when the temperature was the wrong side of zero. But then, I would think, in winter the mountain men took refuge in cabins, or lived in snug tepees with their squaws. Not Frémont. He was out in all weathers, all temperatures. Not only did he endure with his men but he endured better than most. Small wonder that they would follow him through hell and high water. Small wonder that when I came to write a book about him, I would focus on the fourth expedition, that dire and uncomfortable adventure. Most dangers are sudden and stimulating but acute discomfort shrivels the soul.

The fourth expedition was doomed before the start. Frémont left the Missouri an embittered man, the bitterness having its genesis in the aftermath of his third expedition. In 1846 he was sent to California on what purported to be a topographical survey of a new route across the Great Basin. California belonged to Mexico at the time but many Americans had settled there. In 1846 the Americans revolted. There was war with Mexico and, on reaching California, Frémont and his men joined in with gusto, an action which had probably been intended from the outset. The revolt ended with California becoming American territory. In the resulting confusion concerning military control a quarrel flared between two senior officers: a general and an admiral. Frémont was loyal to the admiral but he lost the day, and the young junior officer was taken back to Washington by a victorious general to stand trial for insubordination and mutiny.

Senator Benton backed his son-in-law to the hilt, as did Jessie, although she was pregnant with their second child. Their first, Lilly, was now six years old. Jessie became ill during the court martial, which found against Frémont. President Polk, however, aware of the esteem in which the public held this dashing explorer, remitted the penalty and ordered him back to duty. Frémont, feeling himself dishonoured, resigned his commission.

Now his explorations would have to be privately financed. With his wife and his father-in-law behind him, Frémont concentrated on a fourth expedition: the big one, the one that would redeem his tarnished honour.

Benton canvassed friends and business men in St Louis and raised the money quite quickly. This expedition had high investment incentive. Frémont was proposing to find the route for the transcontinental railway. In 1848 trains ran no further than St Louis. From there one continued up the Missouri by boat to Kansas Landing, which is now Kansas City. From that point the traveller had to walk or ride two thousand miles to the Pacific.

Not quite all the money was raised. Some members joined the expedition agreeing to defer their pay until the end. There were rumours that gold had been found in California and people were blinded by the lure of wealth and adventure. No one questioned Frémont's decision to leave Kansas Landing in October. Crossing the Rockies in the depths of winter was to be the acid test; he said that where he could go with men and mules a train could follow. He said they had to do it in the worst possible conditions that a train would be called upon to encounter. That seems logical but in the event they went to places where no train could ever go.

In 1848 Frémont was thirty-five years old, physically in his prime. He had vast experience, and stamina which surpassed that of most men. He was also proud and obstinate, and he had come to accept, in whole or part, the public's image of him. No one can be as stubborn as a legendary hero starting out in the wrong direction. If he is backed by those closest in his affections he becomes a juggernaut.

There is a photograph of Frémont taken in 1850. The features, observed individually, are strong and well-formed: a large nose, a wide, petulant, slightly drooping mouth which does not detract from his good looks, dark eyes set deep in their sockets. It is a vital but brooding presence. The expression is watchful; this is a man disillusioned and bewildered by the realisation that men can

9

be far more dangerous than the wilderness. *That* doesn't bear malice.

At the start of the expedition the whole family sailed with him up the Missouri to Kansas Landing. The new baby was only a few months old. He had been delicate since birth and he died on the boat. If Frémont was angry and disturbed after the trial, his son's death must have exacerbated his state of mind. Three months later he would write to Jessie from New Mexico: 'I have never seen men so soon discouraged by misfortune as we were on this occasion; but, as you know, the party was not constituted like the former ones.'

If he is writing the truth he is confessing that he chose his men badly, and one notes, without surprise, the significant use of the first person plural.

At first sight the members were well-chosen. Two-thirds of them were seasoned mountain men, and mistakes in judgement would not become apparent until they were well along the trail, the notable one relating to the question of guides. Delaware Indians were engaged but only to guide them across the plains. Frémont didn't know where he might find a guide for the traverse of the Rockies. Alexis Godey was with him from the start but he was employed as a hunter; they would cross two ranges before he began to take the lead.

Many of the men of the Fourth had been with Frémont on previous expeditions. Charles Preuss was one of these veterans: he was the map-maker, a solid German who hated the wilderness but who had climbed, grumbling, to the top of what is now Woodrow Wilson Peak (13,570 feet) on the first expedition to the Wind Rivers, and who had mapped the Oregon Trail on the Second.

The doctor on the Fourth was Benjamin Kern, and with him came his two brothers, Edward and Richard. Edward was a topographer and naturalist, and both he and Richard were accomplished artists, their letters and journals enlivened by sketches of geological features, people, flora and fauna. Only Edward had been with Frémont before. He was an epileptic but for all that, a man of stamina. The Kerns and Preuss kept journals which provided me with basic source material, as did the Kerns' letters home and those by Frémont himself, written during and after the expedition.

Other accounts were written by Thomas S. Martin, a frontiersman from Tennessee and a veteran of the third expedition, and Micajah McGehee, a well-educated but novice traveller, the son of a judge, who came along for the adventure. And there was Thomas E. Breck-

10

enridge who was only twenty-three in 1848 but already a seasoned explorer (he had been on the third expedition), who was to write his reminiscences of the Fourth for *The Cosmopolitan* in 1896. Charles Taplin, another veteran, gave a short but colourful interview to *The Saint Louis Weekly Reveille* in 1849.

The other members did not write accounts, or if they did, they were not published. Frémont made no official report (only some tantalising notes for memoirs which were never written), and Alexis Godey was illiterate, as no doubt were a number of the mountain men among the members.

There were some surprising inclusions in the party. Godey brought his fourteen-year-old nephew, Theodore McNabb, and Frémont was accompanied by his black cook, Jackson Saunders. A British officer in Prince Albert's 11th Hussars, Captain Andrew Cathcart, came, like young McGehee, for the adventure, and there were three California Indians – Manuel, Joaquin and Gregorio – who must have come east at some time, probably with Frémont, and were now going home.

Elijah T. Andrews had been in the Navy for seven years. He was tubercular and may have joined the expedition for his health, although it's unlikely that Frémont knew of his condition, or did he know and take the risk? If so, Andrews' inclusion is some justification for that remark about the party's not being up to scratch. Andrews was accompanied by his father, Amos, as far as the mountains but the older man dropped out at Pueblo.

There were specialists on the Fourth: Frederick Creutzfeldt was a botanist; Henry Rohrer a millwright; Joseph Stepperfeldt a gunsmith. There would have been no call for a millwright on the journey, and not much for a botanist in wintertime; only Stepperfeldt the gunsmith's expertise might have come in useful. It is likely that these men, lured to California by rumours of the great gold strike, were employed as muleteers and dogsbodies.

A man who was to play a major role in their retreat from the mountains was Lorenzo D. Vincenthaler, who had been with Frémont in California and fought the Mexicans, as had all the members of that party which started out as a surveying expedition and ended fighting a war.

The remaining members of the Fourth were made up of mountain men, French voyageurs, and greenhorns; eventually they would be thirty-four in number, counting the leader, and they took about 130 mules.

The diarists and those writing some time after the event occasionally disagreed on statistics: mileages were a case in point, and compass bearings. These small discrepancies were immaterial so far as I was concerned. I didn't expect to follow their trail meticulously, any more than I had trodden in the ruts of the California Trail. Statistics, even places, matter less than people's reactions to them, and these were recorded by the Kerns – volatile, poignant or resentful – and by the stern and succinct Preuss, who hated the weather and the high altitudes, who deplored the food and had no time for squalor and bad manners.

We converged on Kansas City, Frémont coming up the Missouri from St Louis, myself descending the river from Omaha. It was May 9th when I started south, the Jeep stocked with food and water, with books, maps, clothes, and enough sundry equipment to see me through five months and over thirteen thousand miles of a zig-zag journey. (Frémont took about six and a half months to cover two thousand miles.)

There was rain in Omaha, and when the rain stopped the heat came suddenly. It was hot that first Saturday afternoon when we drifted south through Nebraska to a campground on the Missouri called Indian Cave. This was a happy choice for the first night of a western journey: three thousand acres of pristine timber, all hardwoods, cloaking sandy bluffs above the big brown river. On the Sunday I walked the rim of the bluffs and the cover was so dense that only in a few places could I see the water. On the east bank the land was flat as a pancake and intensively farmed. On my side there were squirrels, lizards, and some large raptors, probably buzzards. I was attacked by a large dog.

In the 1840s travellers might have had to contend with grizzly bears, wounded buffalo, hostile Indians, I had to cope with loose dogs. I was to run into this problem all the way across the States with Rotweilers, Dobermans, mongrels. In the West, when you approach an isolated house, you would be foolish to leave your vehicle before an occupant appears. That same year a pensioner was savaged and killed by a couple of bull terriers. On the other hand I was to meet a man in Arizona who, attacked as he approached a house, shot and killed the dog. 'It was him or me,' he said. He was right; a large dog trained by a vicious man is afraid of nothing.

I fended off my attacker with my rucksack until the owner appeared and leashed the animal. We exchanged some hard words and I went on my way furious that this should happen in such a delightful ambience – and on my first day. But, rationalising, I concluded that nasty dogs were part of the job – and the job was to follow Frémont regardless … I crossed the Kansas River at six o'clock that evening and turned west, absorbed again in the land.

Some years before, I had travelled across the western half of Kansas and thought no state could be flatter than this. The world then was a floor of corn under a shining blue vault. It was autumn and there were big coloured butterflies flapping across the road. I had a truck equipped with my first stereo, and a rack of new tapes. The Welsh mists were five thousand miles away and ahead were the southwest deserts and the red rock country. Kansas could be accepted, if not loved.

Five years later I travelled through a different Kansas; surprising and, of its kind, enchanting. This was rolling country, superbly timbered, watered by creeks flowing into another big brown river that was full of whirlpools. A French fur trader, Etienne Veniard de Bourgmont, came through here in 1724 and found it: 'the most beautiful land in the world'.

Frémont told Senator Benton in a letter that here was timber, game and excellent grass. He was following the Kansas River in preference to the Santa Fe Trail – which took a more southerly course – because this river valley afforded better shelter and grazing than the great caravan route. The northerly line, he wrote, would be good for settlement for four hundred miles.

He was right. The land is now farmed and, later, ranched, and always fenced, all privately owned. There are no walks through the lovely woods, and the only way to see something of the country other than as a passing blur from the interstate is to leave it and take to the dirt roads.

On my second morning, always searching – or appearing to search – for the route, ('Did Frémont come by here?') I turned into a drive and stopped at a modest house. A mongrel approached the Jeep, grinning and wagging her tail. Talking firmly to her, I climbed down.

I was plied with coffee and cookies by a retired baker and his wife. They hadn't heard of Frémont ('This is like a history lesson') but they showed me an ancient wagon trail through the woods. They had often wondered who made that trace but had never been able to discover who might have crossed the land before they bought it.

We talked about the old trails. Frémont wasn't making a new route;

13

he had himself returned by way of the Kansas River from his second expedition, the one when he mapped the Oregon Trail. At least one trapper, Jedediah Smith, came this way in 1825, followed two years later by the trader, William Sublette. It would be expected that pack trains and solitary travellers would look for an alternative route to avoid the overgrazed and shelterless Santa Fe Trail; the reason why the great wagons of the trade route didn't follow was that they couldn't. The terrain was too rough.

My hosts were fascinated by all this and I wondered whether I should suggest the local library as a further source of information, but it's one thing to listen to the spoken word, another to concentrate on pages of print. I had no illusions. I knew that curiosity could flare and die with my passing. I would become a part of history myself: 'She told us about Jedediah Smith – him that was scalped on the Cimarron; he came by in '25, and a man called Frémont in '48.' Centuries are nothing to people with an oral tradition.

The couple took me round their garden: three acres of orchard, vegetables and soft fruit, most of which they gave away. They were miserable to find that nothing was ripe enough to give to me and asked if there was anything, anything at all, that they might supply. I admitted that at the head of the list of needed items when I started out there was always the shovel. The baker disappeared into his barn, emerged with a shovel, shortened the handle to my specification, and taped the end. I continued happily through the golden morning.

It was hot, even for Kansas in May. I can never remember what familiar country looks like in a different season from that of the moment so it was impossible to visualise Kansas under snow. Meadowlarks, brilliant in yellow waistcoats, sang on fence posts; killdeer, the common but pretty plover of the prairies, had families of chicks. As I approached the 100th meridian – the line of longitude separating east from west – a small yucca appeared with spires of waxy cream bells.

We had left civilisation. People waved as they passed me on the dusty roads; at night strange owls called and fireflies flickered about the Jeep. Alas, there were ants, but they were diurnal. Providing I didn't put my sleeping bag on the ground until after dark, I could sleep without company. But they were early risers, and if I was to escape their invasion – often painful because many of them bit – I must be out of the bag as soon as the sky began to brighten.

Temperatures fluctuated wildly. Before we left the plains the nights

14

were mild, dropping to a delicious 60° just before dawn, but that was fleeting. After sunrise the heat increased rapidly and, as yet unacclimatised, I found it too hot to walk after ten o'clock. This was no temperate land. I encountered a box turtle in dry undergrowth beside the trail, and the sight of a big bull snake working its way gingerly across hot dust reminded me that I was back in rattlesnake country. All undergrowth was suspect.

At Junction City the Republican River comes down from the north, and above the confluence the Kansas changes its name to the Smoky Hill. Edward Kern, the artist, noted that the country changed: 'Today the road is much broken by deep ravines ... the edges of the bluffs are bordered by a band of lime stone giving the appearance of huge remains of fortifications.'

I must be in the wrong place. I quartered a high upland called the Flint Hills but nowhere could I find anything resembling fortifications. It was rocky certainly, the rock protruding in pale crumbling layers of yellow and beige. Chunks lay in the green spring grass; it would be a bad place for riding.

I came down from the uplands, back to the fertile flood plain, and I stopped at a crossing of the Smoky Hill. Modern roads often follow old trails and Frémont could have crossed at this point. A rancher came along with his grandson in a pick-up. They both addressed me as 'ma'am'. Like the baker, the rancher hadn't heard of Frémont but, chewing thoughtfully, contemplating the river, he observed that the water was high. At other times, in places, it would be only three feet deep; this could well have been a ford in the nineteenth century. He had stopped to see if I were fishing – and because the Jeep had Nebraska plates. Few people remarked on my accent, only that I appeared to come from another state. This emphasised the magnitude of the country; it was thought that I was merely another kind of American. Thus I had a sense of belonging on this side of the Atlantic; it was only a tenuous thread of security but preferable to living in a vacuum: the stranger in a strange land.

I had left the farms behind and reached the ranching country. The road cut across a big bend of the Smoky Hill where travellers of the nineteenth century started to see buffalo. Here Frémont's men killed and feasted, and probably over-ate. Godey, later the guide, now a hunter, was sick, but that could have been the result of drinking bad water. In the twentieth century it was heat and toothache that troubled me as I searched the country for a campground, finally tracing one to

15

a small town and discovering it had been closed by the sheriff because of vandalism.

I took a room at a motel: airless, hot and noisy, but with filtered water and a comfortable bed. The toothache subsided and I greeted the sights of the morning with a less jaundiced eye. Fences, for instance.

Having spent most of my life in rocky regions I was accustomed to what might be termed indigenous fencing: broad palings of Welsh slate, granite in Devonshire; great rough slabs gilded with lichen and clumped with sea pink on top of the Irish Cliffs of Moher. That morning, above the Smoky Hill, I came on rock fence posts supporting wire. The earliest settlers had to be self-sufficient but surely the skill needed to quarry and cut those posts from bedrock was of a different order from, say, building a cabin of logs or chunks of stone?

There was a graveyard in scrubby grass, the graves dating back a hundred years, the names on the headstones still legible. The melting pot that is the States was epitomised by this half-acre: Liebenthal, Schoencher, Pfeifer; McCracken, Antonino, Yocemento.

I stopped for lunch. I was among scattered oil wells, not big skeletal derricks but the little nodding donkeys, except that many of these were immobile. A pick-up approached and the driver got down to pass the time of day and to learn my business. He was a big brawny man, carrying too much weight. A supervisor of forty-three wells, the low price of oil was forcing him to shut them down. This was a depresssed area, he told me; with five children to support, he worked as a disc jockey in the evenings. His wife was a teacher on $9,000 a year – which would have been about £5,500 at the current rate of exchange. The cost of food was high; everything was bad, he said cheerfully, except the fishing. I remembered North Wales, the bottom falling out of slate in the twenties, the fourth generation growing up on Welfare in the eighties, and I thought he had a lot to be cheerful about.

That afternoon an older man, working on odd jobs in town, directed me to a remote campground, saying he knew the place well: 'I have a ranch out there.' At the time I accepted this as an exaggeration but I soon learned that small ranchers, perhaps over-extended and many of them in debt to the banks, unable to get a good price for their beef, were going bankrupt and taking odd jobs in town. Nevertheless no one had the air of apathy that often accompanies poverty. I had the feeling that here depression was temporary and that people were marking time until things took a turn for the better.

16

I misinterpreted the rancher's directions and, lost on the dirt roads, drove up to an isolated trailer, to stay in my seat, eyeing the dogs which waited silently, daring me to open the door. A thin elderly woman with a swollen belly appeared, polite but unsmiling and suspicious. She put me on the right track and closed her door before I had turned the Jeep, retreating behind her closed windows, shutting out the light and the lovely air; retreating – to what?

I passed a feed-lot: a huge corral crammed with cattle on trampled earth; the place stinking of high-protein excrement, bare of shade, and the temperature over 100° in the sun. If I lived close to that lot I would spend my days, perhaps my life, in a drunken stupor.

The grumbling toothache had declared itself over the last few hours in an abscess. This suddenly flared and broke. Drained of energy as well as pus, but free of pain, I sat in the passenger seat that evening and prayed for a storm. The air was hot, heavy and electric; the cottonwoods had a hard burnished look against a smoky sky. I realised that cottonwood leaves, rustled by chance gusts of air, sound like rain. There was no storm.

The evening drew me away from the camp to walk among trees in the gloaming. Deer and rabbits were coming out to feed. They regarded me with astonishment and then faded like shadows into the gloom of spring foliage. Few people would walk here at any time of day. The paths were marked only by cloven hoofs and the dog-like tracks of coyotes.

Until I reached the mountains I camped mostly in state parks. These were usually sited close to a river and often by a dam, the purpose being to provide recreational activities as well as a campground. In May most of the campers were fishermen: respectable elderly men from small camping vans who sat hunched at the water's edge (the wives some distance away, knitting, or reading Mills and Boon) or gathered in convivial parties at picnic tables.

This was an alien world to me who, less than a week from the start of an adventure and despite the reservoirs, the ubiquitous fences, the absence of mountains, felt a kinship with ghosts on a lost trail, a kinship that I could never feel with these stolid and static couples.

The trail. Even Frémont could lose it. He had the Delaware guides for the first eleven days (during which they covered 250 miles) but the Delawares turned back on the Smoky Hill and for a while the course of the expedition was erratic. They had left the river and they returned to it too soon, their progress probably obstructed by bluffs.

17

The clay banks of the river were high and dangerous. Captain Cathcart was chasing buffalo when the herd leapt down a twenty-foot bank into the river. Richard Kern said that 'the Capt. in attempting to follow them nearly drowned his mule; he lost his revolver and powder flask and broke his ram rod, and came into Camp in his stocking feet. He cut a very sorry figure, looking like Don Quixote in extreme trouble.'

On November 3rd Frémont left the Smoky Hill and struck south, making for the Santa Fe Trail. The weather was uncomfortably cold and windy, and they had snow for the first time. They took four days to cover the eighty-five miles to the major trail.

The day I left the Smoky Hill rain was coming up from the south. I was on a dirt road and within the hour I was slithering in the slime which they call gumbo. The country was the same as when the expedition passed: destitute of timber. Like them I crossed Walnut Creek and the Pawnee Fork, and if I took only a day to cover the distance which took them four days (riding hunched against the cold), in late afternoon and close to Dodge City I walked along the ruts of the Santa Fe Trail.

A few acres have been set aside to preserve the ruts: pale lines in the flowery prairie where buffalo grass grows on soil that has never been broken, grass that once covered the plains from the Missouri to the Rockies, supporting vast herds of which only a handful of beasts remain. I have seen them: plump and placid on the Bison Range in Montana and along the Snake River in Wyoming. I have sat in my car and watched them cross the road in the sunset, and I know that, without the shadow of a doubt, the ground did shake when they stampeded.

At Dodge City we were on the Arkansas River. Fort Dodge is now a Soldiers' Home and had it not been, it was not my period (there was no Fort Dodge in Frémont's time). I pushed on to spend the night in the KOA in Garden City.

'Kampgrounds of America' are scattered across the continent. They are not cheap; for the same price ($12 for a tent site) one could get Bed and Breakfast in Britain, but they are cheaper than motels, with the salient advantage that they have laundries – coin-operated but preferable to washing clothes in a motel basin and drying them on coat hangers.

At Garden City the campground was patrolled by large neurotic cats seemingly dependent on hand-outs. One was a loud-mouthed dark tabby tom who hung around exchanging alley gossip with me while the others watched from the darkness. I deposited my trash and put the lid firmly on a bin that was full of beer cans. Perhaps the tabby was drunk.

On the way to Garden City, above a small town and picked out in bright chunks of lime or chalk on a hillside was the statement: CHRIST DIED FOR ME. Such arrogance.

Graffiti abound in the States. Sandstone crops out beside the road and on every facet local youth proclaims its devotion in spray paint. Aspens on woodland trails are gouged by pierced hearts. Ruins are daubed, even the asphalt of the road is utilised as a vehicle for spite or affection. Towns announce their existence monstrously with their initial letter on the nearest – and often the loveliest – eminence. If you live in a place where visibility is infinite and even big mountains disappear only where they sink below the curve of the earth, then the gesture of advertising your tiny community may be a defence mechanism: 'This is my town, where I live, therefore I exist. No doubt about it.' Next year the Scouts will go up and whitewash the letter anew, proving my point, proving *me*.

The majority of Americans have lost their sense of adventure. Few people explore the marvellous back country, and those who do tend to cluster. Parties led by a guide are popular, and the solitary walker is regarded as eccentric, and mad if he's old and lives rough. The ordinary American has forgotten that the first white people in the wilderness were solitary, at the most travelling in small parties, that they had no choice (and many no wish) but to live rougher than any of today's travellers – and they came in winter.

'As my mule had just been shod,' wrote Richard Kern, 'the snow and dirt balled in her feet rendering my position very unpleasant, as sometimes one leg would be 3 or 4 inches lower than the others. Her movements were all kind that can be imagined. I had the pleasure of being thrown over her head and landed in safety on the ground.'

On November 8th they forded the Arkansas amid rushing ice and they were forced to abandon some mules. 'Two were left behind,' they say, or: 'The mules were giving out'. Nothing more. With all the buffalo they were chasing they might have spared a bullet for a mule.

Indians were encountered on the Arkansas and for a while the expedition travelled unwillingly in their company. The natives, Kiowas, Comanches, Arapaho, showed no hostility but they were

19

thieves and God knew what they would do to a weak party. 'There were several Spanish boys and girls among them they had stolen from Monterey 3 years ago – day clear and pleasant. Thermometer 50°.' Without drawing breath Richard Kern disposes of kidnappings and – probably – murder as coldly as Captain Cathcart refers to sex in a letter to a friend on November 17th. He had not yet had a squaw because they were lousy and suffered from 'severe poxes'.

Lice did not deter Frémont from acquiring a tepee on the Arkansas. It would go to 12,000 feet in the San Juan Mountains, the mules dragging its twenty-foot poles. The tepee's great advantage was that the occupants could have a fire inside. At times it was shared with Preuss, the Kern brothers and Cathcart. This snippet of information suggests that not everyone suffered the same privations all the time. But whatever the improvement in the nightly quarters of some, they all experienced the same conditions by day. If they fell in the river at the crossings (and mules fell backwards – probably failing to get a grip on the slimy banks) immersion in the icy water meant that their clothing froze stiff immediately. Frémont's feet were frostbitten on the Arkansas.

Three weeks after they started, one week after I left Omaha, we crossed the line into Colorado. For me the new state was signposted, for them there was no difference; no natural feature marks the boundary between the plains-state and that which contains more mountains than any outside Alaska. As yet not even a hill was visible; but just over the state-line, from a point where a post marked an elevation of 3,600 feet, a wisp of cloud some sixty miles distant on the western horizon marked the presence of the Rocky Mountains.

Two

As THE LAND rose the temperatures dropped. Nights were ten degrees cooler on the Arkansas than they had been on the Smoky Hill. Soon we would be on mountain tracks and I remembered with alarm the Jeep's uncontrolled and uncontrollable slithering on wet dirt roads. I stopped at a garage and asked the foreman to inspect the four-wheel-drive transmission. He could find nothing wrong and sent me down to the river bank to put the Jeep through his paces in deep sand.

He loved it. He was even better in sand than the little Jeep in which I had explored the deserts three years ago. I would put this big Cherokee at a bank: stall, reverse, and then persevere until we had discovered how it should be done. I didn't think I would encounter deeper sand than this. In the event I did but that hour beside the Arkansas gave me the basic knowledge of my vehicle that would stand me in good stead in the months to come.

I hadn't been at fault on the gumbo. Nothing can cope with gumbo short of a tank. I recalled a Montana rancher telling me that if people were stranded by rain on the prairie, they must abandon their vehicle and walk, or stay there until the mud dried. It is the peculiar property of this fine silt-dust of the West, that when it is wet it has as much traction as oil.

Beside me as I ploughed the sand the Arkansas ran high and brown: a big, fast, frightening river in full spate, despite water being drawn off for irrigation. Over its swirling surface clouds of martins swarmed like gnats, busily catching flies to feed their young in the rows of nests plastered to girders under every bridge.

Colorado was suddenly exciting. Kansas had been dull in its western half and very hot; I had drifted across it somnolently in an ambience of sunshine and music. In Colorado there was a busyness in the air and on the roads: an excitement that was subjective. As the clouds in the southwest grew and I knew that late today or tomorrow morning I would see the first snow, people approached me, evidently responding to my obvious gaiety.

21

Mexicans moving house, their pick-ups piled with chattels, stopped in a lay-by and an ancient man with a terrible smoker's cough came over to tell me he'd been lost on the road and had to buy a map at a gas station. He said it with the same kind of incredulity that he might have employed had he been forced to buy a new tyre. It was a milestone: the first map he'd bought in his life.

I was approaching Bent's Fort when I was stopped at road works. The flagman was a woman in her fifties: 'Women are better at the job. A while back we had to stop people for three hours on Wolf Creek and they called us everything except white girls. A man couldn't take it.'

A wagon eased up, its load of tar steaming; probably fifty tons there, including the wagon. The small driver got down and said she must go through before the tar cooled. The ganger was a woman too. Did they run the state? Hardly, when motorists could call them anything but white girls. They just did the jobs that the men couldn't cope with.

Bent's Fort was charming, like something out of *Beau Geste* except for the sage and the cottonwoods and the blackbirds shrilling in the reeds. A man who seemed moderately intelligent asked me what animal was making the noise, and what was the big bird with the sulphur-yellow waistcoat and the black V on its breast? He had just seen his first humming bird. He had reached middle-age without knowing a meadowlark or noticing humming birds. I wondered what his line was. Even a coal miner must spend part of his time above ground.

Shadows were lengthening as I approached the fort and I told the man at the gate that I would return in the morning. I retreated to stare at the great adobe walls and remember all the people before me who had seen it in the evening light. An elderly tabby queen – a dowager cat – weaved her way about my feet and sang throatily. Back at the roadworks I became aware of a bluff to the south, a few hundred feet high. 'Went up the bluff,' wrote Doctor Kern, 'to look at the mountains fine view of Spanish peaks covered all over with snow. ...' I wouldn't see them until the following afternoon.

The Bents, Charles and William, were brothers who went into business with another trader, Ceran St Vrain, and built Bent's Fort as a trading post in the 1830s. The Indians brought in buffalo hides, the trappers furs; Mexican and Navajo merchandise came up on wagon trains from the south by way of the Santa Fe Trail, and continued to St Louis passing caravans of manufactured goods coming west.

In the fifteen years of its existence the fort must have been an astonishing place. Sixty people were employed there: blacksmiths, wheelwrights, carpenters, gardeners, herdsmen. William Bent married Owl Woman, a Cheyenne, and after forming a bond with one nation succeeded in drawing together rival tribes at least so far as trade was concerned, at least within the confines of the fort.

The boom was short-lived. Trade slumped as the beaver were trapped out and fashion forsook beaver hats. There were hostilities with Mexico and the Indians went to war. Goldminers, the army and emigrants polluted the streams and overgrazed the land. The buffalo disappeared. Charles Bent was murdered in Taos, St Vrain left for New Mexico; in 1849 the cholera reached Bent's Fort and William Bent took his family and moved out. Behind him the fort went up in flames.

The building has been lovingly restored, concrete foundations hidden under the adobe. The effect is a little too good: the adobe too smooth and rounded, the cottonwood beams too raw, but these will mellow with time and the dry air. The design is a hollow square with rooms backing on the massive walls. There couldn't have been much room for sixty employees, not to speak of visiting trappers and other guests. When the fourth expedition arrived, Frémont and his men slept in their camp on the other side of the river.

There was ominous news for them at the fort; trappers and Indians warning of a severe winter ahead. 'Still,' Frémont wrote to Benton, 'I am in nowise discouraged by the prospect and believe that we shall succeed in forcing our way across. ... The party is in good spirits and good health ... breakfast before daylight with the thermometer ranging from 12° to 18°, is a somewhat startling change from the pleasant breakfast-table in your stove-warmed house. I think that I shall never cross the continent again, except at Panama. I do not feel the pleasure that I used to have in those labors, as they remain inseparably connected with painful circumstances. ... It needs strong incitements to undergo the hardships and self-denial of this kind of life. ...'

It is a curious letter for the leader of an expedition to write shortly before the hard part starts. One wonders what Senator Benton made of it. Did he interpret those disillusioned statements as a passing yen for the fleshpots and his own warm house? Every explorer craves a soft dry bed, gourmet meals, chairs, and when he has them he is heartsick for the camp fire and a blanket under the stars. Benton wasn't a stupid man and he must have known from the start that his son-in-law led two lives; it is doubtful that he realised that this time was different.

'11 degrees,' wrote Dr Kern the day they left Bent's Fort, 'at 8 o clock over cast and very cold deep snow 1st 3rd of the way ... litt very large camp fires tonight & last night mules getting still weaker – '

Next day cold blasts of air blew from the west alternating with warm currents. They reached Pueblo: an adobe fort built by the mountain men of which Richard Kern wrote: 'A miserable looking place, the inside resembling a menagerie – a compound of Spaniards, Horses mules dogs chickens and bad stench.'

Pueblo is now a sprawling bustling city that promises a refuge after a long hot day on the road, but for me the promise was not fulfilled. I dined in a restaurant where the food was so fast that the next course was brought to table when you were halfway through the last. Nor was my motel of the first order. I called my American clearing house and heard, to my astonishment, the motel operator asking my friends to accept the charge. Then I woke in the night and went to the bathroom to find the door jammed. I was forced to utilise an ice bucket. At seven the manager came and *kicked* the bathroom door open.

The Jeep was tuned for the mountains, I bought a sheaf of maps, *The Hiker's Guide to Colorado*, and the only mango chutney in Pueblo: a tiny jar which left little change from four dollars.

Leaving town I made a turn in error and found myself in a one-way road with four lines of traffic, just released by a light, hurtling towards me. In the middle was a gap just wide enough for a Jeep. I steered straight for it, swung round behind two lines of traffic, found the angle too acute and had to leap a bank, circling a vacant lot to creep back when the surge of cars had vanished in the distance.

We all had problems with transportation.'The mule got off before I was seated and threw me backwards,' wrote Dr Kern. Mules fell down icy or slimy slopes, they tripped, slipped or were just plain ornery; people fell so often it was a wonder that no one was seriously hurt. The doctor mentions one such incident, right at the beginning: 'Bathed in the creek was called out while enjoying it to dress Moran's lip cut in two by a mule.' Moran was one of the French voyageurs. Apart from this, falls were more likely occasions for amusement as when Captain Cathcart nearly drowned with his mule.

24

But by the time they reached Pueblo the mules were running out of energy and now in the southwest loomed the first range – when they could see it through the storm clouds. Shortly the men would be walking and the mules carrying food, until they themselves became food – but first they had to find a guide.

No expedition travelled through the wilderness without guides. These were drawn from the ranks of the mountain men: trappers who had spent years roaming the West in search of beaver. Next in importance to the guides came the hunters. A pack train, with its long string of animals, frightened game, and the hunters would have to range far ahead and out to the sides searching for meat to feed the expedition. They too had to know the country, must possess a superb sense of direction.

Alexis Godey had been engaged as a hunter; he was an experienced and competent man who had been with Frémont on his second and third expeditions, to Oregon and California. In view of his later achievements it's unclear why he shouldn't have been considered as a guide at this point; perhaps, being a modest man, he never put himself forward, thinking that since he didn't know the immediate country, he wasn't qualified to lead the party through it. Whatever he thought, or Frémont, when the Delawares left them on the Smoky Hill, the expedition had a hard time for a while, and all the journals note that when they arrived at Pueblo they were without a guide.

At Pueblo the retired trappers who lived there confirmed the opinion of men at Bent's Fort, warning Frémont that it was madness to attempt to cross the Rockies in a winter that was already showing its claws: in ice on the river, in unusually heavy snowfalls in the mountains. Among the trappers, sixty-one years old and suffering from a bullet wound, was Old Bill Williams. He was reputed to know every mile of the country where Frémont proposed to go.

Old Bill was a legend long before he died. He had been an itinerant preacher in his youth but he had given up Christianity when he married a squaw and went to live with her tribe. He had been a trapper, hunter, trader, guide and horse thief; stealing horses in California to drive them across the Rockies and sell at Bent's Fort where he would gamble, and drink away his profits. Once he stole 1,500 animals but lost them all to thirst in the desert, and to the Indians. He returned to Taos on foot without a horse to his name.

His squaw died in 1825 and he became a solitary man. There is a haunting image evoked by another mountain man who met him on the bank of a river in Arizona. When they parted, Old Bill 'turned north and was swallowed up by the mountains'.

He was a tall, gaunt man with a face scarred by smallpox. He had a long beard, and hair down to his shoulders. He was dirty but vain, signing his name: Bill Williams, Master Trapper. On occasions he wore turquoise earrings.

He rode with short stirrups, hunched over the saddle. He walked stooped and with a kind of stagger. Despite the alertness that he must have possessed in order to survive in the wilderness, he seems to have been uncoordinated, unable to hold his gun steady, and firing at the moment that the line of the barrel happened to be on the target. Amazingly, he was an excellent marksman.

Shortly before Frémont reached Pueblo Old Bill had been employed by an army raiding party to guide them to a village occupied by Utes and Apaches. In the skirmish that resulted thirty-six Indians were killed and Old Bill's arm was shattered by a bullet. It was this wound that he was suffering from when Frémont asked him to join the fourth expedition as a guide.

This was a last resort. Thomas (Broken Hand) Fitzpatrick had guided Frémont in the past, but he was now in the Indian Service near Bent's Fort and (no doubt with an eye on the weather signs) he had declined to go this time, pleading prior commitments. Kit Carson, another of Frémont's former guides, remained in Taos, reputedly ill. Finally Old Bill was persuaded to join them although, says Micajah McGehee, 'it was not without some hesitation that he agreed to go, for most of the old trappers at the pueblo declared that it was impossible to cross the mountains. ... However, Old Bill concluded to go, for he thought we could manage to get through, though not without considerable suffering.'

They left Pueblo on November 22nd. The signs were bad. There had been rain in the night, there was snow after dawn. The cloud was down and when it lifted it was to reveal storms raging on the mountains.

They were to have one last indulgence. On the banks of the creek called Hardscrabble, outside the mouth of the first canyon, on a little level place among junipers and prickly pear, they came to a group of cabins that the trappers used in summer time. There they had chicken and baked pumpkin for supper. Next day they spent shucking corn which was to provide fodder for the mules in the weeks ahead when all the grass would be covered by snow. As for the men: 'We have a

26

small store of provisions for hard times,' Frémont had written to his father-in-law from Bent's Fort.

They were at Hardscrabble on November 24th and the general opinion was that in a few weeks' time the difficulties would be behind them. Preuss said that Old Bill told them: 'to our joy, that it was naturally advisable to cross the mountains before Christmas. But, he said, it was several days until then, and before that time snow was out of the question. The very second day we made our way through a difficult narrow pass, and we had to contend with a lot of snow....'

After Hardscrabble, the mules now being used as pack animals, the men had to start walking.

On May 27th, 1987, I began my search for Hardscrabble. I was looking for a site only, but I had one fixed point: Hardscrabble Creek, which Frémont followed upstream into the Wet Mountains.

Finding the site of the settlement was one of those exercises in detection which lend an extra dimension to research. My informants were often intriguing in their own right even when they could give me no help concerning the route of the fourth expedition. And if people were dull or suspicious or just not at home when I drove into their farmyards and could get no reply, I was becoming saturated in an environment which, as an ordinary traveller speeding along the highways, I would never have known.

The search for Hardscrabble started with a bright hot walk along the banks of an irrigation channel: a false cast, but a pleasant stroll. From the morning's heat I fled to the cool of the local library. Libraries are my prime source of information in strange towns. Their staff are always delighted to meet authors; they are unflagging in energy and unsparing of their time, all of which they see as a contribution to the Work in Progress.

The library at Florence, Colorado, was a cool cave in a baking street, empty except for the elderly librarians and a small boy with excellent manners who was reading *Tracy and Hepburn* because he liked their movies. We discussed *Golden Pond* and wondered if it might have been improved with Tracy in Fonda's role. We were solemnly agreed that no one could improve on Hepburn.

From the library, always hunting Hardscrabble, I was passed to the local historian whom I found in a house beside the cemetery, with a view of the Wet Mountains on one side, Pike's Peak on the other. My host's main interest was in restoring old cars, but he was going blind and had been forced to sell his treasures. He showed me his last Model T Ford which he couldn't see properly, could only run his hands over its familiar contours. Nor could he help with Frémont's route, but he sent me to the postmistress in Wetmore, a hamlet at the mouth of Hardscrabble's canyon.

It was late now so I drove through Wetmore into the canyon and, six miles upstream, turned up a track to pitch the tent by a brook in the aspens. A red-tailed hawk came to perch in a tree, watching me with a proprietorial air. There was a scent of nuts and vanilla which seemed to emanate from a shrub like serviceberry.

Next morning the postmistress sent me to the Draper ranch. Buddy Draper – a youngish man who, with all his family, competed in rodeos – led me across his land to an elevation between two creeks. Here were two shallow pits and ancient stumps where trees had been felled a long time ago. Draper was the third generation on this land; his grandfather, now turned ninety, had been brought here by *his* father at the age of three. That would be only fifty-two years after Frémont came through, and oral tradition had it that where we were standing was the site of Hardscrabble. It could have been inhabited even before the trappers built their cabins. Arrowheads had been found on the site.

Draper left me, merely asking that I close a gate as I came out. I wandered among the cacti and the cottonwoods, looking up at the timbered mountains with their craggy canyons and wondering if aesthetic values played a part in the choice of ground for a settlement. Here there was water, fuel and good grazing; it was an idyllic site but was it lovely? It is possible that my current standards were influenced by those of the settlers; beauty in a wild land was water, fuel and good grazing.

Frémont went straight through the Wet Mountains by way of Hardscrabble Canyon. Even before my journey started I knew that I would have so little difficulty here that the direct traverse of the range would be dull: a paved road all the way. I had recourse then to my normal practice: in order to see the country as they saw it I would leave the road and climb the mountains.

I was fortunate in my first peak. Using a Forest Service map which is on a small scale and without contours I had selected an easy walk of about twelve miles with a high point of 9,622 feet, but there was no indication of the altitude at the trail head. Next morning I was astonished to find that this was at 7,800 feet. There were only two thousand feet between me and the summit.

We had come up a dirt road to a rough lay-by on a spur. All the eastern plains were spread below us, clear to Kansas Pike's Peak loomed in the north – but cloud was thickening at the southern extremity of my range, making my heart sink until I remembered that this would be a normal day in Snowdonia or the Highlands: a good dawn deteriorating to rain. But rain would be snow at nine thousand feet. Glumly I packed my survival clothing.

The trail followed a ridge and was graded for horses although there was no sign of any. It gained height smoothly but rapidly through an enchanting world empty of people but burgeoning with spring. There were not many animals certainly – I saw only squirrels, heard only woodpeckers, but flowers were everywhere. There was a magenta vetch as showy as a lupin, but the lupins here were yellow. There was a blue penstemon, mauve asters, innumerable golden daisies. At the highest level there were pasque flowers.

Meadows appeared among aspens and I came on the remains of a log cabin beside a stream. The rocky knoll of Curley Peak showed ahead, up which I scrambled – unnecessarily, because there was an easy way round, but it was good to feel the rock under my hands.

From the summit the range of the Sangre de Cristo was revealed: peak beyond peak receding southward and all plastered with snow except, I thought, my pass, *their* pass, but I had no time to study the topography. Creeping up the length of my own range came the hail showers: matt white against a naughty sky. I turned to descend, noting only that the northern end of the valley that separated the Wets from the Sangre de Cristo looked interesting: rolling ground covered with pinyon and juniper. There was an impression of a valley remote and hidden from the outside world.

I tramped along the divide, continuing on the loop trail, not going back the way I had come. For a short distance the Sangre de Cristo stood on my right: watching and waiting. Accustomed to the Alps I could not visualise those crests without snow and it never crossed my mind that in a few weeks' time I might be sitting up there, *lounging*, and idly contemplating the Wets, thinking that it had never crossed my mind ...

A little notice showed on a tree: 'Tanner Trail', the only marker in ten miles. You are on your own in these mountains, which is good for concentration.

I came down East Bear Gulch: a jumble of timber and crags; some of the crags tall enough to be termed cliffs, and all of a granite rough as the rock in Cornwall, but pink. Squirrels scampered before me and the place was loud with the songs of birds and water. Streams ran down the path but the soil was thin and the mud just mud, not gumbo.

I came out on a dirt road beside Oak Creek whose canyon was even more spectacular than East Bear Gulch, its red cliffs dull in the shade, vivid in the sunshine, and one steep slab, the colour of crushed rose, scattered with clumps of blue penstemon.

In the bottom of the canyon there was a ranch, an enclave in the forest, where one thin horse drooped in a corral. Lilac was in bloom about decrepit cabins. The ranch house was built of breeze-blocks and covered by a tin roof: ugly as sin but mostly hidden by the lilac which was thronged with bees and butterflies. There were old orchards and ancient fruit trees. The road climbed and I looked down on fields that had once been hedged and were now lush and overgrown. There would have been a time when this was a desirable property, and cherished.

Curley Peak was at the north and lower end of the Wets. Emboldened by the absence of snow I moved south and next day made an attempt on Mount Rudolph, over ten thousand feet high. But I had crossed the magic line and I found the going hard even before I reached the snow. I was probably the first person of the season to go up from this side and there was a lot of timber across the trail from the winter's storms. I reached the snow-line and saw the track of one person who must have come up from the other side. I spent a long time wading through the snow but, unable to see the peak for the trees, I never found the summit.

In the dark, still depths of the conifers, a pair of squirrels chased each other across the snow. A woodpecker gave its demonic laugh. The sky was colourless, what I could see of it, not blue. I turned back, following my own tracks. Behind me there was a stealthy sound. I swung round, searching desperately for the cause. It came closer. I must have looked a picture of terror: frozen, waiting for *it* to make a sign. Then I saw it: a little stone, disturbed by my own feet, slipping down the surface behind me.

Storms threatened again and thunder rolled round the rim of my world. Freezing temperatures were augmented by the creeks which, in full spate, generated their own bitter currents of air. Camping by the

30

creeks, my beds were stony. Normally the camper, with only a quarter-inch of foam between him and the ground, fits himself round the bumps, but in the Wets there were too many bumps. My nights were restless. They were cold too, but mornings were the coldest time for the sun didn't reach the bottom of the deepest canyons until late, and I would be a mile up the trail before I could feel my feet in my boots. Then, suddenly, it was hot and one was forced to think of sunstroke.

On the last day of May I had my last excursion in the Wets. In three days I had become fond of them. With the alien Sangre de Cristo ahead the Wets were sweetly familiar, at least below the snow-line, at least in the morning as I trudged up an eastern slope exposed to the sun. Every day the flowers increased, in fact there were more flowers beside the trail when I descended in late afternoon than there had been in the morning. Yesterday there were calypso orchids, today there were violets and lilies-of-the-valley and today, at ten thousand feet, I lost the trail.

I lost the peak too. Again I was thwarted by the thick cover of Ponderosa and spruce. I wandered about this high ground where, infuriatingly, I could see nothing, building cairns as I went, finding snow again and leaving tracks deliberately (to be lost in forest would be the last straw, although the most likely hazard at the moment), thinking wistfully of the Sangre de Cristo where mountains rose, naked if snowy, high above the upper level of the trees.

I retraced my route by way of the cairns and came down through the lupins and columbines and the borage that Americans call bluebells and which is nothing like. I had failed to find another peak but it had been a good day. Tomorrow was June 1st: an ancient wedding anniversary, the day a friend's book was to be published, the day I would cross the Wets: 'Seven miles of hard toilsome travel.' I would have it easier than Benjamin Kern, but (remembering the stony beds, the icy mornings) I'd had it hard too.

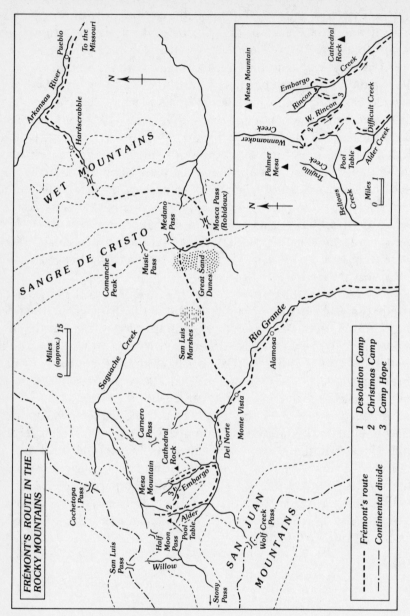

The Fourth Expedition in the Colorado Rockies.

Three

THE DAY AFTER the fourth expedition left the Hardscrabble settlement they moved only a few miles to halt in scrub oak outside the mouth of the canyon. I calculated that they camped a short distance upstream of Wetmore. The postmistress listened politely to my theory and sent me to a man called Breece, another third, or even fourth generation settler.

Mr Breece was a charmer, and a raconteur. He received me surrounded by peacocks, guinea fowl and innumerable cats. Crippled last year when he caught his leg in a mower, unable to ride and forced to sell his cattle, he was delighted to find someone who hadn't heard his stories. We toured the ranch and as we went, he talked.

The big barn had been built (of pine) in 1902, but the great roof beams could have been raised yesterday. Inside, a friendly cat greeted us and an Australian sheep dog stepped forward to stare intently at a litter of squirming kittens. Uneasily I called Mr Breece's attention to the situation and he said that but for our presence the bitch would have selected a kitten to carry around like shopping. The mother cat ran herself to a frazzle chasing after the bitch to retrieve her young.

We stood outside the barn and regarded the surroundings with pleasure. The *old* house, said my host thoughtfully, had been built in 1846. I pointed out that Hardscrabble was established only in 1832. He nodded; his ancestors were mountain men. I stared at him; that would be a great-great-grandfather, a great-great-uncle? He shrugged and switched to his grandfather's relationship with Jesse James.

He saw my expression. Jesse, he explained, wasn't killed in the shoot-out with Ford at St Joseph. 'They took some other man who died and filled his chest with gunshot wounds and buried him.'

After the shoot-out Jesse James came into the Wet Mountains 'to live a human life'. He hauled pit props to the coal mines with a wagon, and lived in a dug-out up the road. Sometimes he stayed at the old Greenwood Hotel, now burned down. One day a big black Buick came by and Jesse asked the people at the hotel to look after his horse, and he took off, and the bank at Westcliffe was robbed. (Westcliffe was over the mountains, in the Wet Mountain valley which I had seen from Curley Peak.)

Jesse used to sit on the step of the barn behind us and watch the chickens. Or he'd go up to the house and sit on the stoop and Mr Breece's grandmother would bring him a piece of pie. He was a bachelor. He would never go in the house. Well, very rarely he did and then he'd go right to the back wall so that all the doors were in front of him.

'Was he armed?' I asked.

'No. He never packed a gun after he came here.'

'But you all knew who he was.'

'We didn't know until he was dead. He was an old, old man. And after he was dead the state dug him up and they knew it was Jesse James by the scars on his chest.'

Mrs Breece came home. Neither she nor her husband knew anything about Frémont.

I left the ranch and entered Hardscrabble Canyon. The chasm must have been extremely narrow before the rock was blasted to clear a way for the road, but the expedition had little trouble. They covered nine miles this day. I found the canyon more impressive than they did, the most sensational features being two colossal pinnacles that must have measured a thousand feet from the canyon floor to their summits.

At a fork in the road called Mckenzie Junction the paved highway went west and I took a dirt road that followed Hardscrabble Creek, to a gentle depression where deer grazed beside the water, a red-tail called through the thin air and a bluebird flashed in sunlight above spring grass. 'Camped in a fine warm hollow,' wrote Dr Benjamin, 'walked in summer coat – passed some beautiful groves of pine which contrasted with the snow made quite a pleasing effect. ...'

After a mile or so I came to rocky narrows where the road was squeezed between creek and crags. They had floundered in this bottom through deep snow, and the packs were stripped from the mules by aspen trunks. I passed a horseman, and shortly I was in a high basin with good grazing and ranches. Frémont camped at the far end of the basin where Hardscrabble Creek has its source.

We climbed the headwall in low gear (although the Jeep was automatic I could feel him selecting the gears) and slowly, inexorably, the Sangre de Cristo rose ahead, their rock peaks bare and tempting: focal points of a chain whose snow summits were mere foils.

34

These were the thoughts of a climber; if one surveyed that range as a guide with thirty-three men and over a hundred mules in the rear, in November, one would be looking for the passes, not the peaks. And there it was, far in the southwest, our goal: Robidoux Pass.

Still high above the Wet Mountain valley I came to a place called Rosita. Old mines were marked on the map, and the cemetery dated from 1870. Only twenty-two years after Frémont passed, this land was settled by miners and a cemetery laid out. 'Rosita Hills' was a new departure. A mile or so below the pass, around the nine-thousand-foot level, the land was scheduled for development. On a swell of windswept grass a new road sign proclaimed Buttercup Drive. A little lower, where a buzzard mewed from a dead fir, came Columbine Crest. Then the cabins started, ornate and tacky, festering on the ravished slopes. Mistletoe Way, said a sign. So much for my remote valley, cut off from the outside world.

I descended without pause to where, straight as a crimson arrow, my road headed across the flats to the Sangre de Cristo.

In the foothills of the great range I made a false cast and found myself among the widely spaced pines of yet another development. It was like Surrey without planning. I back-tracked to the valley, to be arrested for one enchanted moment by a field of wild mauve iris with a peak like a horn in the background. From there I followed the next creek upstream to a camp under Comanche Peak. That evening I recorded the first mosquito. Like the first snowflake it augured ill.

I knew I couldn't reach the summit of Comanche but I was interested to see if I could get as far as a lake at about twelve thousand feet. It was an ambitious project but if the trail followed eastern and southern slopes it should be bare of snow and, whatever happened, I would have started to familiarise myself with the new range, the one that had looked so daunting from the other side of the valley.

For two miles the trail *was* bare, but on the far side of an avalanche chute it climbed a north-facing slope where the snow lay deep and hard, shadowed by trees. I had used the axe on the avalanche chute but I was not going to cut steps for six hundred feet merely to a lake, and there was no way that I could kick steps for that distance. This slope was for crampons, and crampons I did not have. I turned back, to be rewarded by the sight of a western tanager in spring plumage, looking for all the world as if a hawk had stooped and given him a bloody head, the scarlet seeming to seep into the yellow nape; so unlike the acorn woodpecker which appears to be wearing a garish red toupee.

The weather would not settle. I woke next morning to an overcast sky and the cloud ceiling at 9,500 feet. I pulled out and descended to the valley, striking the line of the Fourth and turning south. 'Bitter cold,' wrote Benjamin, 'Ther[mometer] perhaps 8° ... wrapt my leggings around my feet kept them dry but made the walking heavy. Snow deep 1 to 4 feet. ... one continued tramp thro' dry snow – up and down hill all the way – laborious and weakening. ....'

A venison bone on the trail was claimed by 'Broncho' who must have been a dog, but it is the only reference to the animal. He appears from nowhere and vanishes, a mystery.

I followed them up the Wet Mountain valley to an incipient divide which marked the county line between Custer and Huerfano. Now the drainage was south and I was close to that pass which had been so obvious for the last few days. To my surprise I discovered that this was not Robidoux (which is now called Mosca); it was Medano Pass. Mosca-Robidoux was eight miles to the south as the eagle flew.

I went to look at Medano. There was a track all the way to the top, good enough that I didn't have to use four-wheel-drive until just below the summit. On the crest a notice informed me that it was six miles to the Sand Dunes (another fixed point on the journey) but that the trail was for 4WD only. I pondered this. The creeks were in spate and, at the start of the season, trails had not been repaired following the winter's storms. In such circumstances a mountain trail that is an unknown quantity is best inspected upwards; one can become trapped if trying to reconnoitre on the descent.

As I retreated I considered the relative merits of the two passes. That the fourth expedition should have crossed Mosca rather than Medano seems curious, considering the former was a day's journey further south, but there was an established route over Mosca, the trader, Antoine Robidoux, having taken at least one wagon over it. The crossing of Medano had been recorded only once to my knowledge, by the explorer Zebulon Pike in 1807. In altitude Medano was marginally preferable, being about four hundred feet lower. This was all theory on my part; I would have to study the terrain. From the summit of Medano I had seen a twisted canyon which looked long and could well have been very rough in the 1840s.

I stocked up with food and water at Walsenburg and went to visit the sheriff. I'd said I would send photographs back to deepest

Hertfordshire: to Elizabeth who was operating the English clearing house. Her grandfather had emigrated to raise horses on a ranch near Walsenburg, and her mother had been born there.

I was taken to the place by a sheriff's deputy, a large man in a worn check shirt and shades. North of the town we turned off the highway and I dropped back, not wanting to eat the cruiser's dust. For nine miles we sped through open country dominated by the Spanish Peaks to the south, their snows shining in the sun, and suddenly I came on the police car in the middle of the road, stationary, a door wide open. The deputy was walking back, looking excited. What was this? An ambush?

'Now I'll show you your first rattler, ma'am.'

The snake had crossed the road ahead of the police car and stopped on the bank where it waited, part-coiled, weaving and feinting. Even the little prairie rattlers will stand their ground – and good luck to them; it's their territory. It was by no means my first, but it was a fine pugnacious specimen.

There was a big truck at the ranch. The deputy drove back to Walsenburg and the driver of the truck approached and introduced herself. She had married a son of the house and lived here in the 1940s. (Elizabeth's grandfather went back to England around the turn of the century.)

Nine miles from a road I listened to a woman who had spent her married life here and had returned today on what I took to be a sentimental journey. She was a poised and elegant lady who warned me against rattlesnakes and then went to look in the barns herself. Why? To look at the stall where she used to tie her horse, to see if her saddle were still in the tack room, to breathe the dusty, fusty air of a place that had been home for sixteen years and was now given over to snakes? I watched her, projecting wildly, and the feisty old lady who had come with her for the ride and stayed in their truck munching Trailmix, told me in tones that brooked no argument from a foreigner, that the survivors of Frémont's fourth expedition lived on the dead.

They left and the sound of their engine faded. Strange birds called. I went up the knoll they called Indian Hill where they used to find arrowheads. I saw fluorescent scarlet ahead. Plastic litter. I would take it down. But it was a cactus in brilliant bloom.

The view from the top was stupendous. To the south were the Spanish Peaks; the Wet Mountains stood to the north, and in the west was the Sangre de Cristo Range. And all around was the vast spread – thousands of acres – of this lovely ranch: pastures and pinyons and little knolls of pink sandstone like the one I was on. Below me the buildings stood, forlorn and empty without people or animals. Nothing stirred down there; no windmill turned, no horse stamped, saddled and tied to the rail of a corral. The large modern house was an anachronism, and only occasionally occupied by the present landowner, a man from Texas. Among the pinyons were a few scrubby steers, a token herd.

I camped some distance from the buildings in a clearing among the little trees. A light came on from the direction of the ranch and I started along a wagon track to discover who had invaded my space. As soon as I left camp the light was hidden by a rise in the ground but enough of the afterglow remained for me to see if there was a snake in a rut, although not enough to know if one were coiled on weeds between them. The light turned out to be a security device, presumably on a timer, mounted on a pole above the corrals.

Night comes swiftly in these low latitudes and it was so dark on my return that I couldn't see even if the ruts were occupied. I started the kind of rambling monologue that I was wont to use when rescuing sheep on cliffs, the idea being to reassure the animal with the sound of confidence. A quiet approach in the wild, particularly the *dark* wild, could be that of a predator, and I was well aware that out here I was prey.

In the morning the ground about Indian Hill was aglow with evening primroses. The day was warm but not hot. As I drove away a bull snake, some six feet in length, was basking on the road: a bright moment shortly marred by the sight of a dead rattler, its head and tail missing. The rattles are taken as trophies. It's hard to understand why, in a country overrun with rodents, where a horse may have to be shot if it puts its foot in a hole, even ranchers kill the major predator. Not all ranchers; those who like to see lions and bears and eagles on their land will also spare the snakes.

I drove west to the Sangre de Cristo and the road to Mosca Pass. Although unpaved, this was wide and smooth, with posts to mark the lip of the drop. It was a service road to a radio tower above the pass.

On the crest the sun was full in my eyes. A great flatness extended far below and it could have been a plain, a desert, or water for all I could distinguish of its surface. On the other side, perhaps sixty miles away, was a spectral ridge: high ground with two faint gaps. I was looking across the Rio Grande valley to the San Juan Mountains.

I started down the west slope, to be pulled up short by a staggered rail where a horse might pass but not a vehicle. On my map a 4WD road traversed the pass, but the map was dated 1972. The Great Sand Dunes were only three miles below but to reach them by the nearest motor pass would involve me in a drive of well over a hundred miles. In a moment I had accepted the fact; after all I had always known that marked roads might no longer exist, that the higher parts of my own expedition must be done on foot. I decided that, before I started on the detour, I would walk down to the Sand Dunes. It would be good exercise.

As if to confirm this I came on two women who had walked up from the west. There was a cold wind at ten thousand feet and I was driving among the aspens and the drifted snow trying to find a campsite that was both level and sheltered when I spotted two figures sitting in the sun and watching me like deer about to take off. Instantly I was aware of their uneasiness in the presence of this vehicle that circled slowly like a predator sniffing round potential prey. I drove over, climbed down and introduced myself.

The older woman was a local resident who worked in Alamosa, the largest town in the valley. For some reason, perhaps their constant exposure in local papers, local historians are well known, and she gave me the names of two, and directions how to find them. One might be found in the library at Alamosa, the other I must ask for at the Post Office in Del Norte. I had already decided on Del Norte as my base of operations, the place where I would spend the summer. Ruth Marie Colville was the name, and she was known everywhere, I was told.

The women descended to the warm and golden valley, leaving me to a windy night that was to become my introduction in Del Norte: 'This is Gwen Moffat, who slept out on top of Mosca Pass.'

The route across Mosca seemed an easier line than Medano – so far. I had yet to see the west side of Medano. In the morning I strolled down to the Sand Dunes, Benjamin's journal in my pack, stopping occasionally to sit down and read. 'Not a hard day,' he wrote. 'A narrow descent along a little rill ... the travel interrupted more by fallen timber than rocks. ... The mountains are extremely steep covered with Juniper and pine or composed of huge irregular blocks of naked rocks – almost all the way the passage is narrow and winding so as to prevent any distant view but withal very romantic ... near one [o'clock] we sighted the valley very little snow on it – while right in front was a low range of sand hills with a foot of snow on them. Our deepest snow was $4\frac{1}{2}$ feet....'

I stopped when I saw the sand hills. Now I could distinguish the odd house in the valley but there was no sign of the San Juans. A bank of cloud lay on the western horizon and below it was a grey murk that must have been rain shadow. Would Frémont have seen more from this point than I, or less? There had been heavy snow the night before they crossed Mosca, and the storms continued for three days without a break. When they did have a fine morning blizzards still raged on the mountains. He would have seen less than I, and visibility was crucial at this point because from here the situation, never good, began to deteriorate dramatically. Preuss, running several days together in his journal, blamed Old Bill Williams: 'Bill's vacillations showed that he was not very much at home, at least in these parts. Trips lasting all day cost us lots of provisions, provisions which were used up before we reached the place for which they were scheduled. In crossing the second chain [the Sangre de Cristo] Bill definitely missed the promised *good* pass; again we had to struggle a lot with snow and tree trunks [on the descent of Mosca]'.

The 'good pass' could only have been Medano, so Preuss is implying that they had intended to go that way, although no one else suggests that the intention had been other than to follow Robidoux's route over Mosca. And Preuss omits to mention that, after descending Mosca he, with Frémont, Old Bill and two other men, went to examine the west side of Medano. Did Preuss decide privately that the latter was the better route, that Old Bill had made a mistake and was incompetent? But it was an *established* route that they had followed over Mosca. Preuss was a sensitive and fastidious man, repelled by dirt and coarseness. It is possible that his opinion of Old Bill's competence was influenced by the mountain man's personality and behaviour.

I left them floundering down the creek to the Great Sand Dunes. I went back to the Jeep and started the long detour to the south. The day had turned hot and I was listening to *La Traviata*. On such days, with a long drive ahead, I like to go slowly. 15 mph is very pleasant: the ideal speed for a dirt road, good country, and *La Traviata*. To my delight, before I reached the highway that would take me to Walsenburg and La Veta Pass, I came to a sign that directed me to a short-cut through a wild and rocky area.

I passed steep sweeps of granite that would have had climbers drooling in the Lake District but there was no sign that anyone climbed here. Higher, just before the pass, came the horrors of sub-division. 'Paradise Acres' screamed the notice of development and I put my foot down and turned off the stereo and came roaring to the highway where the container wagons passed me doing seventy and I didn't stop until thirst demanded that I pull off the road and drink. When I started again I knew immediately that I had a puncture.

The jack provided with my Cherokee was a fragile tool but it served its purpose, and although the wheel nuts had been tightened with an air pump or by a very powerful man, by dint of kicking the wheel brace I managed to loosen all but two. These were the anti-theft nuts which American Motors install on all the wheels, including the spare. They can be removed only with a key, which the wheel brace refuses to grip unless held in place by one hand. With a hand on each end of the brace I had no room to kick. I struggled for over an hour, the traffic thundering past within a few feet, the sun beating down, the bonnet raised in a mute signal for assistance.

It was a Mormon couple who stopped. They had driven by, turned round and come back. The man loosened the remaining nuts, changed the wheels, tightened everything and stowed the gear. Meanwhile his wife, a diminutive poodle draped over one wrist, washed my hands and dried them with paper towels, clucking over me as if I were suffering from senile dementia. I told them that the hero of my *Buckskin Girl* was a Mormon. I did not tell them that he renounced Mormonism when he fell in love with the buckskin girl.

They were from Texas and the man was the owner-operator of a low-loader (transporting earth-moving equipment). He gave me his card in case I should ever find myself in Corpus Christi and in need of a low-loader. They followed me ten miles, to Fort Garland, the nearest town, making sure that I reached a garage safely.

The Great Sand Dunes, now a National Monument, are obvious from a considerable distance, rising to seven hundred feet, their colour varying from pink to beige according to the light. I pitched my tent in their shadow and walked up Mosca Pass, finding its lower reaches more impressive than the part I had already explored from the top. There was a gloomy defile (I had begun to think like Benjamin) and the trail was exposed above a drop, much too narrow for wagons. Prior to 1898 there was a toll road down Mosca but it must have been in the bottom of the canyon.

Back in the valley a creek, descending from Medano Pass, ran between the sand dunes and the mountains. Above the campground were narrows where the water piled up, to be released in surges like little downstream bores. The creek was shallow but wide and the surges were quite alarming when one was halfway across although the water scarcely reached the knees. There was a series of waves, and a sinister whispering noise. The sand shifted under the feet; water like liquefied mud streamed past on a current so strong that quite large stones were rolling along the bottom. There seemed to be no danger however, even to children. One might lose balance but the water was too shallow to drown and, surprisingly – when I remembered other shallow rivers of the West – there were no quicksands.

I waded upstream for two miles, emerging to walk on hard wet sand, watching the banks crumble under the surges (instant erosion), coming to a fence across the creek on the upstream side of which was a notice: 'All Vehicles Exit Here'.

I sat down opposite a high steep bank and waited. Soon a large truck plunged down the bank, its passengers screaming, hit the water and sped upstream. A Ford Bronco – like my Jeep but less powerful – came downstream, in the water, and rushed at the bank. There was a nasty grinding impact, the Bronco stalled, teetered, just retained its balance (the exit was at an acute diagonal angle) and eased back into the water. The driver withdrew to a sand bar and people got down to inspect the damage. After a while the truck was turned and disappeared upstream.

A trail bike came down and took the bank with more panache than skill. It stopped, fell over, and the rider walked away in disgust. Two big trucks and a small Jeep failed. I walked on; if this were the only way to approach Medano Pass, I was not going to subject the Jeep to such indignities. (But I was to discover that the proper route was at the back of the dunes.)

Above the narrows I met a party of Scouts from Kansas who gave me lunch and asked pertinent questions about Frémont. A courteous group, their good manners were natural, and no veneer assumed for the occasion. At the time I did not follow up a comment made by one of the lads. He said that, coming down from Medano, the water was up to his armpits. Odd that I should not have remarked this, but my thoughts were with Frémont rather than my own projected ascent of Medano Pass.

The trail skirted woodland through which a track ran to a cabin with printed notices warning of 'cyanide capsules' outside, and cyanide guns inside the building. Permissible, I thought, after some consideration. The *notices* might not be illegal.

Across from the cabin the creek ran under a tall dune with a grand slip face, as if a slope of brown windslab had avalanched. On my side of the creek I traversed rough sage land scattered with pines, the pass obvious on my starboard bow. The creek was now like an alpine stream (there were no surges above the narrows) and I crossed it on a fallen tree to follow a game trail up the side of a sand cliff. I treated the sand like unstable snow, at every move alert for a sudden collapse.

For half a mile I walked on the dunes: an undulating tramp that was hot and tiring, but eventually I reached a crest from which I could see the campsite of December 6th, 1848.

The night after they crossed Mosca Pass was bitterly cold and a high wind covered their blankets with snow. Next day they followed Medano Creek upstream (as I had done), the dunes affording some shelter until the wind changed direction. They camped after only five miles and that night they 'pitched tent' for the first time since Hardscrabble. Whether this was tents for the men, or Frémont's tepee, Benjamin Kern doesn't say. Six inches of snow fell in the night and next morning they made only two miles before a blizzard forced them back to their last campsite.

The following morning was fine (although snow was still falling on the mountains) and it was then that Frémont, Preuss, Old Bill and two other men went off to examine the gap that led to Medano Pass. In their absence Godey took the lead.

Four

ALEXIS GODEY DID not know his date of birth, but in 1848 he was probably in his thirties. He was in his prime: lean, physically powerful, and extraordinarily handsome – although no doubt, like all of them by the time they reached the Sand Dunes, starting to show the effects of seven weeks of hard winter travel. A man of great determination, he seems to have been impervious to cold, hunger, and the suffering of others – which can be as debilitating as personal injury. Unfeeling? Godey would save the expedition.

It was a dry but bitterly cold day when he first demonstrated his abilities as a guide. 'He piloted us thro the road in a capital manner,' wrote Benjamin, 'each hair of mule and man was covered with frost, and icicles hung down from moustache below the chin. ... Ther[mometer] in the gap at one o'clock was below zero. King [one of the men who had gone to look at the gap with Frémont] came in at sunset with frosted toes. Very cold. Ther may be 6 below zero. Clear and brilliant night but one of the most horribly uncomfortable.'

The day after my walk on the dunes I went to look at Medano myself. We had not gone far before we were stopped by sand so deep that the Jeep couldn't cope until I had let ten pounds of air out of each tyre. When I came to Medano Creek I packed my rucksack and was about to wade the stream when a family drove up in a small 4WD camping van. They said that if I cared to follow in the Jeep they would wait for me at the crossings. With someone there to winch me out if necessary I had no qualms, and so we started to tackle the numerous crossings formed by the creek's meandering down the canyon.

About two miles from the summit there was a crossing with a sudden drop in the bed on the downstream side (the presence of a drop could be deduced by the existence of a trough and a standing wave) while, on the upstream side, a number of fallen trees were jammed, with one raw and broken snag. You had to steer close to the drop-off to avoid the snag, and the current was so powerful that I was hard put to it to keep the Jeep on a straight course.

Somewhere around here we picked up some more travellers who had been camping in a glade and I hung back to avoid their dust. At the penultimate crossing the others had stopped on the far bank and I didn't notice that they had taken the water at an angle. I took it straight and suddenly a big smooth bank loomed ahead, seeming higher than us. I dared not stop so I put the Jeep at the bank as if he were a horse. He went up it like one too. I stopped and the others gathered round: gypsy faces, lots of hounds, beautiful grimy children. They were charming and friendly, wishing me a safe journey and then driving on: to Denver, they said.

I came to the familiar sign: 'Dunes 6 miles' on top of the pass. Any lingering doubt concerning the Fourth's route was resolved; they couldn't have crossed Medano. It was not the creek crossings that supported this conclusion (the water would be low, if not frozen, in December) but the distance. They took one and a half hours from the summit to the sand hills, floundering in the narrow bottom through fallen timber and snow. They would have had to 'flounder' at four miles an hour, dragging mules round and over obstacles. And Medano is a wide canyon. They went down Mosca.

Having confirmed this to my satisfaction I walked as far as the snow-line and turned back as spots of rain began to fall. I was three miles from the Jeep and the rain increased rapidly. Back at the truck I lost some time changing into dry clothes so when we arrived at the crossing with the big smooth bank the water had risen.

When the Jeep put his nose down I thought he was going to stand on it, like the black beetles that stick their rumps in the air and squirt a noxious fluid at an enemy. But he levelled out and, like an amphibious vehicle, trudged stolidly through what had become a river.

The cloud dropped and the rain came down in torrents. I passed some decrepit cabins at the side of a meadow and crept down steep rocky slopes where miniature flash floods crossed the track or drained down it in streams. At the crossing where we must edge between the broken snag and the drop I stopped. There were six crossings below this one. If I were caught by a flash flood it was better to be caught high than in the lower reaches of the canyon.

I put on my waterproofs again and walked to the edge of the river. It was a shocking sight. The drop-off wasn't detectable; there was just a rushing mass of waves. I shuddered and walked back almost to the cabins looking for a place to turn round. At the crossing the Jeep was blocking the road. Nothing could come through of course, but there was a principle involved. Sleeping on the road I was stranded; if I could get back to the cabins I would have chosen my campsite. I would be in control. Moreover there was a feeling of security in spending the night where other people had lived.

I was soaked. Puddles on the level portions of the trail were so deep that I had to take to the woods, and the woods were saturated. I didn't like the idea of reversing the long mile to the cabins. The ground was steep, the road now in poor shape, and one mistake in steering would have us over the edge. I could find no place where I could turn with comfort so I picked the least constricted. Instead of trees there was a thicket of brambles on the uphill side.

It was tricky. The Jeep was too long to turn on a wagon track with only an extra yard of brambles. There was a bank behind them – and I wouldn't push him into the aspens down the slope in front of us for fear of finding ourselves jammed between the trunks. However, after some lucky juggling we managed to come round. With relief I started to climb the rocky slopes, creeping through the long puddles between gradients in our lowest gear. At last I dared to think of dry clothes again, and of tea.

We came over the lip of the slope below the cabins and I saw that, since our passing, the creek had burst its banks. The meadow was flooded.

My first impulse was to get out and run, but then I saw that the water must rise a few feet more before it could cover the track. I stopped and brewed tea in my waterproofs, drinking it as I sat in the driver's seat. The radio was broadcasting warnings of flash floods. I moved all the boxes from the back of the Jeep to the front seats, put the cooler on the bonnet knowing that a bear could reach it easily, but not caring, and I got into my bag in the back. At 9.40 p.m. the rain stopped.

I rose at 6.30 to grey skies. I ate a leisurely breakfast and reached the upper crossing at 9.30. I looked at the water level, trying to remember where it had been yesterday. I decided to cross when it had dropped twelve inches. I started to read a novel by Dick Francis, blessing him.

By 11.30 the level had dropped, but less than an inch. By 12.30 I reckoned you could say it was an inch. I celebrated with the last of the fresh milk in my coffee and with some crackers. At intervals a weak sun appeared. The wind was in the west. Was that a good quarter?

At 12.50 there was a little rain; at 1.30, more. A heavy shower lasted forty-five minutes. I gave up and returned to the cabins. Leaving the Jeep, I walked to the bad crossing downstream. A new creek, product of the storm, crossed the track, too deep to wade. I bridged it with fallen saplings.

The lower crossing raged and thundered: a frightful sight even to someone on the bank. I went back to the cabins and moved my camp to a lovely site among the aspens. The afternoon was beautiful; I did all my washing, and read, and told myself the water level was falling.

The moon was nearly full that evening, the aspens ethereal in its light. There was a frost and in the morning I had to rub the ice off the thermometer before I could take the reading: 30°. Then the sun rose and I thawed out, along with the birds and the tent. Shortly before I was ready to leave, ominous little clouds started coming over from the west and, panicking, I threw the rest of the gear higgledy-piggledy into the back of the truck.

Because the Jeep had power steering and brakes, to stall on a mountain road could be fatal so, although I wanted to go downhill, first I went up in order to warm the engine quickly. I drove as far as the top crossing where I saw that the level had dropped two inches: ten inches short of what had been my minimum requirement.

At the bad crossing downstream I stopped and worked out my line: a slight dog-leg. The marker was a fallen tree and, in the middle of the current, I must change direction, steering between 10° and 15° to starboard.

The Jeep went through like a bird, very slow and steady – and that was the neatest crossing we did. At the next he put his nose in a big hole, but came out of it, and when I stopped on the other side the plugs were still dry.

I was bothered about my own safety. If we stalled and were swept down, there was no way that I could open a window because they were operated electrically and the mechanism would not function without the ignition. I could think of nothing more horrid than sitting in a truck that was slowly flooding and being unable to open a window. Consequently at every crossing I closed the window on the upstream side and opened the other. In addition I wore my heavy anorak with my money, cheque book and matches in plastic bags in the kangaroo pouch.

47

The water at Crossing Three came halfway up my door, but this was not what canoeists call white water. It was deep and fast but quiet; I could hear the stones on the bottom grinding under our wheels.

At Crossing Four the water reached the bug shield above the grille. Incredulously I looked along the surface to the opposite shore. Could we be *floating*? Upstream the breakers boiled, obstructed by our mass. Again we came through, shedding water like a buffalo, but the engine still running smooth as silk.

Crossing Five was wide and looked deep but the depth was little more than two feet. At Number Six it was bug shield depth again and this time I *knew* the engine would die. On the other side I lifted the bonnet. The batteries and everything else were soaked but the Jeep stood there, humming casually to himself, and I climbed back and eased him down to the last and deepest trial. This one had to be where the Boy Scout was up to his armpits – and that was before the deluge, for Heaven's sake.

Down went his nose again (where were all the holes on the way up?) and as his front end rose I put my foot on the accelerator and sent him up the bank pouring water like a tank.

After that the deep sand of the dunes was an anti-climax.

As the land became more exciting people were more involved with its history. Until we crossed the Sangre de Cristo I had been throwing bread on the waters, often happy with the result even when people hadn't heard of Frémont. Suddenly, in the valley of the Rio Grande, not only had everyone heard of him, everyone knew to a mile which route he had taken through the San Juans. Innumerable canyons were involved, innumerable permutations. One person would maintain that the fourth expedition went up Canyon A and down B, another would be adamant that it was up B and down C, a third would dismiss all other contenders with contempt because it was up D and down E, and he could prove it . . . Every route had its proponent, every proponent his following – but then the professional historians differed too.

I considered the situation. I would listen to everyone, as I had read all the books, and I would go everywhere that Frémont could have gone, but always keeping in the forefront of my mind the basic sources: the journals that were written at the time. Somewhere out there I would cross his route; as a guide I couldn't fail to gravitate towards it if only by choosing the easiest way. In the last resort the route was not important; it was less the country that intrigued me than the relationship men formed with it, with the elements, and with each other.

It was in the Rio Grande valley that my experiences diverged most wildly from those of the Fourth. When I was in the big mountains I had no trouble envisaging their struggle over that kind of terrain in winter. But the Rio Grande valley, all white, with a blizzard raging? The first time I crossed that valley the temperature was over 110°.

I had pulled off the road beside the San Luis Marshes at a place where I could look back at the Sangre de Cristo and forward to the San Juans. Immediately I stopped I had to close the windows as the mosquitoes rose in clouds from the marsh. Then I had to start the engine to get the air conditioner going before I fell prey to heatstroke. From behind the glass (thronged with furious mosquitoes) I regarded the valley.

It had once been desert, now much of it was irrigated and intensively farmed, but where I had stopped the water table was high and the old marshes remained: a sanctuary for wildfowl. Red-headed duck up-ended in the shallows, shovellers trawled; yellow-headed blackbirds trilled in the cat-tails. In 1848 they made supper from cat-tails. Close to the road avocets were sitting on little islands of nests in water that reflected a sky flecked with cirrus clouds.

In the east the passes showed as clefts in the white range: Mosca, Medano, Music. Music looked pleasant, I thought, but it was only a pass; I wondered when the mountains would be clear of snow. And I turned the Jeep round and looked towards the San Juans, as always indistinct – but then they were more distant than the Sangre de Cristo. The great gap of the Rio Grande showed between the foothills. The river rises in the San Juans and runs east before, opposite Mosca Pass, it changes course to flow south, a direction it will maintain, more or less, as far as the Mexican border.

In November Frémont had written to Benton: 'We will ascend the Del Norte [the Rio Grande] to its head, descend on to the Colorado and so across the Wahsatch mountains [east of Salt Lake City] and the basin country somewhere near the 37th parallel, reaching the settled parts of California, near Monterey. There is, I think, a pass in the Sierra Nevada between the 37th and 38th, which I wish to examine.'

The only pass there is Tioga which, at 9,945 feet, is the first to be blocked in winter, the last to be cleared, but he said that he only wished to examine it. He was definite about ascending the Rio Grande to its head.

That letter was written three weeks before they reached the Rio Grande, before they ran into the terrible weather. Some ten years after the event Micajah McGehee, the judge's son who, like Captain Cathcart, came along for the adventure, described their passage from the sand dunes to the river: 'One broad, white, dreary looking plain. ... We camped in the middle of it, without any shelter from the winds, and with no fuel but some wild sage. ... The cold was intense, the thermometer at night standing at 17 degrees below zero, and it was so cold during the day that Ducatel, a young fellow in the company, came very near freezing to death.'

Benjamin Kern suffered considerable pain from a badly frozen foot. He also mentions the crossing of the dreary plain: 'The air filled with snow the sun made a little shadow we soon left the bushes and all was of a dismal white colour all the mountains were hidden. ...' And next day: 'very cold started about 9 with clear weather soon the air became filled with spiculae of ice which hid the sun made the atmosphere very chilly and soon enveloped us in frozen cloud making a singularly white day. ...'

The plight of the mules was pitiful. McGehee says that during that night in the middle of the valley, the animals 'stood shivering in the cold with bowed backs and drooping heads, suffering from their exposed situation and half starved, being now reduced to a pint of corn twice a day, and having no other resource for food, [they] broke loose from their weak fastenings of sage bushes and started off *en masse* on the back trail. ... In the middle of the night, we had to rise from our beds, lifting half a foot of snow with our top blankets, and strike out in pursuit of them through the severe cold. We overtook them several miles from camp. ...'

Two days after they left the sand dunes they reached the Rio Grande at a place where there is now a small town called Monte Vista. The river was lined with cottonwoods, as it is still, and the trees provided them with food and shelter. Where there were bare patches the mules found good grazing. But the river was only partly frozen and they were to have a terrible time crossing it, the mules breaking through the ice and having to be hauled out by the men. The following day they were forced to cross again, but this day was brightened when Godey killed two elk. Game had been scarce in the mountains.

Big rivers change out of all recognition with the seasons and when I reached it in the second week of June, the Rio Grande was a mass of

50

brown floodwater: fast and dangerous. I followed it upstream from Monte Vista to Del Norte, going down to the water whenever a dirt road offered access through the farmland. The cottonwoods suggested a green and welcome shade, but the mosquitoes were voracious. The air around the bridges was alive with frenetic swallows.

Del Norte backed onto the river. There was a wide main street but little more than that. The town stood at an elevation of eight thousand feet and I had envisaged something small and primitive, but there was a Post Office and a library, there was even an antiques shop with some very good pieces in the window.

I called at the Post Office to pick up my mail and to inquire for Ruth Marie Colville. She lived on a ranch six miles west of town. In a cabin close to the river I found a spry old lady with a shock of grey hair and tinted spectacles, wearing sensible trousers and hiking boots.

She had come to Colorado from the East as a young teacher, had married the son of the ranch and set up home in this log cabin. Eventually they built a house, but when her husband died she moved back into her original home. Her children had modernised the interior with care. A sink and a range were unobtrusive, a wooden door opened on a shower and lavatory. In the sitting room a picture window looked across a meadow and the cottonwoods of the river to a range of mountains between twelve and thirteen thousand feet high.

I revelled in Ruth Marie's furniture, her books, her pictures. This was the first place I had come to since Omaha where good taste mattered more than display. She served tea in delicate china, with saucers.

She was entranced by the Jeep and touched by my use of the royal plural. She insisted that this coming weekend I should attend a meeting of the local historical society as her guest. Meanwhile she gave me directions to Old Woman Creek, on Colville land, where I might camp and explore. 'Watch out for the rattlers,' was her parting admonition, not knowing that ants and mosquitoes were my real problem, not snakes.

I had a bumpy buggy night and greeted the dawn grumpily. In new country, without maps or trails, I had no idea how to spend my day. Coffee restored my equilibrium and after breakfast I walked the skyline of the valley, climbing through timber and over rough pink rock to a hill about ten thousand feet high from which I saw strange mountains to the west. They were immense and rolling, like the Cairngorms on a grand scale, and they still bore old snow wreaths.

Their canyons were so densely timbered that I could see no clear ground, but there were patches in the dark trees that I knew were crags.

The morning turned stormy. Thunder reverberated distantly. Visibility was inconsistent. You could see fifty miles when a ray of sunshine lighted on a high snowfield, but in shadow conifers were indistinguishable from rock only ten miles away. Over the next six weeks that country in the west was to become my territory: Mesa Mountain, Pool Table, Embargo Creek. It was the country that had seen the apotheosis of the fourth expedition.

Five

THE HISTORICAL SOCIETY was meeting at the Lost Trail Ranch. For eighty miles we drove upriver, the ground on either side becoming ever rougher and more showy until we reached the ranch above the Rio Grande, which at this point was a torrent cutting through a chasm with walls of yellow clay. A towering escarpment of red rock rose above the ranch, and between the cliffs and the river a track climbed to Stony Pass which was still blocked by snow. When Frémont wrote that he would follow the Rio Grande to its head and descend to the Colorado I had taken him literally and thought that he had planned to go over Stony Pass. He could have done this, following a river system that would eventually debouch in the Colorado, but it would have been a tortuous and impractical route for a railway.

The historical society's meeting was more of a social gathering than an exchange of data; we ate hugely, walked in the woods, took photographs – and the meeting broke up on Sunday morning. As I descended the valley I saw a side canyon and, tired of the highway and of traffic reminiscent of a Sunday in North Wales, I left the road and started to climb.

At the point of departure the elevation was little more than eight thousand feet. By the time I stopped the engine seventeen miles later we had climbed three thousand feet and I was on the southern slopes of those mountains I had seen from the east two days ago. I was nearly at the timber line, among wide expanses of grass called 'parks', which bear no resemblance to the manicured plots in urban areas. They are pristine grazing grounds and those above the upper Rio Grande looked out to snowy peaks seemingly on the same level. They all had names, ranchers' names: Long Park, Middle Park, Divide, Corral.

I could have camped anywhere. I chose to camp in the only ugly place: a corner of Corral Park on Difficult Creek where trees had been felled and abandoned among stony wastes. I thought I camped there for access to good water and to the peak of Pool Table: an easy ascent from which I could survey the country, but next day, looking down on the ridges and canyons from twelve thousand feet, I realised that I had camped on the trail of the Fourth. I had not intended to do so; my intention was to throw a net round their area and work inwards, sniffing out all the possibilities, contracting the net until I was reasonably certain which way they had gone up, which canyon they had descended. Pool Table was to have been a reconnaissance but within a few hours I knew it had been a gravitation. There was nothing miraculous about it and it was no coincidence. I was doing this job because I was a guide, and I was looking at the country with the eyes of a mountaineer.

The birds woke me and I emerged in the bitter dawn with half an hour to go before the sun slipped down the trees to warm my creaky bones. By nine I was following a game trail up the side of the creek and it was still early enough that I could meet a beaver ambling down the bank looking for willow shoots to break his fast.

The game trail ended at a fence on the far side of which was an old and well-constructed cairn of pink rock covered with lichens. I had seen similar cairns on the Parph, the furthest corner of northwest Scotland.

It is not impossible that a man from Sutherland emigrated to the San Juans. In this land of timber and mighty rivers with its extremes of heat and cold, would such a man miss the heather moors swept by Atlantic gales? Few people were as poor as Highland crofters, to whom America would have been El Dorado, but if he was here, this mythical man from the Parph, he would surely have looked up from building his cairn and seen, with a stab of shock, thunder clouds building over Wolf Creek Pass. He would remember other cairns – of Torridon sandstone – and little flowers: tormentil and butterwort and daisies, and he would see, instead of Wolf Creek, long drifts of snow draping the screes of Foinaven above Glen Dessary.

I squeezed through the fence and walked up Middle Park, timing myself. At a steady pace it took me a quarter of an hour so the park was nearly a mile long, probably six hundred acres; you could put a lot of cows on that.

Ahead on the left was Pool Table, a mountain like a mesa with, on my side, a steep skirt, vaguely rocky, which I avoided by timber. There was snow in the shade: steep enough that I found the axe useful but not so hard that I had to cut steps.

I reached the summit to see that the weather was deteriorating.

Keeping a wary eye on the clouds I started to walk the southern escarpment which turned out to be less smooth and less flat than it looked from below. The surface was made up of chunky rocks where one must attend to the footing or risk a sprained ankle. Concentration was difficult among the alpines: forget-me-not, phlox, penstemon. There was an indefinable fragrance that was not flowers nor grass nor rock but something of them all, and warmed by the sun.

The terrain improved. In the centre of the southern scarp there was the remains of a cornice, and avalanche debris below. Thunder rolled and the western sky was black. I calculated that the approaching storm would allow me enough time to walk to the northern edge of the mesa and see the country that Frémont must have come down to after he passed Pool Table. Wannamaker was the creek I was looking for but it was hidden by the swell of a divide, and by Palmer Mesa. If I walked the divide from Pool Table to Palmer, I would be able to look down Wannamaker.... The thunder muttered and growled. I sighed, spared a glance for the high ridges, and chose prudence rather than valour. I have been in too many electric storms on mountains to forget the law of averages. I retreated, traversing slopes of boulders which looked as if they hadn't moved since the last earth tremor, and were poised to fall with the next lightning strike. Ptarmigan shrieked at me; they would have young close by. Now I must watch for ptarmigan chicks in addition to loose rocks.

On the descent to Middle Park I took a more direct line than on the ascent, making for bare ground beyond the timber. Now I saw that this ground sprouted pinnacles of pink tuff – a solidified volcanic dust. There would be nasty gullies between the pinnacles, so I bore left towards the trees and found some soft scree which I ran down, reflecting that I was probably the first person to run scree on Pool Table, and the scree gave out in a tilted grey hardpan like cement. The pinnacles had, as it were, crept round below me and were lying in ambush.

I stopped on a stone that remained stable providing I didn't move, and I worked the axe carefully off my pack (remembering all the people who had taken fatal falls in similar circumstances) and I bent to cut the first step.

Even the pick made no impression. I straightened, pondering. The first pinnacle was some twenty feet below me, its flanking gullies hardly lethal, but if I missed the pinnacle I would be lucky to escape with a broken leg.

I couldn't stay on that stone all day. Keeping the pinnacle below me, on the fall line, I minced down to it, using the ferrule of the axe as a psychological brake and leaving a line on the surface like a scratch on metal.

There followed some strange antics: up and down and across, quick spurts over gullies, retreats to lines of weakness that were nothing more than lines, and finally, steep red soil beside the firs, and a game trail.

I came slowly down Middle Park as thunder exploded on the summit. At least, I thought, the reconnaissance had been productive. Frémont walked along the divide (*walked?* They were being battered by blizzards) – they fought their way along the divide until, virtually exhausted, they dropped down a few hundred feet on the other side, and camped. I had a series of routes mapped in my mind but first I had to go back and fill the gap between the Rio Grande and Difficult Creek.

That gap was Alder Creek – and my road came down the mountain above it but now I could hardly spare a glance for it. The rain had started and I had no wish to be caught on roads where deep ruts, holes and skid marks indicated the trouble other people had encountered during the last storm. I was aware only of a great abyss, but I had the impression that the canyon was full of timber. There was some hard work ahead.

I camped low so that I could escape easily in the morning if the trail were slick. I slept beside a creek and I went to bed in my clothes, hoping to grab the tent in passing and leap into the truck if the water level rose. I was told that there was a dramatic thunder storm in the night but I knew nothing of it, fast asleep in the bottom of the canyon, snug under a canopy of aspens. The creek had a small catchment area and the water level rose less than an inch.

I had been right to descend the precipitous road before the rain. Next morning I had only a hundred yards to drive before we were out of the wood, but in those few yards we slithered all over the place in four-wheel-drive. However, the main 'road' was in full sun and the mud had dried. I came to the mouth of West Alder Creek and, climbing down, started to pack my gear.

After the fourth expedition reached the Rio Grande they followed it west, upstream, towards Stony Pass and San Luis (which was then called Leroux, Del Norte or Williams Pass). Stony Pass was eighty miles distant, San Luis twenty-four, but fifteen miles above the present town of Del Norte, on December 12th, they turned north, up Alder Creek, into mountains where no white man had been before.

There is no doubt that the western course was abandoned at that point because of the amount of snow ahead, but controversy has raged ever since concerning the reason for turning up an unknown creek instead of retreating.

Seven weeks later Frémont would write to Jessie from Taos, charging Old Bill with incompetence: 'The error of our journey was committed in engaging this man. He proved never to have known, or entirely to have forgotten, the whole region of country through which we were to pass.' He explains that they turned north where they did because that was the way Old Bill took them, and at the time they still had confidence in him.

They did not leave the Rio Grande without considerable disagreement. Thomas E. Breckenridge, the youthful frontiersman, wrote that long before they reached the river Old Bill was trying to persuade Frémont to avoid the San Juans by a southern route through New Mexico. At the mouth of Alder there was further discussion, Old Bill, now that they had come this far, advocating retreat and a *northern* detour over Cochetopa Pass, thirty-three miles to their north as the crow flew. At ten thousand feet, Cochetopa was high but, at least in summer, it was a popular route and well-trodden. Breckenridge suggests that Frémont saw the sense in going for Cochetopa, even agreed to it, but that he went up Alder as a short-cut: one side of a square instead of the three that a retreat would involve.

Alexis Godey was to confirm that, in turning up Alder, they were attempting to reach Cochetopa, but he maintained that Frémont wanted to go over Cochetopa Pass from the moment he saw how much snow there was on the San Juans, and that was right back in the middle of the Rio Grande valley, on December 8th.

It would appear that Frémont was gambling on getting through by cutting a corner instead of going the long way round, and Williams agreed to take him. Godey, in a campaign letter when Frémont was running for president eight years later, accepted responsibility: 'If there was blame to be attached to any source, on Bill Williams, our guide, and myself should its entire weight rest.'

Whoever was responsible, a mistake was made and the consequences were disastrous. They need not have been; the situation was by no means unique. Exploration is always a gamble, or a series of them, a matter of calculating the risks involved. 'If we can reach the top of the escarpment. . . . get across the river. . . . ride eighty miles without water. If the weather doesn't break. . . .' Much of the time explorers are lucky; there is no bad luck in the wilderness, only mistakes in judgement. They could have made it up Alder Creek and back to the Rio Grande. They did – virtually, but many were weakened beyond hope of recovery. Had they got over the top their circumstances might have been no different from those of any other expedition that had been forced to live on mule meat while they were lost for a few days.

They started up Alder, and it was possible that this was the worst terrain they had yet encountered. There was no trail. They worked their way along the bank of the creek through shrubs and fallen timber (there had been a big fire in the bottom) and all this was covered with snow deeper than the mules' bellies. When the animals became mired in bog or could not get over obstacles they were hauled across the creek with ropes. Often several were jammed together in a bunch and the men had to wade waist-deep in floating ice in order to free them.

Upstream the canyon narrowed, the creek tumbling down waterfalls in a chasm. They were forced to climb the side of the canyon and traverse above the cliffs. The first night the gradient was so steep that they could contrive level places only by dropping trees across the slope which, supported by standing timber and packed with boughs, provided secure if uncomfortable beds.

The mules, encumbered by the packs, fell on the icy slopes and died in the bottom of the canyon. If they survived, packs were sure to be ripped off in the fall. A great deal of time, not to speak of energy, was spent in retrieving scattered loads, repacking, and finally reloading animals on the terrible slopes, and all this in bitter temperatures, struggling with knots and buckles when their hands were numb.

Nothing has changed in Alder's canyon since 1848. When I saw it that June morning I knew there was still no trail in the bottom (by now I had large-scale maps) but I did hope for game trails. A region so thickly timbered must be full of deer.

There had been a cabin at the mouth of the creek, and a meadow from which a path ran along the bank but only for a few hundred yards. The vegetation was wet and in no time I was soaked to the waist. After the path gave out progress was like forcing one's way through a jungle, but without a machete to hack a way. There were game trails, but they were much overgrown. The water was deep and very swift. A dark red buttress came down to the creek (they would have crossed at that point) and I started to traverse on the rock. I came to a tiny bay occupied by a garter snake which slipped into the water and was immediately swept away by the current.

I followed the creek for several miles reflecting that if I were wet and uncomfortable, how appallingly miserable they must have been, with the thermometer around zero, and forced to drag the mules across the river and through the snow.

After three miles I started up the side of the canyon. We were approaching the narrows and the expedition would be trying to get over the rocky buttresses. I climbed, traversing on terraces, gaining height as I linked the ledges with interesting pitches but remembering, as I crossed a gully, that they would have had to scramble up these gullies pulling reluctant pack animals; there was no way they could have climbed the rock. It was not difficult to see where the mules fell.

The buttresses rose several hundred feet above the creek, then the angle eased, and here the Forest Service had built the road which I had descended last night. I walked up it for some distance and went back into the forest when I judged I was past the narrows. Upstream now I could see the canyon widening to a V-shaped valley, and within two miles Difficult Creek came in from the right. Now they were on easier ground – but they had left a number of mules in Alder Creek, dead or dying.

If the temperature rose, the snow fell. They had two inches on the night of December 12th. In the morning the thermometer stood at 20° ('mild', Benjamin called it), but the snow in Difficult Creek was fifteen feet deep. Benjamin's stockings froze to his feet. And now, a few miles up Difficult Creek, past my camp of two nights ago in the corner of Corral Park where I had met the beaver, they had the long mile of Middle Park (before the cattlemen came and built the beautiful cairns). Ahead of them was the divide: that series of white whale-backs where the crescendo approached its climax, and Christmas came at the end of a week of storms at twelve thousand feet above Wannamaker Creek.

Six

I CAME DOWN from the high country, visited Ruth Marie, and was bidden to a party the following night. I camped in the foothills; a country of rock reefs so fine that in one place a great arch had been eroded by the elements, its roof plastered with the nests of crag swallows. After five minutes in my camp among the pinyons I knew why swallows and flycatchers were in such abundance. The ground, the air and the vegetation swarmed with ants, mosquitoes, wood ticks (bloodsuckers like sheep ticks) and small black flies that crept into every orifice, but most particularly the eyes. To crown my discomfiture, in the glorious sunrise when all but ticks and ants were in abeyance, I shut my finger in the car door.

I sat down before I fell, and it was the ants, biting like fury, that brought me sluggishly to my feet, wondering if – because it didn't hurt so much as I thought it should – there was something very wrong indeed, like instant gangrene.

Doped with paracetemol, and with Ruth Marie's party that evening, I had an easy day in the foothills, drifting down the wagon trails, watching the antelope watching me, strolling in cottonwood groves where flattened grass spoke of recent occupation by some big beast – lion, I wondered? More likely bear. But there were only the antelope leaping away like African buck on the television screen, and bluebirds, and the vultures wheeling over a long and empty combe called English Valley.

I arrived early at Ruth Marie's cabin, longing for a shower, to find the bathroom occupied by a strapping woman who divided her life between professional photography and working at a 'de-tox centre', which I understood to be something to do with drink, drugs, or both. She owned a pick-up and, accompanied by a cross-bred Keeshond called Cody, she spent her leisure time, such as it was, searching out subjects for photographs in the high country.

A Scot arrived: a kind of latter-day GI bride, fragile and lovely in a cotton jump suit. Looking like a child herself, she was accompanied by a son of six, a solemn and mature small niece, and mother-in-law from the wilds of New England. Then the *pièce de résistance* appeared, and Ruth Marie's eyes were on me. This had been the lure: five nuns, from different orders. They wore Levi's and western shirts. They wore no make-up but their hair had been cut by stylists, and all had the innocent confidence of young and cherished children despite their years of working among under-privileged people, mostly in Latin America.

The party went like a bomb. All the guests were environmentalists, and most were Peace people. They were not parochial but were unfamiliar with the European scene: unaware that Britain (which they had thought led the field in conservation) still put lead in petrol, and dumped toxic chemicals in the Irish Sea.

Their attention was flattering, their intentions impeccable. The party broke up at nine-thirty and Ruth Marie appeared to have no idea that it was anything out of the ordinary. I had attended innumerable ranchers' parties where conversation was anathema, where food was merely fuel and the entertainment was television. Ruth Marie's gathering had its roots in an older and more sophisticated culture.

Fortified, re-charged, next morning I drove round to attack the San Juans on their eastern front, following a creek called Carnero. I needed to look at Cochetopa Pass, and Carnero was a short-cut that also promised a diversion.

This was in the shape of Storm King, a mountain of eleven thousand feet which, in a land of proper nouns often dull or derivative, attracted me by its name. Hellgate was a case in point. Innumerable western canyons are guarded by 'hellgates' and one might, without recourse to a thesaurus, think of a dozen options: Charybdis, Scylla, Tawny Port ... The Hellgate of Carnero was a portal of columnar red basalt on one side, bulging overhangs on the other, that deserved a more distinguished name.

But Storm King, for all its suggestions of romance, had no presence. Hidden in trees, with no trail that I could discover, it must be approached on a compass bearing, although finding the summit was no exercise in navigation because the mountain was isolated. I climbed through the trees and when there was nothing higher, I was on the summit. This was the Wet Mountains over again, with the advantage that here there was no snow. We had come a long way since the Wet Mountains. Three days before midsummer, the snow-line was above eleven thousand feet.

Storm King was remarkable for little other than its mediocrity. Even the view was mostly the near hills smothered by timber, and only on the far horizon: beyond Monarch Pass to the north for instance, could one see peaks that might top fourteen thousand feet. Some small claim to interest (lying in wait for the unwary hiker) was a band of ragged rock that barred my passage on the descent.

I was coming down on a bearing when I was diverted by a bird with a beautiful song. I stalked it to a grassy shoulder (which struck me as an odd feature to find on what was otherwise steep ground) when I realized that this was the top of an escarpment which I had seen from the valley. I followed its lip, the grass giving way to timber and stony ground, which made for rough walking. The only way down was a line of weakness involving an overhang where I had to lower myself, not without first calling a warning to whoever might be in occupation of the cave below the overhang – but there was no occupant.

Next morning I crossed Carnero Pass and came down Houselog Creek, a wide, shallow valley, its sides topped by the familiar red scarps broken only by short gullies. This brought me to a valley where the features were repeated but on a larger scale: a hilly, grey-green sage country, brighter green in the bottoms from new grass and willows where, in places, meadows were covered with blue washes of iris. There were a few ranches, very far apart, and one was much aware of space. The road was almost empty of traffic and there was no development. The absence of dramatic scenery had saved these mountains from exploitation, but for how long? I wondered how women liked living on those isolated ranches. When they were middle-aged and the children had gone, would they sell the land and move to the sun belt? Then there would be no one to buy the land but the developers. Perhaps I was privileged to have seen the valley before the blight crept up the road to Cochetopa.

I left the state highway after a few miles and took a side road to the original Cochetopa Pass. This had been built as a toll road in 1869. Sixteen years before, it had been surveyed by Frémont on his fifth expedition.

We climbed to 10,032 feet and descended to Cochetopa Park: a wide and empty basin with no habitations, and so large that it dwarfed its own backdrop of mountains which resembled low and stylised waves. Then the basin fined down to a valley, the reservoirs started and fishermen appeared, then dude ranches. The country became more exciting so far as the scenery was concerned, but more crowded. The

West has taken to tourism as the Highland crofter took to Bed and Breakfast.

For two days I traversed new passes, drifted down cliff-shadowed canyons, lunched by blue water, slept in dark woods. I found that people tended to coalesce more than in England. In Colorado the majority of cabin owners sit tight at weekends or visit each other; few people explore the countryside or drive after dark. Once, exhausted, I slept beside the road and no one passed in fifteen hours.

We crossed Pinos Pass and Slumgullion, and came to Lake City: a tiny place whose dubious claim to fame is Dead Man's Gulch, the site of Alferd Packer's peculiar activities.

Packer was about thirty-two years old in 1874. An epileptic working in a lead smelter at Salt Lake City, he had frequent fits. Like many westerners of the time however, he was versatile and, although a shoemaker by trade, he was at different times soldier, prospector and guide. In November 1873 he contracted to lead a party of miners from Salt Lake City to the goldfields in Colorado.

That winter was exceptionally severe and the party lost most of their food when crossing a river, but they managed to reach an Indian camp where they recuperated. On February 9th, 1874, against all advice, Packer left with five of the original party to take a hazardous route through uninhabited country to Los Pinos Indian Agency.

The journey should have taken no more than two weeks. Fifty-five days later Packer came into the agency, looking plump and in possession of a considerable amount of money. He was alone. His story was that he had gone lame and his companions had left him. He thought that by this time they would have reappeared in civilisation.

Packer continued his own journey and reached the town of Saguache where he spent a lot of time and money in a saloon. Suspicion was aroused, there were threats of lynching, and under questioning he broke down and made a sworn statement.

He said that he had left the already starving party in order to climb a mountain and reconnoitre the route. After being away most of a day he returned to find one man at the camp fire roasting meat, and all the others hacked to death. The survivor – who had gone mad and was cooking human flesh – attacked Packer with an axe. Packer shot him in self-defence. He moved his camp some distance from the scene of the massacre and survived by feeding on the bodies until a crust formed on the snow when he managed to get out and reach the agency.

He guided a search party to the area but refused to approach the original camp. The searchers found that the victims had indeed been killed by an axe; one even had the fragments of a blanket driven into his skull. One man had been shot in the back.

The inquest brought in a verdict of murder against Packer, the presumption being that he killed his victims when they were asleep. He managed to escape from custody but was located nine years later in Wyoming, living under an assumed name. Brought back to Colorado he was tried for the murder of one man, Israel Swan. He was found guilty and sentenced to death by Judge M. B. Gerry at Lake City, to be 'hung by the neck until you are dead, dead, dead, and may God have mercy upon your soul!' Folklore has it that the repetition served as a safeguard against two failed attempts to hang a man.

Hearing the sentence, a drunken barman was to interpret it in terms which have become part of the Packer legend: 'The judge, he says, "Stand up y'voracious man-eating son of a bitch. Stand up.... There was seven democrats in Hinsdale County, and you've ate five of them, God damn you. I sentence you to be hanged by the neck until you is dead, dead, dead, as a warning against reducing the democrat population of the State. Packer, you Republican cannibal, I would sentence you to hell but the statutes forbid it."'

That trial was nullified on a technicality. Three years later he was tried again on charges of manslaughter relating to all the victims. He pleaded not guilty, but was found guilty and sentenced to forty years imprisonment of which he served fifteen.

By the time he was released in 1901 nostalgia for the Old West was rampant and he found himself a hero. He died in 1907. Since then Packer clubs have sprung up, Packer Massacres are re-enacted, Packer sandwiches devised. One of his biographers speculates that a combination of lead poisoning, convulsions and dreadful conditions may have resulted in automatism and Packer never knew what happened at Dead Man's Gulch. He confessed to cannibalism but until the end he always maintained that he was innocent of murder.

Cannibalism was not unknown in the West. In 1846 the people of the Donner wagon train, stranded by winter on the wrong side of the Sierras, ate their dead. It was said that a trapper would eat his squaw before he ate his horse, and there was Liver-Eating Johnson, the mountain man. ... I came away from Dead Man's Gulch pondering the taboo against eating people, and coming to the conclusion that, like sanctions against incest, it was well-founded. Once you start eating the bodies of people who have died naturally, it's only a short step to killing them in order to survive. There was a leading case in 1884 in the British courts ... but it must wait for its context: when Frémont's men were *in extremis*. The fourth expedition was not all that hungry as yet; they still had the mules, those which had survived the ordeals of Alder Creek.

Returning to the Rio Grande, I camped beside the river, preparatory to going to look at that San Luis Pass so confusingly termed Leroux, Williams or Del Norte.

I woke to the glorious morning of Midsummer's Day. Green humming birds whirred about the Jeep, even through it, attracted by bright colours (they would hover about my shoulders when I was walking, examining my shirt). By nine I knew it was going to be a hot day, and a hard climb. I had forgotten the altitude and the snow.

Willow Creek descends from San Luis pass, the stream squeezed in the bottom of a spectacular canyon above the old mining town of Creede. On the Forest Service map a Jeep road was marked to within a mile of the pass.

If the creek had to squeeze down the canyon, the road was in worse straits. It was not actually built on piers but it was overhung, not by rock, but by old mine workings. The drops below were hair-raising, the angle appalling. I had taken one look at the first gradient and engaged my lowest gear. Nothing appeared to be stable, and that included the mine chutes that depended above the road like Swords of Damocles threatening to disgorge hundreds of tons of ore released by the vibrations of our approach. There were great rock faces above and below; there was the roar of the creek in spate – for the mountains were still wreathed in snow. I opened both windows, and the roof; if we were to go over the edge, I wanted as many escape routes available as possible.

After two miles or so the gradient eased to relatively gentle slopes covered by firs and aspens. The sun shone, the birds sang – and notices warned of Heavy Truck Traffic Dead End. Not a happy selection of phrases, one might think, but it was Sunday and there was no traffic. The reason became clear when I reached locked gates beyond which marmots had taken possession of the Equity mine. Marmots ruled, whistling rudely at me as I tramped up a drifted trail that by-passed the mine workings.

The skyline dipped to a number of depressions and here and there were vestiges of paths between drifts and snowfields. From below and with a small-scale map, the pass could not be identified, and that made my work doubly interesting. I must walk the whole skyline in order to do the job properly. For a moment I allowed myself the familiar joy of knowing that this was the epitome of authorship: walking a ridge in the Rockies on a halcyon summer's day – but it was a momentary indulgence, and dangerous to prolong it. I was alone in big mountains and no matter that it was shirt-sleeve weather now, a night above ten thousand feet would be hellishly uncomfortable. I must watch my footing.

I guessed that the main pass was to my north so I took an easterly line and struck the remnants of an old trail which brought me to a saddle on the continental divide. It was at this point* that I realised that (if Stony Pass were excluded) the San Luis was the only pass the fourth expedition could have crossed that would bring them down to the Colorado River. This was obvious when one related the terrain to the map. I was lucky with the weather. It was not enough to get high to find out where you were, you must be high on a fine day, with good visibility and, ideally, warm, so that you might sit in comfort and survey the world.

From a rocky knob on the divide I could identify very few peaks – and how many maps would one have to carry to do so? There were distinctive features: Uncompahgre Peak about Lake City, Wolf Creek Pass to the south over which the highway ran to New Mexico. Close at hand was San Luis Peak on a spur of the divide, of little interest. I was amused: a fourteen-thousand-foot peak of little interest? But I was imbued with my subject and it was the pass and the trails that claimed my attention.

The first depression, the place where I came out on the ridge, must have carried a sheepherder's path originally; on the north side a faint line dropped steeply over screes. Another dip, about a mile to the west, would have been the main pass, with the more frequented trail, but neither was much used now. From the ridge it was obvious that sections of the main trail had been washed away. San Luis Pass was not popular but I liked it the better for that. It was wild and lonely, and I saw no other person from the time that I left the road until I returned in the evening.

It's possible that the mountains were quiet because the season had not yet begun and I was in the vanguard of the walkers, but I doubt

* See map, p. 32.

that. Throughout the summer, more often than not I had my peaks to myself; only when I went to fashionable mountains did I encounter parties and even then, if I were to extend my walk to the next mountain, a hundred yards beyond the first summit I was on my own. I gravitated to the lonely peaks and passes and on San Luis I had the best of all worlds: solitude and a rioting spring.

Every day I thought the flowers were at their best and every excursion above ten thousand feet surpassed the last. It was not only the alpines (superior in colour and mass to those of the Alps) – moss campion a foil to the vivid cushions of stemless forget-me-nots and phlox – there were large yet fragile columbines: lavender and white; there were alpine sunflowers and drift after drift of the purple sky pilot which is supposed to smell like skunks and even if it did, would be a herbal smell. There are worse smells than skunk.

I continued along the skyline to a high point where the main divide turned west and a ridge took off to the south. That was my way but before I descended I swept the panorama with the binoculars and in all that great expanse I could see no houses. I could not, or would not, identify with the fourth expedition, at least at this moment, not only because I was in the wrong place, but because I had no wish to identify with anyone at twelve thousand feet in the depths of winter. Summertime was another world.

How many people, I wondered, had stood in this place and looked at the same view before starting down, men who were part of a long pack train perhaps – or a solitary rider, leading one pack mule, and over a thousand miles from civilisation? Old Bill travelled alone and often came here. Like all the mountain men, Old Bill was a trapper: a trade that took its toll not only of beaver but of lions, bobcats, eagles; any animal that was caught by the foot to die in slow agony. Some would gnaw through their legs, or break them off as they froze on a cold night but a one-legged eagle or a three-legged lion would have no chance of survival, would die, starving and more slowly than in the trap. It was an obscene trade, but there was no question that the stamina and stoicism of those old mountain men, often travelling alone, was formidable.

San Luis was at twelve thousand feet and the pass had been clear of snow. In a state of euphoria I drove to Wolf Creek Pass and struggled to the summit ridge through a mile of wet snow and mire. There were magnificent hiking trails westward from the top but they were deeply drifted. I was at a similar altitude to San Luis. I concluded that the difference lay in the absence of trees on that pass and the open nature of the ground, whereas here a scatter of timber and a rocky ridge must be sufficient to hold big drifts. Drifting too could have resulted in heavier deposits of snow here; on San Luis there was no resistance to the blizzards, and the tops would always have been relatively clear.

I looked at the mountains: the San Juans, Stony Pass, the ghosts of the Sangre de Cristo across the valley of the Rio Grande. A walk from this spot would be a walk along the ridge-pole of the West. I filed it for future reference, and glissaded down the shadowed snow slopes to the Jeep.

There was no mail for me in Del Norte. I rented a room at a motel and dined in a restaurant where the décor ran the gamut from exquisite quilts to Mexican dolls glittering with Lurex, but there was no nasty air conditioning, and windows were open on the wide and almost empty street.

Next morning I collected some mail and, parked in the shade of a tree opposite the Post Office, I sat in the passenger seat and worked on my correspondence. I had already shopped for a week's food, had filled the water containers, fettled the Jeep and had my hair cut. I put the outgoing mail in the letter box, drove out of town westward, and turned up Embargo Creek bound for the high camps.

Seven

THE FOURTH EXPEDITION followed the Rio Grande for fifteen miles and turned north up Alder Creek. I went nine miles and turned at Embargo Creek because this was the way they had come down.

I had been looking up Embargo on my first day in the San Juans, when I walked round the skyline of Old Woman Creek. I remembered that bird's eye view when rock was indistinguishable from trees. Now I was part of the picture: an ant crawling up a dirt road through pinyon and juniper woodland to the narrows of a most spectacular canyon.

An isolated pinnacle rose above the trees and beyond it a line of crimson palisades repeated the pattern so characteristic of the San Juans: a depression – valley or canyon – the sides of which were crowned by long escarpments, although in this case just one side. The effect here was highly dramatic because nothing could be seen of the ground and the scarp reared like a great sea cliff fronting a bottle-green ocean of conifers. The rock: vertical, overhanging, fissured, was unstable. No one climbed here; it was a haunt of falcons and bats, of owls and snakes. It was a pristine wilderness and I adored it. I pitched the tent among yellow lupins on the bank of the stream and within two days that place was home.

Two of Frémont's camps were on a tributary of Embargo Creek: Christmas Camp, upstream and close to the headwall, and Camp Hope lower down. The highest camp of all, Camp Desolation, was a mile beyond Christmas Camp, over the headwall. That last mile was as the crow flew; I had no illusions as to how far I might have to travel in order to link the two. I had the relevant maps ($2\frac{1}{2}$ inches to the mile), I had copies of the journals; in Caryn and Peter Boddie's *The Hiker's Guide to Colorado* there was a description of a trail that promised to lead me right to 'Frémont's camps' – and I had thousands of words of notes. One camp was actually marked on the Forest Service map, but that map was half an inch to the mile and bore no contours. I had no illusions about that either. Frémont's camps would be found by my own efforts.

I wasn't a stranger to this kind of investigation. Finding the camps would be an exercise similar to determining the site of an accident in the days when I was collecting material for my book on search and rescue. Similar but not the same; most of the accidents I was concerned with then had occurred recently. In addition I knew the country, knew exactly what I was looking for, and if I needed more information, informants were usually available in the persons of survivors or members of the rescue party concerned. In comparison that research had been simple.

After I had pitched the tent, and with some five hours of daylight left, I set out on a reconnaissance. A hundred yards above my camp the Jeep road was barred by a locked gate, on the far side of which the trail was like a tank proving ground. An earth mover had been at work gouging the banks, pushing the aspens aside so that they leaned like drunken mannequins on the lower side, while some on the upper bank had fallen to block the road. Progress was arduous and I resolved that nothing would bring me this way again, even Frémont, less because of the difficulty of climbing over fallen trees than because of my anger that this was allowed even on private land. Title to land is no licence for destruction.

After two miles I came on a shoddy cabin in the process of construction from chipboard and felt. Caterpillar tracks led to a raw and ugly dam across a creek. Miserable, I wandered uphill and suddenly came on a trail, a proper trail, my trail, marked only by horses. Shortly it fined down further and there was a fork with a neat little wooden sign: 'Frémont's camp.'

I returned down the terrible road, hating it no less, but coldly. Fury sapped energy and inhibited concentration, and I would need both tomorrow, for work *and* personal safety. So I viewed the road dispassionately on the way home, and twelve hours later I ignored it. I carried a heavy pack and I walked fast, monitoring my body as if it were a machine, and the day proper began three miles out, at the little wooden sign pointing me along the path to the real start of the day's work, where I could relax and become human again.

The trail angled downhill to cross a stream after which for several miles, it followed a creek without a name. No country can become familiar until its features have names so I called it West Rincon Creek because Rincon was another headwater of Embargo, over the spur to the east. 'Rincon' is Spanish for 'corner'; in this context it was used for a recessed valley.

Trees on the route were lightly blazed but, anticipating that I would be returning late and in the gloom, I left twigs on the path marking salient points. The trail was poor, sometimes giving out completely where it twisted uphill or took a wide detour to avoid a fallen tree. Occasionally the ground was marked by old horse tracks but mostly the path was used just by deer and elk.

The day was warm and I was glad of shade, but this was a brief respite. Above eleven thousand feet the trees started to thin out, and I could see willow thickets below marking the course of the creek. The forest ended and I stepped out at the foot of a long meadow where another notice indicated 'Frémont's Camp' as if it were at that spot.

After a moment's consideration I dismissed the notice. I felt things could never be that easy, and I was pretty sure that this sign was in the wrong place. In any event I wasn't going to spend time here; the priority was to get high, to find the furthest camp and work back. Camp Desolation lay on the far side of the divide, Christmas Camp – and I looked up the meadow with the light behind me – Christmas Camp must be *there*, under the headwall. Camp Hope should be in the vicinity of this notice certainly, but lower down the creek because they had been stopped by a big buttress, and not a scrap of rock was visible from where I was standing.

I followed a faint line up the meadow and in the middle where the path crossed a dry patch surrounded by bog, another sign said 'Frémont's Camp.' This was ridiculous. They camped in the open, in *winter*? Where was the shelter, the fuel, dry ground and branches for beds? Less than half a mile away, at the head of the basin, there was a scatter of timber. If they camped in this meadow, they camped there. I would come down that way. At the moment I was taking the easiest line to the divide in order to avoid the big snowdrifts.

After a few hundred feet the slope eased and the ground was rocky, interspersed with stunted pines and – curiously – more willows. I came out on the divide at a cairn. It was of the same type as the one below Pool Table. I remembered my theory about the man from Sutherland, but I was better informed than I had been when I came on that first cairn. I had discovered that the tops were threaded by stockways (the British would call them drove roads) of indeterminate age, and Ruth Marie had told me that an old Mexican trade route came up one of the headwaters of Embargo heading for – where was it – Cochetopa, fifteen miles to the north? The builder of the beautiful cairns could have been a Celtic Highlander, but it is intriguing to recall that a Celt might trace his roots, be he Scottish, Welsh, Irish, Cornish or Breton, to Iberia. But so could a Mexican, in part – the Spanish part. I was amused, then another thought struck me. Why were there so few cairns? In good visibility they were not needed; if the cloud were down they were useless, set as they were at intervals of several hundred yards. Perhaps cairns could be used for purposes other than to mark a path in mist. These were built so well they might have been altars. They could be marking graves.

I was crossing a ridge so broad that for a while there was nothing to see but grass, then the cairns brought me to the lip of a big canyon running northwards. I sat on a rock. This must be Wannamaker, and somewhere within visible distance was Camp Desolation.

The Fourth stopped at twelve thousand feet and they camped in trees. Below my perch a bay of timber lapped up the mountainside while, further left, towards the head of the canyon, was another. The twelve-thousand-foot contour ran through the upper fringe of each bay, in fact the contour was the timber line. But the slope was extremely steep and no one had remarked on the angle. Benjamin Kern said that they half-erected the tent. There was nowhere on these slopes where I could have found a space level enough for my pup tent. Had I made a mistake and, in following the cairns, drifted off course and this was not Wannamaker? I looked for fixed points, places I could identify: Pool Table, San Luis Peak, Uncompahgre. It was impossible to relate the map to the terrain, and the only fixed point was the sun. The summit of Mesa Mountain should be to my north if I had followed the map correctly, but all I could see to the north were slopes rising so gently as to appear almost level. What would they look like on a winter's afternoon with the light failing? How hard did the blizzards drive across these scoured and stony wastes?

Panic stirred at the back of my mind. I pulled my wandering wits back from the unknown and terrifying view, from the canyon that could be a canyon in a nightmare, even from these slopes which might be a figment of my imagination. I contracted the world to the pin point of existence: I, and started from that point outwards. Here I was lost, so I would move and hope to find out where I was. Usually, in such a situation, I would go to the highest point to hand, so I stood up and looked north, but the summit was invisible (it was over two miles away, on a whale-back), and instinct said that Desolation Camp was in the opposite direction.

The sky was clouding over and I kept an eye on those clouds but I stayed high, utilising an old stockway occasionally, but taking short-cuts, treading solid snowfields, plunging through willows. I crossed a stream below a long drift like a glacier tongue and, zig-zagging up the slope beyond, I looked back to see a trail climbing a depression to disappear in the snow and behind, beyond the bays of timber where I had felt a *frisson* of panic: dropping into the canyon, stood a great lump of a mountain which I knew without doubt was Mesa. So this *was* Wannamaker Canyon and I had never been lost at all.

Grim now but open-minded, I turned to the slope, determined to find Pool Table and Bellows Creek. Bellows bounded Pool Table on the north; its head was just across the divide from the head of Wannamaker.

The cloud was thick now but still high. There was no sun. I came to level ground, but always the ridges were whale-backed so that you must go miles off your route to see anything that lay below. I descended to a saddle, expecting at any moment to see Pool Table on my left. A tiny sign – infuriating at any other time – pointed to *Trujillo* Creek. Bewildered, I didn't consult the map; that would have made the situation even more incomprehensible. I looked northward and saw showers advancing. I felt a little sick. I plodded on; if I was going to die on this bloody divide I would first find out where I was. Occasionally I lifted my eyes from my boots to stare hopelessly at the view and finally, almost at the top of the next mountain, I looked back – and there was Pool Table: lower than I, inconspicuous but familiar and at right angles to where I had been looking for it.

I was nearly at the top of Palmer Mesa. Without a glance at the summit I turned back to a place from which I could look across Wannamaker to those bays of timber that I found so puzzling. Then I studied the place on the divide where Godey must have emerged and halted, searching for a place to camp. He wouldn't have been able to see that steep timber, I thought, groping in my pack for Benjamin's journal. I knew it backwards but one could misinterpret a phrase. Even punctuation could be misleading, or the lack of it.

They had come up Middle Park and, close to where I encountered difficulty in descending Pool Table through the towers of petrified dust, they had reached a ridge. They had thought it led to the continental divide but, for all its height, it was a subsidiary ridge, the traverse of which would have brought them down to the east, the wrong side of Cochetopa Pass.

The crossing of this ridge, from Difficult Creek by way of Bellows to Wannamaker, I would walk in less than three hours in a few days' time. It took them three days. The snow was so deep that men had to be sent ahead to clear a road, compacting the snow with mauls. The resulting trench was sometimes eighteen feet deep between its walls. Where there was no wall and a mule stepped out of the track, the animal sank from sight and was abandoned. The surviving beasts were so hungry that they were eating their blankets and ropes, the pads of the pack saddles, even each other's manes and tails down to the flesh. The trail resembled that of an army in retreat, with harness, pack saddles and the carcasses of animals strewn along the way.

As the mules died they were butchered and eaten. At this point the men were suffering more from cold and exhaustion than from hunger. On the day that they made their first attempt to cross the divide and were beaten back by a blizzard, many had their faces, fingers and toes frost-bitten but, curiously, this was not third degree frostbite. No mention is made of anyone's losing fingers or toes, nor of gangrene, but the pain of those frozen parts thawed by the camp fire must have been excruciating.

'That old fool Bill lay down and wanted to die, just at the summit,' wrote Preuss. Bill Williams nearly froze to death on his mule that day. We remember that when he left Pueblo his arm was shattered by a bullet. The man was never fit, from beginning to end, which is why one assumes that it was Godey, not Old Bill, who was in the lead when they crossed the divide.

December 17th was comparatively mild and the wind had dropped so they made a second attempt to cross the ridge, men going ahead as before to break the trail. At 10 a.m. the animals followed. Benjamin Kern's mount was now loaded with mule-meat, which was too much for her failing strength. She stopped on the hill and the load had to be removed. She 'was unpacked and started loose ahead gave out half way up the hill – I reached her to encourage her – She stopt and trembled cries of go ahead we're freezing I gave her a slight push with my knees she fell over off the trail and died.'

They came over the hill and down the other side, the Wannamaker side, to camp in deep snow 'on the water shed of the Rio Colorado.'

In fact they were still on the east side of the continental divide, still lost, and unaware of it.

That evening the mules were driven up the ridge to a place where the wind had swept the slope clear and grass was showing, but when they reached the spot the snow was as deep as ever and the 'grass' was the tips of willow twigs. Most of the mules never moved from there or if they did, it was only a short distance in search of food. When the blizzards abated and the men came back to see if any had survived, they found trails leading to small holes in the snow which, wrote the veteran, Thomas Martin: 'showed their last resting place, perhaps fifty feet below.'

The worst blizzard started on the night of the 17th. One attempt was made to escape next morning by way of Wannamaker but, the storm increasing in force, the men returned to the camp, Camp Desolation, where they stayed until December 24th.

Benjamin did not move from that camp for seven days, and six of those he ran together in one entry: 'During these days of horror desolation despair and almost continued heavy winds intense cold and snow storms we lived in camp fluctuating between hope and despair....'

On December 20th an attempt was made to establish another camp, but the men were driven back by a fresh storm which was to continue all day. Someone counted the mules. Of the 130 with which they had started there were 59 left alive. Next day yet another attempt was made to escape and again it failed. That evening was clear but bitterly cold. They saw the sunset, saw too that all the country to the north was buried under snow.

It may have been that evening that Frémont decided to retreat for so he implies in his letter to Jessie from Taos: 'It was impossible to advance, and to turn back was equally impracticable ... I determined to recross the mountain more towards the open country, and haul or pack the baggage (by men) down to the Del Norte [the Rio Grande]....'

The retreat started on the 22nd with men packing baggage back over the ridge and establishing a new camp on the south or Rio Grande slope of the divide. They continued to move the equipment on the 23rd, and on Christmas Eve Camp Desolation was abandoned. The weather must have improved greatly by Christmas Day because Benjamin returned alone to the old camp and he had no difficulty at all with the snow or the conditions.

On Christmas afternoon Camp Desolation was a bleak and terrible place. A fire was still smouldering beside the remains of Frémont's riding mule which had furnished their last meal in Wannamaker. The only sign of life apart from Benjamin was a raven. He packed a few articles of equipment and hurried away, to rest at the top of the hill where the mules had been abandoned. Some were still alive but too weak to move. When he had rested Benjamin picked up his load and started along the ridge towards the new camp.

I walked down the south slope of Palmer Mesa in the direction of Wannamaker Creek where it emerged from the long drift like a glacier tongue. Beyond that were the groves of willow that I had forced my way through as I descended from Mesa. That must be the place where the mules were abandoned.

I stopped at the twelve-thousand-foot contour and looked down the canyon. My eye traced the imaginary contour past the steep bays of timber, round the headwall, across the creek, towards me. ... I veered left, dropping down the slope a fraction because twelve thousand feet seemed too high ... we would still be exposed to the wind, and the wind was rising, sweeping through the dead grass. Thunder rolled. The sky in the north was black. Desperately I searched Wannamaker and just below me, only a few hundred yards away, I saw the tips of tall trees, not climbing but massed. The trees were on a level with each other.

There was a shelf in that place, and several clumps of pines. 'We unpacked on a small point, and camped in the snow in a small pine wood to the left,' wrote Richard Kern.

There was the level ground, the shelter, the fuel, and there were the bleached stumps of trees cut off six feet or less above ground level ('camped in $4\frac{1}{2}$ feet of snow'). I picked up a lumbar vertebra: pitted, porous, very light ('polly [a mule] was brought into camp and nursed in hopes of saving her'). In utter hopelessness I looked around me. It had been misery to exist, said Benjamin, who had my compassion where others had my admiration or my pity. In the mornings, he went on, they had to scrape as much as eight inches of snow from their beds with saucepan lids, and their blankets froze to their hair. I was sick at heart for Benjamin who had survived all this but never reached California.

Thunder crashed as I turned the old bone in my hand and I looked up to see the summit of Mesa taking the brunt of the storm. I didn't care. I was not going to die today.

I climbed south out of Wannamaker, following Benjamin on Christmas afternoon, to stop by the willows where the mules waited for death with lack-lustre eyes. The thunder exploded and rolled up the canyon, rain curtains drifted languidly southward, someone sighed – a mule? Benjamin? The sun emerged fleetingly to floodlight statuesque pines against the purple storm.

I walked along the divide, feeling spots of rain, feeling the ground shake under the impact of the thunder. Instinctively I kept off the crest, but I was beyond fear. The storm satisfied me. To be in a position of danger absolved some of the survivor's guilt.

I didn't choose a way into the head of West Rincon Creek but came straight down the deep wet drifts where they had floundered. Below us more trees appeared (those I had noticed this morning) and I entered the grove and walked through the bare brown trunks, through a lifeless calm to the southeast corner, which would be sheltered from the bitter northerly wind, from blizzards yet to come, where there would be level places for thirty-four men to eat and sleep. I found the place and I looked around and there were the tall stumps of trees that had been cut for fuel 137 years ago. I had found the Christmas Camp.

When it was all over and most of the facts were known about the retreat from the San Juans, there would be controversy over the fact that the mules were left behind. This wasn't based on humanitarian considerations, but on the folly of leaving meat when the only food in abundance that Christmas was mule-meat. Godey, in defence of Frémont's action, was to point out that the dead mules were under twenty feet of snow. It was also thought that they had enough provisions for the short journey to the Rio Grande (which was only fifteen miles) and there they would find game. But the real reason they didn't slaughter the remaining animals for meat was that the men had all they could carry with the baggage: the equipment, scientific instruments, books. There was Frémont's personal trunk for instance, containing volumes of law by Blackstone. He intended to study law on reaching California but it is curious that he didn't send these weighty books round the Horn with his household goods and farm implements, doubly curious that they were not abandoned with the mules. There was so much gear to be transported that, without their pack animals, the men had to take it in relays from one camp to the next.

When Benjamin was returning loaded to the new camp on Christmas afternoon he met the gunsmith, Joseph Stepperfeldt, coming along the divide to pick up a load from Camp Desolation. How empty those high white wastes must have seemed that December afternoon with the light failing and just a solitary figure in the distance to prove that one was not the last person left alive in an inanimate world. After all, one might think, seeing that figure approach, only the pack animals had been lost. Conditions were such in the West that although losing pack and riding animals was a serious matter, it need not be deadly serious. Many of these men had been on foot for so long that walking a few more miles to the Rio Grande could be viewed as no more than a nuisance. Why, from the slopes above Christmas Camp they could *see* the Rio Grande. Such might have been their thoughts, in the euphoria of escaping the blizzards, at least for a day or two. It was I, on the slopes above the mile-long meadow, seeing the linear smudge of the cottonwoods that marked the river, I who remembered that this meadow and the whole of Embargo Creek would have been deep in snow, as would all that timber that shortly they would have to negotiate. From Christmas Camp I could walk to the Rio Grande in four hours. They took eighteen days.

If there were differences of opinion concerning the outward route, once Frémont gave the order to retreat he was in control, and although he made mistakes his orders were accepted. He left food behind in the shape of mule-meat, and energy was expended on salvaging equipment, but he did appreciate the dangers of their situation. They were about 130 miles from the nearest settlement, at Red River (now called Questa); they were 150 miles from Taos. He knew game was scarce even on the Rio Grande; he knew some of the men were very weak. It takes a good leader to diagnose the condition of his followers. Frémont was extremely fit, as were Godey, Preuss and one or two of the others. But the bulk of the men were now faced with a double, even triple descent of Embargo as they relayed the equipment to the river. Frémont needed pack animals and more food so he selected four men to go ahead, fast and unencumbered, to procure mules and provisions at the settlements and return, meeting the rest of the expedition on the Rio Grande. He reckoned that they would be back within sixteen days.

Bill Williams was with this party but not in charge. Frémont appointed Henry King as leader. King had been on the third expedition and had fought as a captain in the Mexican War; no doubt it was on the latter grounds that Frémont thought him better fitted to lead than

Old Bill. Tom Breckenridge and Frederick Creutzfeldt were the other members: the Missouri frontiersman, also a veteran of the third expedition and the Mexican War, and the botanist who had never been with Frémont before. This party left on December 26th carrying light loads: one blanket each, some mule-meat, macaroni, a pound of sugar and a few candles. They were armed with rifles and a shot gun.

Breckenridge says that before they left he asked Frémont to take care of $1,200 in Spanish doubloons and that, if he should die, to send it to his father in St Louis. Frémont told him: 'If anything should occur, and it is lost, I will see that the loss is made good to you.' Breckenridge goes on to say that Frémont left the sack of gold behind at one of the camps, and he was never reimbursed. No one else makes any reference to this gold although Preuss does say that King was 'furnished with $1,800 in gold.' This would seem reasonable because King would need money for the mules and provisions, but the 'Spanish doubloons' lie in a corner that will always remain murky, lit only by the small light of Breckenridge's reminiscence.

When King's party left on December 26th Godey went part of the way with them reconnoitring the trail. People were very busy this day; loads were being brought into Christmas Camp and then ferried down the long meadow. They built a sledge but, in Preuss's words, it 'came to grief'. They were unable to make snowshoes. They had nothing to make them with. (In 1846, when the first big snowfall of the winter stranded the emigrant train led by George Donner a few days' journey from the crest of the Sierras, their first relief party got out on snowshoes made from ox bows, which are the loop-shaped collars of wood that depend from the yoke across the oxens' necks. It was members of the Donner party, including a number of children, who survived by eating the bodies of their companions.)

The night after Christmas (when they had gorged on mule-meat) Benjamin was taken ill with severe vomiting and was too weak to carry his own gear to the next camp on December 26th. He rested, and recorded a fine view of the Rio Grande and the mountains beyond. The weather was now so mild that there was a slight thaw. On the 28th everyone moved downhill, Godey going ahead to find the best route, and returning to report that they should not follow the creek; they must go over a spur in order to escape the narrows of a canyon. They camped by the running creek, in aspens. Supper was mule-meat sprinkled with corn meal. This was Camp Hope.

One might almost have thought that, with the running water, wood for fuel – aspens now, so light and airy in contrast with the grim conifers – nothing said of blizzards or cold, and next morning: 'a fine warm day', that it was metaphorically as well as literally all downhill – except for that tiresome spur to toil over.

Never again would they have such terrible weather as they'd had before Christmas, nor would they have to fight their way upwards through canyons choked by snow and timber as Alder Creek had been choked. But they were in retreat and the fire went out of them. Listless, without the splendid goal ahead, no longer members of a glorious expedition led by a charismatic leader, they were flotsam. And their plight was recognised: Frémont had sent out a rescue party, or one that should implement a rescue. Before, they were surviving by their own efforts; now they relinquished responsibility. Their survival depended on the rescue party and their only hope was that it would arrive in time. Not all of them felt this way but many did. The descent of Embargo Creek was a winnowing.

Godey never succumbed to depression. He must have been an inspiration over that fifteen-mile stretch, going ahead to find the route, casting about like a hound dog looking for the line, retracing his steps to divert them this way or that. It would be Godey who found the camps but not Godey who found the game. There was none. When the mule-meat ran out they went hungry.

Micajah McGehee remembered the journey for the dreadful conditions and the exhaustion of the men rather than their state of mind. They were slow: 'on an average, at our best, scarcely making a mile a day, for wading through the deep snow was very laborious. It would bear us up for two or three steps with our load but, at the next step, we would break through and go in waist deep when we would have to scramble out the best way we could, and try again … our labor became very exhausting, for we were now on short allowance, and our starvation also ill fitted us to endure the cold.'

Richard, the middle Kern brother, was at first unaffected by these conditions. In his short diary entries the days are 'pleasant', 'warm', 'beautiful' from the 26th December (29th: 'warm and sunny with birds singing. Mule soup') until New Year's Day. On New Year's Eve the day was 'pleasant with occasional summery clouds'. He mentioned the load carrying but didn't deplore the additional strain. Richard was an ebullient young man and he gives no hint that he suffered or was depressed during these days that so sapped the strength of his companions.

80

On the other hand Edward, the youngest of the Kerns, writing to Antoine Robidoux, the trader, on February 11th, 1849, from Taos, had darker memories. The descent had been 'a severe undertaking in the cold, and no positive hopes ahead of reaching any place, even should we have been able to get out our effects. By hard labor we worked our way gradually down.'

It was Edward who was the object of his brother Benjamin's one reference to dejection before they reached the river. It was on January 3rd, ferrying loads, that Edward gave out 'being weak and dispirited'. Benjamin must have turned back for another load because when he reached that night's camp he found Edward 'sitting in gloom by the fire dug up our provisions smoked pipe eat supper cheer Ned [Edward]. . . .'

Apart from this entry the men who kept journals (Preuss and the Kerns) or wrote letters and accounts, don't mention depression. Only Frémont, writing to Jessie, speaks of 'men so soon discouraged by misfortune'. Was he projecting his own fears or was he referring to that section of the company who left no record of their thoughts? Probably it was something of both; he carried a heavy responsibility in the task of getting his party out of that wilderness and there must have been occasions when he doubted his ability to do it. It's to his credit that he never showed it at the time.

Nor did anyone else, at least as far as the Rio Grande. Their differences lay in their physical strength. Richard Kern seems not to have noticed anything extraordinary in the descent, Edward had only one afternoon and a night of despondency; Benjamin had energy to spare at the end of the day to try to rally his youngest brother's spirits. But up and down Embargo Creek, other men who left no written records were killing themselves as they did the work of draught animals carrying and dragging loads through the snow.

Eight

As I came down from the Christmas Camp on that June day I felt nothing. I was drained of emotion. For hours I had been searching for Desolation Camp; even physically it had been tiring, in particular working my way through those willow thickets. And to add to the constant strain attendant on being alone on big mountains was the threat of bad weather.

When I found the camp above Wannamaker relief was counterbalanced by a merging of attitudes, behaviour, minds. Until that point the day was a matter of converging lines, but in the pine grove above Wannamaker the lines came together to run a course that was not the same but similar, one shadowing the other. The traveller who descended the long meadow remembered the horrors of Alder Creek and the abandoned mules, but she also had knowledge of the horrors to come, and refused to contemplate them. Late in the afternoon, any afternoon, winter or summer, eight miles from camp, fifteen miles from a road, the solitary voyager has no wish to be reminded of mortality.

At the lower end of the meadow, by the sign that said 'Frémont's Camp' I gave myself half an hour, until five, to find that site, the site of Camp Hope. Now I had to discover the steep ground that forced them to abandon West Rincon, when they had to climb the spur to the east and descend into the main canyon of Embargo. 'We came towards the Cañon where it was so steep one fell down very often,' wrote Benjamin. The valleys only appear to be wide and open; once you are down in them, you find the precipices among the timber.

I worked through the ubiquitous willows to the far bank of West Rincon and followed game trails downstream between the timber and the water. After a quarter of an hour the ground became steep and stony. The crag had to be close at hand, but it would be a one-sided canyon; on the far bank there was only timber, with my trail of the morning running through it.

They had camped at a point close to where the buttress halted further progress, and before they turned to scale the spur. I looked for stumps. There were some but they were too old for me to tell if they had been cut by an axe. One log was charred; would a camp fire char that deep or was it the result of a lightning strike?

My time had expired. I went back to the meadow and started down the trail. The forest was in deep gloom but after I had gone some distance a sunlit buttress showed through the trunks on the other side of the creek. Having verified its existence I turned to concentrate on my own route. In the same way that climbers are vulnerable when they take off the rope, walkers will lose the way as they come down the trail at the end of the day. I knew I was going to make mistakes, and I did, usually where timber lay across the path and I had to make wide detours. Lost, I would go back to the fallen tree and start again. I didn't make mistakes at the places that I had marked with twigs arranged as arrows on the ground. I would approach these with surprise, recognising my own handiwork, and I would focus on my surroundings with such intensity that these were places where I was least likely to make a mistake.

I returned to the glade without incident, and the Jeep had the air of a patient and waiting animal. Vehicles always have this appearance after the owner has had a day on the hill. You may be halfway up a cliff, bringing up your second man, and you look across space to a speck at the trail-head, or you climb a dune and see a glitter miles away in the sage – and the reason why you have always pretended that this object was animate is obvious. Something is waiting for you. It cannot love but it reflects love. That evening, parked by the tent among the yellow lupins, the Jeep was home.

Next day I spent in camp studying journals, letters and maps: correlating what they had written and I had done. In the intervals between work I performed domestic chores, my every movement observed and sometimes commented on by squirrels who must have had a drey close to where I drew water from the creek. I knew they were a pair because, while one would berate me every time I passed a particular tree, the other would spiral up the trunk fast as dark light, and as silent. The tirades of its mate made me jump but I continued about my business smoothly, and after a day or two I was accepted as just another big but harmless animal, like the deer.

I was grateful for trees in the bottom of the canyon. During the day off, I was driven into the shade after breakfast but I left the thermometer in the sun, and the mercury climbed to 114°. In the afternoon clouds came over, making me wonder if an afternoon storm were the norm in summer time. The thermometer dropped to 90° and the atmosphere seemed delightfully cool. But winter ruled in my mind. I was back in the last century, reading Ben Kern. No wonder he omitted words and nearly all his punctuation; the wonder is that he wrote as well as he did, that he kept a journal at all. Half the time his hands must have been frozen.

Next day I took the trail up Embargo Creek. An old route, often giving out altogether, it could well have been the Mexican trade route that was in use before Colorado was ceded to the United States. (After that an embargo was placed on this transmontane trade, hence the name of the creek.) The only recent tracks were those of elk and deer and some large carnivore, probably a bear. Within a mile I came on a beaver pond and lodge. The animals had felled immense trees, some three feet in diameter; the site looked like a development project. It was curious to think that ancestors of these beavers could have blocked Frémont's trail when he came past. At some point the Fourth had come to Embargo from Camp Hope and Rincon. I would try to discover that point when I returned this evening. At the moment I was heading for Mesa, hoping for a fresh angle on the high camps.

There were no bridges in this canyon; I crossed the creeks by way of saplings or fallen trees: flimsy or wet with spray but adequate providing one were careful. I was gaining height all the time however, and the creeks shrank accordingly until they could be leaped. Now the trail went through thinning conifers, and willows sometimes ten feet tall. The footing was greasy chunks of rock.

At last I emerged from the brush to a meadow where a herd of elk was feeding. Some had young and they were mostly cows; so since they were grazing across my projected route I gave them a wide berth. It was not wide enough for one mother who must have dropped her calf in the meadow. Even when I diverged so far as to be walking away from Mesa, she was still loping back and forth in front of me, emulating a plover with a broken wing, but with less sense than a plover who knows she has only to draw you away a few yards and the chicks are safe. All the time the disturbed herd milled and watched from a distance, their high-pitched squeals of warning to the calves driving me frantic, as they were designed to do. I crossed another of their grazing grounds and picked up their flies, and I cursed all elk.

I toiled up Mesa wondering why my legs were tired, forgetting that Mesa is nearly thirteen thousand feet and that my camp was at 9,500.

The summit was so flat that it looked and felt like a mile square: more like a table than Pool Table, or any Cairngorm.

I moved across the plateau (the old cairns were here too) and I came to one tall stone man on the lip of a canyon called Bear, and knew that I had reached the summit. The sun had gone behind clouds. It was noon; this must be the afternoon storm building up. There had been high cirrus at dawn and that had deteriorated to a milky haze with a halo round the sun. A shower was falling on Wolf Creek Pass. Three miles away, across Wannamaker, the grove on the site of Camp Desolation looked blandly innocent.

It was now that I realised how easy it would be, on Mesa Mountain, to turn round and not know which way one were facing. Constantly I checked fixed points: Pool Table, Wolf Creek Pass, Palmer Mesa. I thought of the cloud dropping, of rain, hail, snow, and I shuddered.

As I started down there was a storm on a peak on the far side of the Rio Grande. A warm air stream was fighting a cold front from the north. I hoped I could reach the forest before the rain came. It is difficult to navigate in trees but today I had the creeks for bearings, and timber is shelter. As long as you have matches you can survive. I remembered then the nights on alpine peaks, in the Highlands, in winter, waiting for the dawn without any more warmth than my clothing. I had lost my sense of proportion.

The elk had left Embargo's high basin and it was empty but for the whistling marmots. The threatened storm didn't materialise and I forgot weather in the confinement of the forested canyon, in my attempts to find the route of the Fourth in a place where there was no trail and never had been. Somehow they reached Embargo from Camp Hope: over two spurs and the main Rincon Creek; they pushed up, were forced up, by that stratum of red rock which cropped out in precipices like Cathedral Crag and the palisades above my camp, in the buttress below Camp Hope and, no doubt, in rough crags every-where on the same level but obscured by trees.

This passage, of less than two miles, took Benjamin two days. As McGehee wrote, a mile a day was the average, and everyone was covering the same ground at least three times, going back to the last camp for second loads. There was no concerted movement downhill.

At eight in the morning of December 30th Benjamin started over the first spur carrying a pack, but he gave out a quarter of a mile from the next camp (he must have met someone returning for a load) and he crawled back to the last on his hands and knees. Supper was meat from his own riding mule. The weather that day was fine and warm ('sun burnt very much'): a mixed blessing, progress through the softened snow would have been even more strenuous.

The following day, New Year's Eve, was mild but overcast with a little snow in the late afternoon. Feeling much stronger, in the company of his brothers, Captain Cathcart and two of the Indian boys, Benjamin camped on Embargo Creek, two of the brothers having dragged a bale weighing two hundred pounds into camp. At that place – which must have been close to where I pitched my tent – they passed the crimson palisades: 'fine large rocks,' said Benjamin, 'standing perpendicular along the sides of the Canon – Snow here not more than 2 ft deep quite rejoicing these as all the other messes [parties] about 3 miles ahead so that we have quite a feeling of novel loneliness –'

Next day the Kerns continued towards the main valley, but the country was cut up by creeks, and between water courses it was hilly. Again Benjamin talks of crawling uphill on hands and knees. With the aid of homemade harness the brothers pulled great packs behind them. Six inches of snow fell in the night of January 1st and it continued to snow throughout the next day. The Kern party went back to bring down loads which had been left upstream.

On January 3rd the Kerns made a selection of the more valuable of their possessions, and burned their books. That night Raphael Proue, a veteran of Frémont's earlier expeditions, came in to the Kern fire: 'a weakly and melancholy object'. Benjamin doesn't say where he came from and by this time no one was interested. They were concerned only with shelter and food. It was the night of Proue's arrival that Edward Kern was so sunk in gloom: a fine cold moonlit night. Benjamin had a good bed from which he saw several mice: 'Looked at them with a hungry eye long for a mouse trap.'

Throughout the first week of January the more able men in this rear party struggled up and down the middle reaches of Embargo, ferrying loads, increasingly fatigued and always hungry. There were more snowstorms but as they continued to make progress towards the Rio Grande they began to meet other members of the expedition returning for abandoned equipment.

On January 6th Benjamin wrote: 'Waked at 4 a.m. Preux who camped with us had made a fire looked out and found the snow falling rapidly at day day [*sic*, i.e., dawn] 5 inches Snowed and blowed till one o clock employed all day in sewing – Men passed on with loads & camped one mile below us. Col [Frémont] camped on the river Jan

2nd Saw several snow birds. Ned shot at one in hopes of having something to eat – Hibbard came along about 3 o clock with some goats meat* which he killed yesterday a very welcome addition to our provision No news from below Dick blowed his flute a little to cheer us up washed my feet hands & face shirted[?]

JAN 7th'

Benjamin's diary ends there. It was never resumed. The Kern party, going backwards and forwards relaying equipment, had taken ten days to advance eight miles.

I left the brothers burning their books. My own provisions were running low; I had plenty of tinned food but oil for the lamp was in short supply. At latitude 37°, even at midsummer the nights were too long for me to spend all the hours of darkness in bed. So I worked late, and for that I must have light. The fuel was nearly finished – and I was dirty. I bathed and washed my clothes in the creek but after a week my hair was so matted with sweat and dirt and insect repellent that I could no longer comb it. I would not immerse my head in those icy streams and I couldn't use a shampoo. Any form of soap is taboo in the wilderness; clothes were washed by leaving them in fast-running water, weighted with stones.

I was forced back to civilisation then by health hazards, or so I rationalised. Basically I needed to be with my own kind. However self-sufficient a traveller may be, there is something aberrant if he prefers his own company to that of his fellows all the time. Man is a social animal.

On a Sunday afternoon the mountains brooded in the shadow of drifting showers but Del Norte sprawled in the sunshine. The museum was new, airy, spacious: purpose-built for items displayed as only Americans can display them. There was a gorgeous patchwork quilt over a hundred years old, a square grand piano which had come round the Horn, a buckskin tunic all beaded and fringed that looked as if its owner had reserved it for gala occasions. There were agates and arrowheads, and dresses which had been handed down for generations. The curator was a Yale man who, with his wife, ran the local antiques shop, the one with the good pieces in the window. This, the Golden Fleece, was on the main street. The Allisons owned most of the block:

* Probably antelope.

87

an early twentieth century hodge-podge on two floors where a plan was needed in order to find your way about.

Mark Allison was tall, thin, bespectacled, balding. He carried me off from the museum and installed me in his guest room complete with four-poster bed and a Victorian shower bath. The apartment was above the shop and everything in it looked as if it had been selected for its intrinsic beauty or rarity, and everything fitted, nothing clashed. Furniture, furnishings, *bric à brac,* pictures, rugs, beds – all were pleasing in their own right, and all made a design for gracious living that was a world away from glossy magazines and Sunday supplements.

Interest didn't stop at the doors of the apartment (doors from Old Mexico). Extending over most of the block, the first floor was a maze of passages and rooms and lofts, the passages crammed with pictures and looking glasses – and flats from a theatre. Above a restaurant (once run by the Allisons, now leased out) was a former Masonic temple (with the original turn-of-the-century wallpaper) where the local repertory company had staged *Guys and Dolls,* their first and only production. The auditorium, now thick with dust, housed gymnasium equipment and the relics of Mark's flirtation with picture framing. Someone had left a Navajo hat on the stage.

Another huge room was filled with antiques that couldn't be accommodated in the shop, and somewhere in this intriguing caravanserai was a bright study lit by a skylight, permitting no distractions. No street was visible, no people or lovely alluring mountains. That study was the place in this luxurious warren that I coveted most. But it was Mark's study, and Mark had literary aspirations, and one's study is sacrosanct; I was put to work in a loft and my working surface was a glass-cutting table.

The proofs of the jacket of *Snare* arrived – my latest crime novel – and the artist had interpreted my own rough sketch as if he had read my mind. Framed in the copper wire of the snare was a moonlit loch, and the words 'A Miss Pink Mystery' were in crushed rose on funereal black. The Allisons and I celebrated appropriately with a California *rosé* called Blush.

Next day, euphoric but somewhat hung over, I said goodbye and set off for another marathon in the high country. I was expecting nothing at the Post Office but I called there out of a sense of duty and was handed the proofs of *Snare* itself and a request to correct and mail them back as soon as possible.

Back at the Golden Fleece Greta Allison soothed my panic and summoned Mark, who came galloping across the main street from the museum with his retinue of Old English sheepdogs, swept the glass-cutting table clear and told me to treat the Fleece as home for as long as I wanted. He vanished and, in a sudden vacuum of silence, in a small town in Colorado, I composed myself to read the proofs of a novel set in the far north of Scotland.

The experience could be alienating but, like an old homicide detective coming home to his family after a day of violence and squalor, I had learned to compartmentalise. Working on two, and sometimes three books at the same time: different countries, different seasons, different sets of people, not to mention different crimes, I would leave one world abruptly, pause, listen to an opera, have an evening with friends: eat, drink, talk, all the time allowing the new subject, inviting it, to infiltrate my mind. That morning with *Snare* I had none of these aids. A few hours ago I was in two feet of snow on Embargo Creek with Benjamin; now, emerging like a developing print on the paper of my mind, was a crofting community at the end of the road on a sea loch in Sutherland. I sat there at the glass-cutting table and let it come.

My birthday came and went unnoticed but when the proofs had been mailed to London, in a burst of rebellion I drove out across the valley, back to the Sangre de Cristo: that lovely range which had been part of my life for six weeks (although recently only background) and where I had never reached a summit.

I had no map other than the small-scale Forest map and on this I discovered a loop trail which went close enough to two mountains that I should be able to reach the top of one of them. Since there were no contour lines and the altitude of few peaks was given, the walk was something of an unknown quantity. I did know that Comanche Peak was over thirteen thousand feet, and that since I camped below seven thousand I would have a rise of six thousand feet, at least. This wouldn't be strenuous in Britain but here heat was a factor – and the possibility of my legs turning to rubber as they had on Mesa. That I could deal with; the heat could be dangerous.

So I left my camp at seven o'clock while the canyon was still in shadow and it was cool enough for me to be grateful for the warmth of a jersey. For several miles the trail followed the line of the creek through aspens and conifers, and then it split. I could see one variant, or rather its destination; trails were invisible in the bottoms where

89

timber was thick as in an Exmoor combe. The variant went up a long glen to a cirque below ridges fretted with pinnacles. It was a far cry from Mesa Mountain.

My route went left to Venable Pass, while between the two a third trail came down from Comanche Peak: the route of descent if I could complete the loop.

In starting early I had avoided the heat and now, although I had to remove my jersey, the air was quite cool – and it needed to be: soon I reached the timber line and there was no more shade. There was a depression called Groundhog Basin, a place of willows and little patches of grass where a big green gentian grew, and a magnificent thistle with a downy head that was so heavy the blooms bent double as they reached maturity. The basin was a mass of scrub through which the trail ran purposefully, hedged by the willows. I was on the headwall before I discovered that there was a tarn hidden in that jungle.

I reached Venable Pass at eleven. It was not a razor's edge but you could look down both sides at once. On the east the trail descended to the Venable Lakes, and beyond them, over five thousand feet below, was the Wet Mountain valley which I had left so long ago that it seemed to be in another age. And there was the Wet Range with Curley Peak and Rudolph, familiar mountains because I'd been on them, and *there* was the gap of Hardscrabble Canyon where the snow had lain so deep in 1848.

The snow here, in the summer of 1987, was confined to northern and eastern slopes, and the only contact I had with it was one old hard drift above the Venable Lakes where I must lose height to turn Venable Peak.

I was working south now, but the peak straddled the crest of the Sangre de Cristo and it was just a stony plod to the summit whereas if I turned it on its eastern flank I would come to something called the Phantom Terrace. That sounded interesting so I cut my way diagonally across the big drift, came on the trail again, traversed round and up, and saw ahead a broken wall with a terrace that was reminiscent of the Dolomites. There was rock on one side, exposure on the other, even a mild *mauvais pas* where the soil had eroded. Everywhere there were flowers: columbine, saxifrages, moss campion. The terrace was a walk, not a climb, but had you given all your attention to the plants, you could have walked over the edge and fallen several hundred feet.

The trail, which threaded the tops like the dance called Shepherds'

Hey, returned to the crest and passed over it to contour an unnamed peak on its western slope. There had been cloud over the Wets and now the odd wisp materialised above the Sangre de Cristo, but I could take bad weather on this kind of mountain where the way was clear. These were like alpine peaks without the glaciers. I might have been uneasy had it been late in the day but I had calculated on thirteen hours of daylight. One-thirty was the halfway mark.

I reached the next pass at noon, and Comanche Peak stood a few hundred feet above me. The col was a sharp crest, and a cold wind forced me to take shelter in a kind of ditch between the remains of a cornice and the top of the divide.

As I ate my lunch five people came up from the east, leading horses. We waved to each other and after a while I left my pack and trotted up Comanche remembering only as I approached the summit that I was well above thirteen thousand feet. My legs were going fine today, and here we were at the top. From below the horsemen sent up a cheer. I thought wryly of my active seniors in the Alpine Club and felt no cause for congratulation, but plenty for pleasure. I had filled a gap.

Below me was that Comanche Lake which I had tried to reach at the beginning of June, when I was turned back by hard drifts. There was no sign of snow in the corrie now. And there was no wind on the summit; I stayed there for some time watching the riders retreat, edging their mounts down the exposed trail, for once in my life not wanting to be on the back of a horse. There were always horses, but I would never again sit on Comanche Peak on a day spared from work and the rigours of the San Juans. It wasn't merely where I was, but why I was there, and what I would be returning to – the whole ambience; this was the importance of the day.

On my return from the Sangre de Cristo I went to look at the little town of Moffat, in the middle of the valley, but it paled in contrast with its namesake in Scotland where, in a nearby burn, Dr Buck Ruxton threw packages in the 1920s wrapped in an edition of a Lancashire paper distributed only in Lancaster. That oversight contributed to his being hanged, for the packages contained the remains of his wife and maid whom he had dismembered in his bath. Moffat, Colorado, could never compete with that.

It was trying to rain when I went back to the San Juans and I stopped and turned the Jeep to see grey veils of gauze hanging in the north

91

with pale mountains behind, like a stage but only weakly lit. The same faint light washed the mountains I had just left, which were clear of cloud and two-dimensional, without shadows. Comanche Peak looked small but friendly (the main peaks of the range are over fourteen thousand feet). I sat there in the middle of the valley, listening to Alfredo pour out his passion for Violetta – *Oh, quanto v'amo!* – wishing that I had been an opera singer. Sighing, I turned west again and headed towards Mesa Mountain which was still marked by its long snow wreath. Why did Frémont choose to get lost there, among those dull little hills?

As I drew nearer and the tall ghosts of the Sangre de Cristo sank in the mirrors, and the San Juans loomed ahead, I remembered the sweep of the plateau, the whale-backed divide: featureless, without shelter, and in the warm glow of the westering sun I was cold. I wanted to go home: back to the Sangre de Cristo, to proper alpine mountains where I knew I was safe.

Nine

HIGH SUMMER CAME to the San Juans. On Friday nights people flocked to the canyon campgrounds, and serenity was shattered by motor bikes on trails, by drunk drivers, by ghetto blasters, by gunfire. Hunting (that is, shooting) would not begin legally until the autumn but any time was open season for coyotes, and there were poachers everywhere.

Many people carried firearms for self-defence, with a disregard for the rules that would have appalled a sportsman. Guns were carried loaded, with a round in the chamber; they were kept loaded in vehicles, in houses where there were children, but then there was a casual attitude towards children anyway as if, like pets, they were appendages. Like the loose dogs, they explored unattended, climbing into vehicles, begging for candy. Every year children disappeared from campgrounds; that summer there was a poster exhibited throughout the southwest asking for information concerning a small girl who had vanished recently from a camp in California.

Some camps were worse than others, as if people gravitated with prior knowledge while others kept away. If there was one woman with black eyes in a camp you could be pretty sure you would see others. And where, in Britain, one would be wary at the approach of a man when one was talking to a woman with a bruised face, in the West compassion was superseded by revulsion. The men were charming.

I started to work a five-day week, coming in to Del Norte and the Golden Fleece at weekends, where life was urbane and civilised. On Monday I would go out again to camp high, climbing new mountains, exploring new canyons, or stretches of old canyons where I had not been. I was tidying loose ends. The Fourth were struggling down Embargo to the Rio Grande and I was cleaning up behind them, preparatory to leaving the San Juans.

I needed to see more of Alder Creek. When I had ascended Alder and been forced to leave it at the narrows, there had been no trail and the day was strenuous, but there was a trail running *down* the canyon as far as the narrows. I had passed the start of it several times and

93

thought it tempting. As the summer wore on and I planned one more sweep of the area around Pool Table, I pitched my tent at the head of Alder in a glade about a mile from the road. I had reached the glade by creeping across the meadows and through the forest, following an old loggers' way that died eventually in a mass of secondary growth. There were fresh tracks of bear about. A bear could be dangerous; they can wreak expensive damage on a vehicle, ripping out doors to reach food. Their sense of smell is acute. There was no way I could eliminate cooking smells and, when water was scarce and supper dishes could not be washed until breakfast time, there were many occasions when, even with the dirty pans in the back of the Jeep, I went to bed with the ice axe *and* a hunting knife beside me.

The upper canyon of Alder Creek was hot, and flooded by beavers' pools. The trail was often water-logged and I crossed the streams by way of dams. The bottoms were a lush and colourful jungle of monkshood and mimulus, and a tall ivory lily called the wand lily. There were snakes everywhere: the slim shy garter snakes with bright lateral stripes in yellow or orange. Around noon I found a pool where I bathed and washed my clothes, sitting on a rock surrounded by water where the ants couldn't reach me while I waited for my washing to dry.

Above the narrows the trail angled uphill away from the creek and within a mile it came out on the forest road. I turned, retraced my steps and somewhere here I was on Frémont's trail again. (I had been on it for part of the morning, but coming downhill when he was going up.) The Fourth had their problems with the snow, but my problem this day was felled timber. Where the beavers had been busy the ground looked as if an incompetent logging crew had been at work.

I returned by a slightly different line from that of the descent, although the beavers' operations involved so many diversions that no route could have been retraced. As soon as I came on a few yards of clear track, I would see more raw yellow stumps ahead. There was an odd smell associated with the felled aspens: a green, sappy scent that carried a long way on the stagnant air.

The afternoon grew hotter, the air heavier, the ground more stony, holding and reflecting the day's heat. I made a kepi from my shirt to protect the back of my neck but I was walking unsteadily, occasionally stumbling. I was close to heat exhaustion. I slowed down mentally as well as physically, concentrating on not falling, thinking only of the priorities: the visible trail and the next step.

I stopped at the mouth of Difficult Creek and even the formula that *they* had it worse could not persuade me to follow them. An ascent of Difficult would extend my route by another mile of canyon with no trail, not to speak of two or three miles of rutted road across the great parks: Corral, Pool Table, Deer Park. Flies had accompanied me out of the woods and their continuous attentions made me feel sick. I continued up the main line of Alder Creek.

On a scree slope close to the last meadow pika shrilled at me and, standing still, I found I could distinguish them by their movements. Pika look like fat rabbits with short ears. They are the same colour as the rocks among which they live and it occurred to me that if they were *always* the colour of their environment, then one might have red pika on sandstone, cream on limestone, even rainbow pika in the Grand Canyon.

As I considered the pika, humming birds appeared like whirring emeralds, feinted at me and darted off to perch on a bush when there would be a brief flare of the gorget: a ruby flashing in the sun. I wondered vaguely if I would have perceived either pika or rubies had I not been drunk with the heat.

I walked the divide between Difficult Creek and the Christmas Camp: the walk I had failed to do when the storm drove me down from Pool Table, the walk where the Fourth laboured for days on the divide, dropping into the head of Bellows Creek to escape the blizzards, climbing out again to a saddle and the descent to the shelf above Wannamaker.

Heat had prevented me from following them up Difficult Creek, but on the divide I had a taste of winter. The day was cold enough for survival clothing and there were flurries of hail above twelve thousand feet. I made a detour on the return, going east to look into Divide Park, another lonely stretch of grassland: good pasture, but no cows grazed there, only deer and elk. I crossed a ridge from Divide to Middle Park and came down to the Jeep and drifted through other parks – always staying high, around eleven thousand feet – to a place where the road ended above a big rock canyon on Bellows Creek. Palmer Mesa was above me on the north, while nine miles to the northwest I could see the snowfields of Half Moon Pass above Wheeler National Monument. This was a geological curiosity that, until the snow melted, could be reached only on foot. I had been saving Wheeler for my next off-day.

My bed was lumpy. There was a hard frost and I drank my breakfast coffee with the thermometer at 27°. I left camp carrying a heavy pack, and within half a mile I had to wade Bellows Creek which was deep and icy.

No navigation was needed on this route and although the trail traversed a huge park for three miles where the line was ill-defined, the way was marked infrequently by posts. In the distance I could see the Monument: an assembly of tall towers above timber. Towards the end the trail led me through a mile of forest, on the far side of which the whole of Wheeler was revealed: the towers standing at the highest point with sharp and shapely pinnacles below, and at the base: cowled and sculpted shrouds. All were made of dust.

I reached the Monument at noon when shadows were short and the sun glared. I didn't stop but went straight past the petrified images and up through forests which thinned to lush alps full of Indian paintbrush and the cream wand lily.

The snow below Half Moon was scattered with boulders. The boulders moved. A herd of elk was lying there. I stood still, so close I could hear them. Tormented by deer flies they were in a state of constant agitation, extending their heads to scrape necks and chins on the snow, rising to their feet to kick. One young cow, driven beyond endurance, was bucking. Squeals of frustrated fury came up the slope for persistence this insect rivals the clegg, the Scottish deer fly.

I was downwind of the animals so they were unaware of my presence until I was very close and then they took off, floundering through the snow, raising a cloud of dust as they reached the dry ground. A well-grown calf got up from willows beside the trail, nearly ran me down as it leapt past, and cantered after them.

I came up to the pass and on the other side was an unfamiliar view of ragged buttes called Twin Peaks. A moulting raven perched on a rock and waited for lunch crumbs. I climbed about the bare pink slopes photographing the alpines: sunflowers – with the sun on the snows of Wolf Creek Pass behind their yellow rays – saxifrages, the last of the dwarf forget-me-nots. I realised sadly that my summer was almost over. The harebells were in bloom: the flower that marks the end of summer, whether in Wales or the Rocky Mountains.

I went down and photographed Wheeler, and the wand lilies, and I started the long walk home: through the forest and the great park.

Ahead was Bellows Creek and Pool Table; there was the divide, and the mesas where we had climbed and drifted, hurrying before the storm, fighting the blizzards. There were the places where we had camped: on creeks and terraces, in meadows and lonely canyons, on hard rock and by beaver pools among the wild iris. I had grown to love this place, which I had thought of variously as dull little hills and the ridge-pole of the West. I didn't expect to come back but, looking at the land that evening as the shadows deepened on the gaunt mesas, not coming back was of no account. I would take it with me, but only the good part: the days, like Wheeler, that prepared me for what was coming.

From the valley of the Rio Grande I looked up Embargo Creek and thought of the Kerns seven miles above the confluence, burning their books, but thinking that once they reached the big river there was nothing between them and the settlements but a long walk down the ice – and food. There would be game among the cottonwoods; the worst was over.

The worst was yet to come. The mouth of Embargo Creek was the halfway mark in the journey, theirs and mine. At this point I had planned an interlude. I felt a peculiar kind of guilt at leaving them just before the storms came raging back, but their sufferings were too grievous for me to face without a break, and this was the place to take it: before we started down the Rio Grande. On a practical level I needed to discuss the illustrations with Malcolm McWhorter, who was developing and printing those I'd taken myself. The McWhorters had a cabin on the headwaters of the Colorado.

Northern Colorado wasn't a closed book to me; I had crossed it from east to west eight years ago: from Denver to Dinosaur and – a bonus to this current diversion – Frémont had been there. I would intersect not only my first trail across the West, but that of the second expedition returning from mapping the Oregon Trail. With Frémont had been Preuss and Alexis Godey.

I started north on a Sunday morning. The road was lined with tall sunflowers and the Sangre de Cristo were a grey frieze to the east, bare of snow except in the deepest gullies. The sky was a vast cloudscape and the air was filled with the scent of sage.

As I chugged north the Sangre de Cristo lost height but strange ranges appeared ahead, and suddenly I was back beside the Arkansas. I remembered it as a deep brown torrent; now it was a sparkling stream which we followed to Leadville. This was an old mining area, a land of deep gorges and range beyond range of mountains: a confusion of high ground. Our road was a succession of passes. I saw one town perched like a Himalayan monastery on the edge of a precipice, a sign announcing that the whole place was for sale: streets, houses, stores, 1,200 acres in all.

The weather had been building up during the afternoon, but for weeks it had done that daily in the San Juans; I disregarded the portents and climbed to over ten thousand feet in the Holy Cross Wilderness.

We rose by way of wide zig-zags through the aspen woods with glimpses of a deepening gorge below, of rock in red striations, of mountains at the heads of V-shaped and timbered canyons, of an indigo sky.

I pitched the tent below another Half Moon Pass and the storm struck before I could eat. Rain poured off the roof into the open back of the truck where I was preparing to cook, and until the storm passed I had to sit in the front reading the *Rocky Mountain News*: an organ which devoted a surprising amount of space to advertisements for salacious telephone conversations.

The rain was heavy. My groundsheet was no longer effective and the interior of the tent was soaked. I would have to sleep in the Jeep tonight.

I had time to start cooking before the next storm approached, but not time to finish. I was driven back to the passenger seat with a dish of parboiled onions, hard pasta and raw tomatoes. The thunder claps were deafening.

The storms continued until after dark, but in the lulls a strange bird called, like a bird in a rain forest. I was quite contented; I had two gallons of drinking water, I was close to a stream; I knew that the route of descent would dry quickly because it was merely a skin of mud on bedrock. I could wait for days for the weather to clear *except* – and this was always a problem – the reading matter would not last for days.

I was pleased, if not particularly surprised, to wake and see the tops of the firs gilded below a cloudless sky. Now came the task of clearing up. I felt like a flood victim (for seven years I lived in a house where springs rose in the kitchen during heavy rain). After a flood, getting rid of the mud is more difficult than drying out. Because I had slept in the Jeep a lot of things – cooler, chair, lamp, water containers –

had to stand outside the truck, and these were now plastered with mud. I cleaned them in the stream but drying out would have wasted a morning. I bundled everything in bin liners and forgot about them.

A delightful little path took me up through flowery meadows full of gentians to Half Moon Pass and a rocky knoll from where I had a good prospect of Holy Cross Mountain, which, although a con-glomeration of scree and loose rock, made a change from the sweeps of the San Juans. Everything was new. I looked into empty valleys with their unfamiliar creeks, my eye wandered from range to serrated range, cool and arrogant in their demands on my attention – but I saw the black clouds massing and I turned and started down as the first rain began to fall.

It was a week of storms, but they were interspersed with heat that could dry a tent in five minutes and the road in half an hour. The surface was a little slick as I descended that morning, but once I came out from the cloud shadow the road steamed, and woodchucks and golden mantled squirrels chased each other shrieking through the sunshine.

I crossed the great canyon below the town that awaited a buyer and turned up a chasm where a sign directed me to Shrine Pass: nine miles. The sky ahead was appalling. I thought of flash floods and trusted that the road would soon leave the creek. The storm broke overhead and then I thought of trees falling, of landslides. There were a few boulders in the middle of the road and I had the distinct impression, as we squeezed past on the river side, that clods fell away from the bank with our passing.

The rain came down in opaque torrents and the windscreen wipers couldn't cope. I stopped in a clear space below a vegetated slope high enough above the water, I hoped, to escape a sudden surge.

When the rain eased we climbed to beautiful meadows and Shrine Pass, where I looked out on a galaxy of ranges chequered by storms and sunlight. I had seen vast vistas in good weather; I had seen the Grand Canyon in storm, but I had never seen fronts fighting it out over a mountain arena as I saw them that day above Colorado.

Chased by the weather I drove down the valley of the Blue River with which I sensed not so much a familiarity as a rapport. Disturbed and fascinated, I stopped and looked at the map. Eight years ago I had crossed the mouth of this valley and looked south, along the surface of a river, its spring floodwaters skeined in the sun, and I'd wondered what was there, beyond the ranges, in a far hinterland. What had been there were the San Juans and the Fourth. And now I realised that I was also on the route of the second expedition; in 1844 Frémont followed the Blue River as he returned from Oregon. It was June and the valleys swarmed with Indians: Utes, Arapaho, Sioux. He was asked by the Utes to join them in a battle against their enemies, the Arapaho, but he refused to intervene. He saw the battle from a ridge as he passed by, and wrote in his official Report that 'horsemen were galloping to and fro, and groups of people were gathered about those who were wounded and dead, and who were being brought in from the field.'

At the mouth of the Blue River I came to the little town of Kremmling. After supper I drove west from the main street and looked up at a brown escarpment which, as the subject of a slide, had often started my talks on the West: a magical, evocative slide. I stopped and looked up at the scarp in the rain-washed light. The reality still had magic.

The temperature stood at 97° in the shade next evening at the moment that I saw the sand start to lift upriver. My camp was on the bank of the Yampa which joins Green River in a canyon in the heart of Dinosaur National Monument.

When I saw the sand begin to move I just had time to put the stove out and close the back of the Jeep before we were engulfed in swirling waves of brown grit. I was flattened against the spare tyre, my eyes screwed tightly closed.

The wind blew a gale for half an hour and I ate another half-cooked supper. Lightning struck the rim of the mountains repeatedly, feinting now and again towards the river. There were a few loud claps of thunder and big isolated drops of rain. The sandbars and cottonwoods that lined the river were achingly bright in sunshine against a sky of darkest slate.

I am fond of the Yampa and although, eight years ago, I had been awed by the wall in Dinosaur's quarry, with its prehistoric fossils, it was the river, not its graveyards, that enchanted me. It flows west through sage country towards high ground that seems to bar further progress. At one time this mountain wall would have been an effective barrier, but now the Yampa pierces the mass at Cross Mountain. From this point, apart from the occasional park or 'hole', the river is a succession of pink rock canyons until it joins the Green between Jenny Lind and Steamboat Rock: headlands a thousand feet tall.

100

As the crow flies, from Cross Mountain to Steamboat would be twenty-five miles, but the river must cover fifty in its convolutions. From the air the creviced plateau looks like a brain. There are places where the water, flowing generally west, runs east at an ox bow, and the distance across a tall reef is so short that you can, with imagination, see the reef crumble before the next flood.

Cross Mountain marks more than the first of the Yampa canyons; it is the start of over a thousand miles of chasms that culminate in the Grand Canyon, and end less than two hundred miles from the ocean at the Gulf of California. It is a significant mountain. East are the bleak sage lands, ranchlands, the Rockies; west is the red rock country. I would climb Cross Mountain in order to see the river as it approached across the plain to cleave the sandstone barrier like a water axe.

The climb was threatened at the outset by a young black cow who, unaccustomed to seeing a person on foot, came snorting towards me, tossing her head. I was already tense because, in order to approach my mountain, I had to cross a damp and overgrown draw and there was no doubt that it was full of rattlesnakes. But as I turned the cow back and others lifted their heads from the willows, I saw that they formed a shield. I drove them in front of me to the foot of the mountain, scaring every rattlesnake within miles.

I scrambled up a gully to emerge on the lip of the canyon. Below me cataracts whispered under friable walls. On my side the edge was so loose that I couldn't see the face until I walked out to jutting points from which I could look back. The walls were about eight hundred feet high, with steep scree below that. The rock was in shades of red and the water was green. The air, as always above rivers and canyon rims, was scythed by the wings of swallows.

The ground was moderately smooth, but progress was a matter of zig-zags. As inlets gouge sea cliffs so the gullies that seamed the canyon walls expanded into draws at the top, some running far back in the mountain. I counted nine which I had to negotiate, either climbing down and up the other side, or walking round their heads. Fortunately the ground was arid and bare under the pinyons. Drought and heat had shrivelled all the vegetation and a rattler would have been obvious; moreover snakes don't like heat. I walked in the sun.

From Cross Mountain I saw the flood plain of the Yampa to the east, and the high ground beyond could have been the continental divide. Westward were the Utah mountains beyond Flaming

Gorge – but these were background. No mountaineer ever went to the top of a mountain solely for the view. Scenery is only a word until you can relate to it. A far range may be the one where Old Bill Williams disappeared in 1837, a cottonwood ten miles away is above the spring where I found the pug mark of a lion. In that canyon I saw my first ringtail cat. Scenery is two-dimensional until you have been there, and then it becomes a part of you.

I looked east up the Yampa to the Great Divide and it was scenery; I looked west and thought: I will write a book about the Yampa one day.

I passed a ranch called Solace before the Gates of Lodore. 'No Service for 50 miles' a notice said. I would have an aeroplane if I lived here. You might be able to buy sugar and spices within fifty miles, but typewriter ribbons and books? A veterinary surgeon, doctor – coffee? I doubt if you can find a well-roasted coffee between Denver and Salt Lake City.

The Gates of Lodore is the gorge by which Green River leaves Brown's Hole, which is a lush park with cottonwoods where trappers wintered since 1826, and Indians before them. When Frémont came through Brown's Hole in 1844 the second expedition crossed the Green in a boat made of skins. Frémont bought it from Antoine Robidoux who at that time was running a trading post in the lonely Uinta mountains to the west. The boat was a great asset. In June the snow may have gone from the land but the melting of high snowfields made torrents of the big rivers and many animals were lost at the crossings.

At the Gates of Lodore, Green River plunges into its own great canyon system (one of them; there is another at Flaming Gorge, upstream). In the cool and sunless evening I strolled down to the mouth of the first canyon. A wren was singing on the opposite wall: a canyon wren that starts high and descends on a dying fall. A deer came across a sandbar to drink at the river which, in late July, was slow and brown with quiet whirlpools. The air was warm and humid, and now and again a few spots of rain fell but there was no thunder.

Next day the appearance of bad weather intensified, but I was leaving it behind. I had diverged westward to Dinosaur in order to avoid bad weather in the Rockies, now I headed east and found that the depression had moved. Four days ago it had been in the north, now it was in the southwest. One morning I came to the corner of Colorado, crossed into Utah, then over the state-line to Wyoming, and I climbed to a high wild tableland where I stopped on a pass for lunch. I drank cold water and ate bread and cheese with the windows closed and the Jeep shaking in the wind. Southwest, beyond Flaming Gorge, all of upland Utah was in the storm shadow except where showers drooped like badly hung net curtains.

Below my eyrie was an escarpment and below that, the empty basin I had travelled through this morning following dirt roads: a place of red earth and grey sage and no people. Northward, the tableland was only marginally populated. After lunch I passed a ranch but there were no more houses until I came to Rock Springs, thirty miles away. I passed the ends of dirt roads: Salt Wells Creek Road, Bitter Creek Road, Lower Sage Creek Road, and they must have led somewhere, but although the faint red lines faded into infinity, nowhere did I see a habitation or a cow, or a vehicle trailing its scarf of dust. It was a land of sage and pinyons and weather, not scenic but possessing an intriguing if daunting character.

Rock Springs came and went: a sprawl in the sage, raw as a landslip. I turned east on the interstate I-80 that, westward, followed the California Trail. I was tired and several times in the last few hours I'd found I couldn't remember what had happened in the last few minutes. I turned up the stereo, battened down the cargo and opened the windows wide, Beethoven's Choral roaring a challenge to the elements.

The storms crept up and encircled us so that we moved in the wide eye of the weather. At one moment, in the half-circle that I could see with comfort, I counted four separate storms, each with its phalanx of lightning ripping through a palpable gloom to stab mountains humped like mammoths.

I crossed the Red Desert and turned south into the Medicine Bow Mountains. A strong wind blew still and I needed shelter for the night. I found it in a forest campground where there were two other occupants: a man and a girl. After I pitched the tent they approached, obviously distressed, and asked me what beasts were making the noise. I listened but heard nothing. The roaring, they said, the terrible roaring; it was right by their camp. They had been pitching their tent when it started and they had been sitting in their car ever since, with the doors locked. Then I had come along. They regarded me hopelessly, convinced I was deaf – or too deaf – when suddenly a nighthawk boomed above us. The couple clung together, twittering.

I explained. They wouldn't believe me. I pointed at the now silent nighthawks hunting above the trees, I talked about wing coverts and

103

aerodynamics. No, they said, that wasn't a bird; it had to be a lion. Or a bear. I told them to watch the birds dive and they would see the wings judder as the male zoomed upwards. I'd never seen this myself but I was trying to soothe them.

They went away. The nighthawks boomed intermittently. After a few minutes I saw a tent advancing up the road, then I saw two pairs of feet underneath it.

They moved their camp as close to me as they could manage without violating my space, and although they spent the night there, they must have resolved not to close their eyes. They were talking when I fell asleep, they were talking at six in the morning. I got up and put the kettle on. They got up and, without cooking, without washing, without looking at me, they threw everything in their car, struck their tent and drove away in the cold grey dawn.

The sun came up and started to burn off the mist. I drove through the ranching country of North Park where a mountain called Parkview dominated the southern horizon. It was a scree mountain, but shapely, and I had time to kill. Malcolm was working on a book; I'd said I would arrive at the weekend and today was Friday. I would go up Parkview. Why was it named so unimaginatively when the pass beyond was 'Troublesome'?

The scree slopes were dull but I was rewarded by a fine panorama from the summit: Winter Park on one side, which was my destination, North Park on the other, through which I had followed Frémont. The second expedition found buffalo in the park, killed some for meat, and then climbed over the range on which I stood by way of a pass at nine thousand feet. This wouldn't have been Troublesome, which was high, around 9,700 feet, but Muddy Pass away to the west and a thousand feet lower. Who, I wondered, named Troublesome, and why?

Around Parkview the weather was deteriorating, cloud scraping the tops of the highest peaks. I had come up the mountain by the easiest ridge; I descended by a short steep slope that, just above the timber-line, was covered with blue drifts of harebells.

Ten

THE CABIN STOOD in woods above the Fraser River and at the side of Winter Park. The south wall of the main room was mostly glass and looked out across the tops of trees and across the park to the continental divide where snow still lingered on the peaks above Berthoud Pass.

My days assumed a gentle rhythm that was not unexciting. I felt the creases smoothing out as I became civilised again. In the mornings Malcolm worked on his book while I answered my mail; no chore when the background was music not heard for a long time: tapes or the public broadcasting station at Denver – or just the sound of someone else tapping away at a distance.

After lunch we packed our camera bags and took off, Malcolm at the wheel (it was bliss to be driven instead of driving): the goal a flower for him, a picture for me, dinner for both, eventually. The fates conspired in our favour. The storms had passed, or if they stayed, did so only on the fringe of our world, presenting us with good effects for telephotos: for dramas that didn't concern me except as a matter of cumulus and shadows, with nothing more to do than wait for a gendarme to be sunlit against a dark precipice. But where we were the sun shone, and we had our dramas too.

I knew without doubt where we would find fringed gentians. I had seen them once in my life, Malcolm never, but I took him to a stream I had glanced at in passing, and it was lined with fringed gentians in full bloom. We photographed them from every angle and then drove along miles of dirt roads for a meal preceded by a quick run to Cameron Pass where we looked beyond a black rock cirque to a mountain called Richthofen which I liked, and filed for future reference.

We drove to Rollins Pass. I maintained we wouldn't find *alpine* gentians below eleven thousand feet, so he took me up this precipitous dirt road that ended on the divide, and the slopes were covered with the ivory trumpets of alpine gentians.

From Rollins Pass the divide swooped northwards to the Devil's Thumb and the Indian Peaks. How many hidden corries lay below that scalloped ridge with all their high lakes, their attendant flowers and animals? I drooled over that ridge, but then every time I'm on a high point I want to go to the next one. Mountaineers have nomad souls.

We walked and talked and took photographs, and dined in those of the local restaurants which had stayed open after the skiers had gone. In the intervals between photography and gastronomy we worked on the illustrations for my book. I wasn't happy with the pictures I had produced so far but Malcolm was encouraging. Taking up a new and intricate activity in later life can be overwhelming at times, but I had to persevere because there was simply no one else to take the pictures. If you travel alone you do your own illustrations.

Malcolm left to attend a wedding in Texas and I was taken under the wing of a neighbour and his Malamute bitch. Art, who was seventy-eight, skied and walked, and he knew food and wine and good mountain manners. After a day on the hill we drank our beer on a balcony above a stretch of water with a backdrop of mountains. I remembered other summers and coming down to a Welsh pub after a good climb, in summers when you could sit outside in the sunshine and drink your beer. Above Grand Lake we sat among the blue rinses and the stiletto heels, our sweat trickling through the dust, my eyes misting from long exposure to the sun, and the drink going down like water. The same routine, just a different continent.

I went to Rocky Mountain National Park, but it was so crowded that fumes from the traffic got in my throat. I stopped at a Visitor Centre to inquire about the situation in the campgrounds and a volunteer ranger was so rude that I got in the Jeep and drove on and left the Park. Next morning found me tramping up the great rock cirque below Cameron Pass that we had been photographing five days ago.

Richthofen was attractive from a distance, but on approach it was only too obvious that this was yet another big scree mountain. I wasn't deceived by the lovely lake in the foreground with its rock island spired by firs, its stony shores that made a classic picture; the climber in me looked at the background, and the background was three thousand feet of scree.

There was no trail of course; there couldn't be on terrain that is

106

always in motion. Besides, I thought grimly as I stepped off the last grass slope, who climbs scree mountains?

It was like the worst Scottish stone shoot but three times as long, or so it seemed. I reached a saddle at noon, kicking up a snow wreath, using my stiff fingers as grapnels.

The ridge was cold. I put on a jersey and the plastic mac I had brought instead of an anorak to save weight.

There were two thousand feet between me and the summit and shortly after I had started again I heard thunder rolling in the Rawah Wilderness to the north. I stopped and ate my lunch. By the time I had finished eating the showers had reached Cameron Pass, three miles away, and the thunder was closer. It had been a truly ghastly ascent, strenuous in that strain derived from the need to concentrate on every move, and everything moved. Rock climbing would have been considerably less dangerous. The chill on the ridge at noon warned me of conditions were I to be benighted with a broken ankle or a trapped leg. Some of the boulders balanced on those scree slopes would weigh more than a ton.

I studied the sky. No lightning yet despite the apparent proximity of the thunder. Perhaps that was merely echoes of distant peals. I calculated the risks and went on, climbing a rock rib to a false summit. The ridge to the true top was like a ridge on Skye, but one side was less exposed than the other. I trod the knife-edge knowing which side I would go over if the storm broke. I was thankful for small mercies; at least I could get off on one side. In the Alps I could have been a sitting duck on the skyline.

Something was singing at my back. That would be the cameras, full of electricity. My hair was blowing too freely for me to judge if it were standing on end. I gathered myself and made a fast dash for the summit, finding a little gully and scrambling up it to a thin and tapering cairn. In the stones there was a cylinder containing a register. I was turning the pages to find out who was the last visitor when thunder shattered the world. I capped the cylinder and leapt for the gully.

I bolted along the ridge and over the second summit and found patches of scree to crash down. By the time the next clap of thunder came I was a hundred feet above the saddle. I glissaded down the snow and the next peal exploded when I was way below the ridge, and by that time I could afford to stop running and try to pick out a descent that would utilise the highest tongues of grass.

The storm passed without rain and I lingered by the lake among baby pika and gentians and grass of Parnassus. It was still quite early. I would buy a six-pack and some king prawns and a wedge of Brie and I would go home to the empty cabin and sit on the balcony drinking beer in the sunset. After that I would read the latest Ruth Rendell until exhaustion drove me to bed. It had been a hard day.

I had the cabin to myself for a while, me and a bat they called The Count who spent the days behind a shutter in the utility room. Since I had been robbed of the peaks of the National Park I looked closer to home for amusement. I went back to Rollins Pass where the alpine gentians grew and walked the lovely scalloped ridge to the Devil's Thumb: a six-hundred-foot pinnacle on a mountain from which the ridge continued to the gap-toothed crests of the Indian Peaks.

There was a bitter wind on the top (but the plains beyond Denver sweltered in the sun). On my progress from Rollins I had been looking at the corries below: bare stony basins with water in the depressions and snow banks under shadowed cliffs. To reach the heart of a mountain you have to go down: walk the sand on the edge of lapping water, smell the marsh, hear the pika. From above the corries are flat: grey and black with the odd smudge of green willow. As the mountaineer descends, weaving carefully between the outcrops, the features grow in stature as the larger world recedes. Obstructed by canyon walls, the plains vanish; a spur hides the canyon, big boulders descend from the spur, you pass one the size of a cabin with orange and lime lichens on the rock.

The corrie that was flat from two thousand feet above now spawns depressions connected by miniature valleys, isolated by moraines. Only the fact that, having studied it from above, the observer carries a map in his head, enables him to work through the confusion, a process that may take a long time – but there is no hurry.

My corrie had two lakes on different levels, and led to another corrie and another tarn below the pass. It had tangles of low willow and dwarf fir which I had to climb through. Underfoot there was loose rock and mire, but there were also patches of scarlet Indian paintbrush. When I stopped, and the pika ceased their calling until I should move again, in the profound silence under the great cliffs I could hear a stone settle back as something passed or, like me, paused and watched.

The local 'big' peak was Byer's. There is always one that seizes popular imagination: Tryfan, Ben Nevis, the Grépon, Byer's, the last because it dominates the southern view from the main road to Berthoud Pass. So I went to Byer's, approaching it from an unconventional angle through empty forests to a pass called Bottle. Then came trackless timber through which I climbed on bearings to a caravan route thronged with people all making for the summit. Parties overtook me, spurting uphill on their toes, unsmiling and virile. I overtook them, collapsed beside the path, sometimes on the path, looking sick. Plodding at a guide's pace I overtook everyone and ate my lunch on the summit mobbed by ground squirrels with an alarming weight problem.

Below me the long file toiled upwards, all pretence of virility dissipated. The first man arrived, his companion bereft of speech. The first man asked me to identify the peaks so I took out the map. 'Well,' he began loftily, 'You're going to need bearings – ' but I was groping in my pack for the compass. His face lit up. 'Oh, look! A *compass!*'

They left and I stood up. The mob was close upon me. I looked in the other direction, at Bill's Peak, almost the same height as Byer's which was 12,804 feet, but with a drop of eight hundred feet between. Bill's was a solid grey mountain with white streaks of serpentine running across its face. It had no distinction, but there was this ridge connecting the two, and a north ridge down the other side from which I might be able to reach a lake in timber at the head of a trail that would take me back to the Jeep. In the Rockies you can walk above the timber-line without a trail, but you need bearings and a lot of time to negotiate untracked forest, and I'd had my fill of that kind of timber for one day.

I left the summit, and immediately I was on my own. I dropped down to the saddle and started up Bill's Peak. A rock crashed down its face. I looked but kept moving. The cause could be an animal but it was just as likely to be erosion and gravity. There are innumerable odd noises in wild places, by day as well as night. Sometimes, when high and miles from any building, I hear a door close, but I assume that this sound is inside my head.

There was a path on Bill's Peak, coming in from the south. I joined it, traversing above strange corries containing lakes. I had brought a large-scale map from the cabin and I calculated that the ridge from Bill's to St Louis Peak, four miles to the south, had seven tops on it, one of which was 12,686 feet, and none had a name. If I lived here I would name everything.

The ridge dropped to a pass where another trail came up from the

Williams Fork of the Colorado. Was this river named for Old Bill? Beyond its valley were the Williams Fork Mountains. Williams is a common name in Wales and there were many Welsh emigrants in the nineteenth century. All the same, Old Bill knew this country well; he could have named the peak I was on and trodden this very trail (an Indian trail?) that came up from the west and plunged into a timbered basin where Lake Evelyn showed black as water in the bottom of a well.

The path descended, skirted the lake and, below the outlet, turned into a full-fledged fisherman's trail. I relaxed. I was a mile or two from the Jeep, the weather was good, I had hours of daylight left. I started to dream.

There was a sudden eruption of noise, and something large fell at my feet. The racket was squirrel curses, of course, and the fallen object was a big mushroom. The squirrel remained some fifteen feet above my head, beside himself with rage. I stood on tiptoe and wedged the mushroom on a branch as a gesture of conciliation, but he continued to rave until I was long out of his sight.

The cabin was at nine thousand feet. Suddenly the heat was gone and although the sun was warm on the balcony, a cold breeze met one at the corners of the house. This was only the second week in August but already there was a feeling of autumn in the air. Here and there the aspens were turning yellow, and in the woods the leaves of the holly grape were crimson. Janet arrived, my hostess, talking of the steamy heat in Texas. 'It was hot here a week ago,' I said.

For a few days life was gentle and sophisticated again. We walked, but not to the summits; we went to the lakes and looked at the last of the flowers; we watched birds and we talked. We dined out and we had gourmet meals at the cabin. And twelve days after I had left the Rio Grande I returned, to find a shallow river with exposed shingle banks, and water that could be waded almost anywhere, which was just as well. I was going to have to wade it.

Eleven

IN THE FIRST week of January 1849 the fourth expedition struggled down Embargo Creek, at the end so strung out that there were seven miles between the first and last group, and that excluded the four who had been sent on to the settlements. As Frémont followed this party he was surprised to see, by the spacing of their camp fires, that they had taken four or five days to cover ten miles. This was disturbing and he decided to wait on the Rio Grande only as long as it took the stragglers to catch up with him, before starting down the river, hoping to make good progress on the ice. He reached the Rio Grande on January 2nd and was relieved to find that there was considerably less snow here than there had been in the canyons.

Seven miles up Embargo Creek the Kern brothers burned their books and were joined by Raphael Proue. For ten days the Kerns maintained the same camp, marginally improving their accommodation by building a shelter out of saplings. They were occupied with bringing down baggage from above, but their strength was failing. Benjamin wrote no more after January 6th (except a date: 'JAN 7th') but his brother, Richard, continued his diary with terse entries: 'Sat Jan 6th in same camp. Sunday Jan 7 Same camp. Monday Jan 8th Same camp.'

There were now three main camps: that of the Kerns, Frémont's on the river, and a large party between them who were themselves straggling. The food was almost finished. The last of the macaroni had been rationed out and they had eaten all the candles. Now they were subsisting on what was left. They boiled anything that was made of leather, or roasted it until it was soft enough to chew.

About five miles above the mouth of Embargo, where Baugham Creek comes in from the northeast, the land is flat and open, without shelter. Micajah McGehee, in trying to cross this stretch with Elijah Andrews, was overtaken by such a fierce storm that Andrews gave up and lay down in the snow. McGehee got him on his feet again and they managed to reach a cave. Having made Andrews comfortable,

111

McGehee went outside and, in the teeth of the gale, fought his way to a position above the cave where he succeeded in dislodging some dead pinyons. The resulting fire brought in Captain Cathcart and Richard Kern who had literally nothing to eat. At this time McGehee and Andrews each had a cup of boiled macaroni and a cup of sugar: four cups of food between four men. It was a feast. Andrews placed it on the fire but as it was warming he tipped it over and everything was lost in the flames.

The storm continued to rage, confining them to the cave for two days. McGehee, a man of parts, poking about the rocks, discovered a roll of leather thongs which could have been intended for fastening snowshoes. They might have been left by another member of the expedition who had sheltered there. A second find was an old wolf's den with some dry bones. They pounded the bones between rocks, cut the thongs into pieces and, boiling these ingredients together, they lived on the resulting stew for two days, until the storm eased and they could make their way towards Frémont on the river.

Groups were forming and dissolving at this time as people tried to get out, or holed up, or went back for baggage in the spells of quiet weather. On January 9th, on a sunny day, Raphael Proue was trying to make his way across the last bleak stretch when he stopped. Richard Kern says his legs froze. The veteran, Lorenzo Vincenthaler, leaving the big party to go forward to Frémont's camp, found Proue collapsed in the snow and covered him with blankets. When he returned that night Proue was dead.

This, the first death, must have shocked them terribly. They were still retrieving baggage and, during the ensuing days, they passed and repassed the body but they could spare neither time nor energy to dig a grave.

McGehee's cave is at the end of a spur and only a few hundred yards from Embargo Creek. The entrance is obvious even from the modern dirt road, and that is a mile away across the flats. There is an old trail close by but this may have been made by settlers quarrying stone from the spur. Nowadays the place is deserted except for the cliff swallows which have built their nests under the overhanging roof. It is a commodious cave and probably saved the lives of a number of men. There are five miles between it and the river; on a summer's afternoon you could walk the distance in little over an hour.

I stood in the entrance of the cave and looked south towards the

112

cottonwoods of the Rio Grande. After weeks of canyons and ridges, of following them and catching up, losing them and finding them again, I could only feel despair.

Proue had died close by on the flats. I had no doubt why Frémont adopted the attitude of his letter to Jessie from Taos: 'The spirits of the camp grew lower. Proue laid down in the trail and froze to death. In a sunshiny day, and having with him means to make fire, he threw his blankets down in the trail and laid there till he froze to death.'

Even before this death Frémont knew his party was on a razor's edge of disaster. The weaker ones would succumb first; the strongest stood a chance of survival. A few of them were so much fitter than the rest that their strength must have been obvious, and would shortly be demonstrated. Frémont's problem was to sustain the spirits of the large company in the middle, between Proue and the strongest men. Panic is infectious: that leaden apathy of ultimate panic when men stop thinking; when they feel that the blizzard is warm, the ground soft, and they lie down to sleep.

With the spirits of his men already low Frémont had to try to counteract the effect of Proue's death. So Proue 'gave up'. He 'laid down in the trail'. The implication is that he is a weakling, the runt of the company, different. *They* would have lit a fire and revived, not thrown down their blankets and waited for death. They would have kept walking; they would keep walking. Frémont would have needed to convince himself of this. He was a sincere man, and he was the leader. This conviction persisted, even in the face of what was to come.

Proue died on January 9th. Frémont had expected the party under King to be back by then, with a string of mules loaded with food. When they didn't return, and despite their slow progress down Embargo, he convinced himself that they had met with disaster. He was unable to believe that, once they reached the Rio Grande, three experienced mountain men (Creutzfeldt was not a mountain man) couldn't make good progress down the frozen river. He thought that they must have been attacked by hostile Indians. Both the local Utes and the Apaches were fighting American troops on the upper Rio Grande and four unmounted white men would stand no chance with a war party who could kill them just for their guns. And if they had reached the settlements and were returning, a laden pack train would have been a far greater prize than a few guns.

But food was essential and Frémont decided on a second relief party to be led by himself. On the 9th he summoned Lorenzo Vincenthaler from the rear and appointed him deputy leader. As it turned out he could hardly have made a worse choice but it was probably made by default. It appears that Frémont trusted only Godey and Preuss and these he would take with him. Of the remainder, the Kerns were not at the river – but he could have sent back for them; communication was good during the fine days. On the 10th men were salvaging equipment from a camp above the Kerns. Perhaps there was already bad feeling between Frémont and the brothers, perhaps he felt that if one were left in charge, the three would form a clique that would carry bad decisions by weight of numbers. The Kerns, after all, weren't experienced mountain men. So he chose Vincenthaler, who was strong physically (he had no trouble going down to the river from several miles up Embargo to receive his orders, and returning the same day) and he had been with Frémont on the third expedition and fought in the Mexican War. The Kerns were to suggest that he was a toady and that Frémont succumbed to flattery. William Brandon, the historian, wrote in *The Men and the Mountain* that his was 'a bourgeois soul, crammed with little moralities to make up for the lack of big ones.' We can judge him only on his subsequent behaviour as recounted by his companions, and no one would have a good word to say for him.

He had his orders on the 9th and, returning to his party, found Proue dead. On the 10th Frémont would have learned of the death and now he would wait no longer for the stragglers. On the 11th, leaving Vincenthaler in charge and carrying provisions only for two or three days, he started down the river with the four strongest men: Preuss, Godey, Godey's nephew, Theodore McNabb, who was fourteen, and the black cook, Jackson Saunders. That Godey and Frémont should have proved two of the strongest is not surprising, and Preuss was solid as a rock. But all we know of Jackson Saunders, apart from his fitness, was that he was a free man, not a slave (Frémont was anti-slavery) and that he had joined the expedition as Frémont's chef and orderly. One of the few references to him concerns this moment when a floodlight touches him and passes on, momentarily illuminating Theodore McNabb.

Although Theodore was Godey's relative, Frémont would never have brought him on the expedition had he not been an exceptional lad. All the same, in the nineteenth-century West children grew up more quickly than those back East. It was natural selection; surrounded by hazards, even on a farm, the child who didn't learn quickly didn't survive. He was bitten by a snake or kicked by a mule, fell in

114

front of the mower knives or was lost in the woods and overtaken by an early snow. At fourteen Theodore went to the wilderness no earlier than many mountain men. The suspicion that Frémont included him in the relief party because his youth rendered him vulnerable if left behind is not valid. (Cabin boys had a low expectation of life after shipwrecks.) It is invalid because the relief party travelled fast and couldn't have done so had one member needed assistance. Frémont took the best men and that included Theodore.

Frémont left the tepee behind, pitched at the mouth of Embargo Creek. That he still had the tepee at that point means that even if he didn't trouble to pitch it during the five nights that he spent between Christmas Camp and the river, men had to drag the poles and carry the heavy skin of its cover. When he started down the river his orders were that the men were to finish packing all the baggage to the river, and to store it in the tepee. When they had done this, they were to follow him south. 'My instructions to the camp were, that if they did not hear from me within a stated time, they were to follow down the Del Norte [the Rio Grande].' This, contained in the Taos letter to Jessie, differed from McGehee's narrative: 'He left an order that we scarce knew how to interpret, to the effect that we must finish packing the baggage to the river and hasten on down as speedily as possible to the Mouth of the Rabbit River [about 80 miles downstream] where we would meet relief, and that if we wished to see him we must be in a hurry as he was going on to California.'

Whatever he said, it would have been relayed through Vincenthaler who may have twisted the order under the impression that the implied threat would have the effect of making the men move faster.

The Kerns' party arrived at the river in the early afternoon, two days after Frémont left. They had spent most of that morning breaking trail through new snow. They had made an attempt to get down the previous day but Richard Kern had fallen in the creek and, aware of the risk of frostbite and gangrene, they retreated to the last camp. Cathcart shot a small bird. Richard doesn't say how small, but even a grouse would have been only a mouthful each.

As they were plodding towards the river they met some men going back. When this party came down again everyone was assembled under Vincenthaler. On the 16th – leaving some equipment still way up Embargo – they started walking down the ice, but they moved only two miles and camped. One of the California Indians, Manuel, returned to Embargo.

The weather was good enough to hunt (although for three days they found no game) and walking was easy on the ice – or would have been for fit men. But Manuel was so close to death that for some time afterwards the others thought he had died. It is possible that he never had any boots; he may have worn moccasins and eaten them. Whatever footgear he wore, by the time he reached the river his feet were so severely frostbitten that the soles had sloughed away. He was suffering such agony that he begged Vincenthaler to shoot him. Failing in this he turned back to Embargo. The other Indians, Joaquin and Gregorio, accompanied him, built a fire, and left him in the tepee.

In their absence Henry Wise, a veteran of the third expedition, dropped back. The Indians, hurrying to catch up with the main party, came on his body lying on the ice under the bare cottonwoods. They covered it with brush and snow, a touching but futile gesture when coyotes are capable of moving rocks to get at bodies.

The men were very depressed. During that night*, in the camp only two miles below Embargo, a man called Carver, a veteran of the Mexican War, went mad. Raving and shouting, he insisted that if they would only turn back with him, he could save them all. When daylight came he took the back trail, and the next person to see him was Manuel, still alive in the tepee. By the time he reached there Carver was carrying meat which he said was part of a deer he had killed – but no one else had seen game and he had passed Wise's body. He continued up Embargo Creek, his stated goal a camp seven miles upstream. He was never seen again.

On the Rio Grande the main company, of twenty-one men, moved six miles further, always looking for game and finding none. Next day, January 18th, they moved only a mile or so to give the hunters a chance to scout ahead, but still they had no luck. Another veteran of earlier expeditions, a French voyageur called Tabeau (sometimes called Sorrel), already blinded by the glare of sun on snow, had a violent convulsion. Next day he travelled with them until his strength gave out. Benjamin and Edward Kern sat and smoked with him for a while but they couldn't persuade him to go on. They overtook the party and when Tabeau's friend, Moran, learned what had happened he put down his pack and returned. Their bodies would be found by

* According to McGehee. Richard Kern has Carver leaving them six miles downstream, the third day out from the mouth of Embargo.

1 John Charles Frémont

Courtesy of the Bancroft Library

2 Jessie Frémont

Courtesy of the Southwest Museum

3 Alexis Godey

Courtesy of the Henry E.
Huntington Library

4 Charles Preuss

Courtesy of the Henry E.
Huntington Library

5 Old Bill Williams

A contemporary sketch by an
unknown artist

6 Dr Benjamin Kern

Courtesy of the Henry E.
Huntington Library

7 Richard H. Kern

Courtesy of the Bancroft Library

8 Edward M. Kern

Courtesy of the Bancroft Library

9 A canyon in the San Juan
Mountains

*Courtesy of the Henry E.
Huntington Library*

10 Olive Oatman

*Courtesy of the Arizona Historical
Society Library*

11 The Sangre de Cristo
Range

12 The mouth of Willow
Creek in the San Juan
Mountains

13 Cathedral Rock, above Embargo Creek

14 Petrified dust pinnacles, Wheeler National Monument

15 Iron Mountain in the
Colorado Rockies

16 The Devil's Thumb,
Colorado Rockies

17 The Rio Grande in New Mexico

18 14th to 16th century ruins, Bandelier National Monument

19 Multi-storey dwelling dating from the 12th century, Chaco Canyon,
New Mexico

20 Storm over New Mexico

21 Apache hide-out, Chiricahuas

22 The foothills of the Sierra Nevada, California

23 Half Dome, Yosemite National Park

24 Tuolumne Meadows, Yosemite

25 The author in the Colorado Rockies

26 The Jeep

Godey, one lying beside the ashes of a fire, the other sitting against the bank.

The men were dying of starvation, not of cold. The days were sunny and although they would have had low temperatures at night (no record was kept after Frémont left) they would have had nothing like the cold of the mountains and the terrible wind chill. All this they endured without tents and with only blankets for covering. Nights on the Rio Grande, not to speak of the days (Tabeau blinded by sunshine on snow) must have seemed comparatively warm.

Where the river starts to turn southeast someone shot a deer. At this point, had Frémont been with them, or Godey, or if one of the Kerns could have stood up to Vincenthaler, they might have held together. As it was, Vincenthaler apportioned the deer unequally, giving two shoulders to eleven men and reserving all the rest for the smaller group of which he was one.

The Kerns were in the group that got the shoulders, so were the two Indians, Gregorio and Joaquin. The day after the deer meat was eaten the Indians joined Vincenthaler's party. McGehee says that the reason they did this was that they were afraid that in the last resort 'certain men' would kill and eat them.

Accounts differ concerning the final disruption of the company. Thomas Martin, the veteran who would dictate his account in 1878, said that they split up and reformed before Vincenthaler abandoned them, but all accounts agree that, after the deer was shot, Vincenthaler said it was every man for himself, and he went ahead with those of the men who could keep up with him.

The remainder, including the Kern brothers, staggered on for four miles and stopped. There were nine in this party. Besides the Kerns there were Cathcart and McGehee, two veterans: Taplin and Stepperfeldt, Andrews – who had nearly died before McGehee found the cave on Embargo – and the millwright, Rohrer.

They remained in the same camp for six days, too weak to continue, indeed some had been hard put to it to get that far. Benjamin had collapsed on arrival; Andrews fell before he reached camp but had managed to give a weak cry which they heard, and people went out to bring him in to the fire.

Next day those of the weaker members who could still move about grubbed for snails and earthworms, but without success, while the others hunted, hindered by snowblindness to such an extent that they could scarcely see to shoot. In the next few days they shot two grouse

117

which they consumed completely, including the entrails and feathers. Part of a wolf's body was found on the ice and they ate that, even managing to eat the skin and hair, after roasting it. McGehee says they ate the bones too, probably pounding them as they had pounded the bones in the cave. A handful of rosebuds was discovered, and Benjamin found some bugs in the river where the ice had been broken, but his most substantial meal was three or four inches of rope which he moistened with a teaspoonful of oil: 'Next morning felt somewhat refreshed.'

They ate their moccasins and a leather bag. They were not uncomfortable. Edward Kern was to write to his sister: 'I felt happy and contented sitting nearly all day by the fire in a kind of stupor listless and careless of when my time would come.'

The coyotes howled outside the circle of the firelight and by day the ravens sat in the leafless cottonwoods and waited for the next man to die.

Every morning they grew weaker and even the task of collecting sticks for the fire exhausted them. On January 23rd Andrews died. He had never recovered after his collapse on reaching camp. Next day Rohrer was failing fast.

They covered Andrews' body with a blanket and sat beside Rohrer. When he died, they said, they would make one more attempt to advance. They had two fires: Taplin, McGehee and Stepperfeldt at one, beside the dead and dying; the Kerns and Cathcart at the other. The day after Andrews died 'someone' came over from the Kerns' fire and suggested that, rather than leave the body to the wolves, they should eat the flesh themselves; it was going to waste. The speaker, whom McGehee doesn't identify but who had to be one of the Kerns or Cathcart, said that he would 'undertake to do the butchery, as you may call it.'

There was some discussion, McGehee saying that he recognised that opposition to the proposal was based on convention and prejudice, nevertheless, he thought they should try to hold out for three more days: 'then, if I do not approve, I will not censure it.'

They agreed to do nothing unless they were unanimous, so they continued to sit there, occasionally firing signal guns, until Rohrer died.

They did not move on. Two more days passed, days in which they imagined they heard answers to their signals. They would stand up and listen, only to sink down again, and wait. The last day was recalled by Benjamin, writing from Taos on February 20th to an unidentified friend called Joe: 'On the 28th of January about 12 in the morning During a snow storm as we sat silently around a little willow fire Taplin suddenly exclaimed by God There is a halloo. Tis but a wolf again we said – rising to his feet he said Christ there's a man on horseback over the river, we gave a shout you may be sure, almost in an instant Alexis Godey was with us.'

The relief had arrived.

Twelve

FOR MORE THAN twelve days Manuel lay in the tepee at the mouth of Embargo Creek. I could find no record of the date rescue reached him, but he left the main party on January 16th, and Godey couldn't have arrived at Embargo before the 28th because he only reached the Kerns that day. (He slaughtered a colt to provide them with food and pushed on upriver.) How did Manuel survive? One answer is that he might have sunk into a coma, similar to that of an animal in hibernation. But an animal has built up fat reserves by gorging during the autumn. When Manuel holed up he was neither fat nor fit. The other possibility (given that the state of his feet wouldn't allow him to reach Wise's body downriver) is that the madman, Carver, himself carrying meat when he reached Embargo which may have given Manuel an idea, did *not* disappear into the mountains but died close by. No enterprising journalist tried to trace the Indian, or if he did, Manuel eluded him. A journalist would have had many questions, but now, so long after the event, they may be condensed to one: if Manuel was not in a coma, what did he eat?

On Helvellyn in the Lake District there is a memorial to a dog which remained by his dead master for weeks until the body was found. I was guiding the Army one day and they were much affected by the dog's faithfulness. How was it possible, they asked, that he could have stayed there, starving. I pointed out why he didn't starve and that lost me all the goodwill I'd engendered to that point.

Somewhere at the mouth of Embargo there could be evidence of what happened there in 1849. The tepee would have rotted in a short time, but are there human bones in the dense growth of willows? Of course, if there are, there is no proof that they are Carver's; they could be the bones of a settler, or of a lady who visited him, or even those of an investigator who came here after 1849, and disappeared. The mouth of the creek is a jungle that could hide many sins.

It is so overgrown that the place where the creek enters the Rio Grande can be discovered only by wading down the river. No one

120

ever camped there, but in the corner of a pasture close by is a grove of cottonwoods. The tepee would have been pitched here, where the trees afford both shelter and fuel.

The Rio Grande would once have been lined for great distances with cottonwoods, even now it gives that impression. Only on closer inspection, following the banks, do you realise that in places the trees have been cleared, probably when the first settlers built their cabins. There are enough left to give an investigator a good idea of where the Fourth camped, because they would have preferred places where the swath of trees broadened to woodland. The second camp, the one where Carver went mad, could well be in a wood by a bridge two miles downstream from Embargo.

I stopped the Jeep by a gate leading into the wood. I walked over the rank grass and through the trees to the river. It was a still grey afternoon with wisps of drizzle in the air. No birds sang and the river slid past quietly. On dry shingle spits against the banks, great tree trunks had been left by the floods, their branches draped with dead vegetation like the wrack of ocean tides. The grove was a sombre place and, despite the fact that no mountain was visible, only the banks and the river and the cottonwoods, it could never be taken for anywhere else but the middle of a huge continent. The very air breathed of space.

Richard Kern said that the third camp was 'below the big rock'. Historians have taken this to mean in or near Del Norte. 'Just the thing,' said Ruth Marie, bearing me off to an *al fresco* luncheon in the town's park on the bank of the river. I walked to the edge of the water, and I looked back at the park. Did *they* camp here, and hunt in vain for food (snails, earthworms) where now the Twin Mountain ladies in pastel pants suits helped themselves to sparrow-sized portions of turkey and ham?

I said my farewells in Del Norte and started down the river. Using the same system I had employed when I came across from the Great Sand Dunes, I went down to the water by paved road or ranch track but now I walked along the banks. I took fishermen's paths where they existed, bushwhacked when there was no trail. If I didn't see the actual camps I knew roughly where the sites were; the diaries gave the distance between each.

In the winter of 1849 there would have been little variation in the three camps below Del Norte; even in the middle of August they looked similar. There was the low river, the shingle spits, blackbirds and swallows. Once there was a host of yellow warblers, brilliant as canaries.

I crossed the river close to where the two French voyageurs, Tabeau and Moran, were left sitting on the bank. Eastward now is the town of Alamosa, downstream of which the Kerns camped: the place where Rohrer and Andrews died – poor tubercular Andrews who came along for his health. Other people had done the same thing and been cured, but they made their journey in the summer time.

Below the Kern camp there is now a wildlife refuge, the river running inside its western boundary. The trail that passed down the valley to Taos would have kept close to the river, as did all trails in the West where, a few hundred yards from water, without irrigation the desert takes over. Rainfall around Alamosa averages eight inches annually. I turned into the refuge, left the Jeep, and followed a track that may have been nearly three hundred years old, dating back to 1694 when the Spaniards entered the valley. Before that it would have been an Indian trail. Few people used it now, that much was obvious from the abundance of wildlife and the reaction of three mule deer which stared at me in amazement before springing away like antelopes.

The river was open here, the occasional cottonwood or big old willow standing out like a tree on the plains. The refuge was vast; although it was in two units, each unit was around twelve thousand acres. Most of the sanctuary was marsh; it was full of birds but on this hot afternoon many of them were in the shelter of cat-tails and reeds where they could be heard crooning to themselves. Avocets paddled in the mud (they seem not to mind heat), and Canada geese were grazing on the far bank of the river. I could hear duck and killdeer and snipe calling, while all around me scarlet dragonflies zipped above the sloughs and gorgeous butterflies sailed by, big as humming birds. I saw five garter snakes in less than two hours.

I drove for miles down the eastern boundary of the refuge and camped some fifty feet above the marsh, so close that I could hear the duck, and yet I was on arid ground surrounded by prickly pear. After the sun set I followed a trail through the reeds using the torch occasionally when I saw a dark patch on the dust. Nighthawks boomed, snipe were diving, a great horned owl called. The dark was busier than the day.

I must have been two miles from the Jeep when I heard coyotes behind me and remembered that I had left the cooler on the ground.

It was stocked with luxury foods which I had bought that day. A bunch of coyotes would have no trouble getting inside a cooler. I hurried back, forgetting about rattlers but pursued by mosquitoes (I had forgotten the repellent), increasingly concerned when the Jeep didn't show above the sage. The fear of losing my food gave way to that of losing myself – not a dangerous situation but hideously uncomfortable when wearing only a cotton shirt and Levi's. The temperature would drop to the mid-thirties in the small hours. It took me half an hour to find the truck. The coyotes retreated before me and left the cooler intact.

Next morning the mosquitoes had gone and I went down early to the marshes. The birds were out, feeding among the dikes and ponds and the old ox-bow lakes. There were bitterns and snowy egrets and black-crowned night herons. All the ducks, and the big blue heron, had families, but the oddest objects, sinister until identified, were a number of very large fish prowling through the water weed, their long, gleaming backs momentarily exposed. For a moment, from a distance, there were monsters in the marsh.

Deer flies moved in on me, tested the repellent, found it innocuous, and started to stab. I fled to the car. They followed me into it. I opened all the windows but I had to increase speed to 25 mph (too much on that road) before they relinquished their grip and were whipped out by the wind.

On a bluff above the river was an untended cemetery. The last marked grave was of the mid-1940s; the earliest was that of Anna Hansen, who died on February 21st, 1878, aged fourteen days. She would have been born to the first settlers; the cemetery was on Hansen Bluff.

I looked at the river and wondered if there was as much marsh and as few trees when the fourth expedition came through. Could it be called an expedition at this point? From the mouth of Embargo they were in five parties: Manuel at the tepee, the Kerns, and Vincenthaler and his company. In front of them were the two relief parties: first King, then that led by Frémont.

Leaving Embargo, Frémont went fast down the Rio Grande, averaging sixteen miles a day. He told Jessie that he was inspired by anxiety for those left behind.

The second day out his party came on the tracks of a horse in the snow. This was the first time they had seen similar tracks since they left the mules on the divide, which must have seemed a long time ago.

In fact they were still within sight of Mesa Mountain, which was little more than thirty miles distant as the raven flew.

Their immediate reaction as they considered those hoof prints was that the rider was associated with themselves. Frémont had told King that if he encountered difficulty in obtaining supplies at the settlements, he was to despatch a messenger upriver to inform the expedition of the delay. Thinking that this track had been made by such a messenger who had mistaken the rendezvous and turned back prematurely, Preuss says that King 'was up for quite a few curses.'

They had some shocks that day, as might be expected since they were approaching the fringes of habitation. Within a short time they came on the tracks of a number of horses, and of Indian *travois*. These are tepee poles dragged behind a horse and supporting a frame on which baggage is carried. The sight of the tracks made them uneasy, but since they turned and went downriver Frémont had no choice but to follow although there was a strong possibility that these were hostile Indians.

On the fifth day out from Embargo they met a solitary Indian who turned out to be the son of a friendly chief known to Frémont. The man was wretchedly poor, but not by the current standards of the relief party whose last two meals had been of coffee and sugar only. At the Indian camp they were fed with corn mush and venison, and Frémont made a deal with the chief's son whereby in exchange for a rifle, two blankets and further rewards when they reached the settlements, the man should guide them there, and provide four horses to carry their baggage.

They were poor horses and walked more slowly than the men. On the day that they left the Indian camp they made only six or seven miles, but the slow progress enabled Godey to hunt and to bring in a deer. Towards sunset they saw a wisp of smoke rising from some cottonwoods by the river. Hoping that this was King's party, returning with supplies from Taos, they left the trail and approached the river.

They found Breckenridge, Creutzfeldt and Old Bill Williams. That was all. No mule train, no supplies, no King. They had never reached Taos, had never got any further than this spot. Creutzfeldt was so wasted he was unrecognisable and Breckenridge had to tell the newcomers which one he was. King, said Breckenridge, had starved and his body was some six to eight miles upriver. Preuss says: 'King had died of exhaustion four days before, and the others had eaten part of his body.'

Their story was simple and differed little from that of the stragglers coming down the river behind Frémont. Food, of course, had been the basic problem, or the lack of it. By the third day their meagre rations had been consumed and breakfast was two tallow candles between the four of them. Over the next ten days their only meat was one small hawk and the carcass of an otter which they found on the ice.

Their lower limbs became so frostbitten that they had to remove their boots and wrap strips of blanket round their feet. They kept their boots and ate them.

They came to a great bend where they were forced to leave the river and cross a fifteen-mile neck of land to avoid an Indian encampment. Old Bill said he had seen smoke in that direction, and told them that this was a Ute camp. Utes were after his scalp as a result of his involvement in the recent army massacre of Indians when he received the wound in his arm. So, already suffering from the onset of blindness, they embarked on the snow-covered desert where there was no shelter and no fuel. At night they huddled on one blanket and pulled the others over their heads. Sleep was possible for only a few minutes at a time. The blankets grew smaller each night as the strips on their feet disintegrated and had to be replaced.

Their boots were gone now and as they walked they chewed on their knife scabbards. When those were finished they started to eat their belts.

King collapsed and was left behind. When they camped that night Creutzfeldt wanted to return but Old Bill said that he had looked back and seen a raven circling. The circles had grown smaller until the bird alighted. King was dead, Old Bill said, but Creutzfeldt went back all the same. When he returned he was badly shocked. He had thought King was asleep as he approached, but he had been mistaken and now he could talk of nothing else but death.

The following day Creutzfeldt collapsed. Old Bill lit a fire and sent Breckenridge ahead saying he would follow. In Frémont's unpublished memoirs he quotes Kit Carson as saying: 'In starving times no man who knew him walked in front of Bill Williams.' But Creutzfeldt survived, and without a mark on him.

After leaving them Breckenridge saw five deer. The animals had not seen him but he must bring one of them down with one shot because they would take fright after he fired. But hitting a beast would be a coincidence because he couldn't see them properly. He rubbed his eyes with snow but he was trembling so much that when he did fire it was a matter of pulling the trigger when the barrel happened to be pointing at one of them. Too weak with reaction to walk, he crawled up a bank and found a deer dead on the snow.

He cut it open and ate the liver on the spot. When he returned to the others Old Bill fell on the meat like an animal and even Creutzfeldt revived, and ate a portion raw. They continued to the river, built a fire, and it was next day, as they were roasting deer meat, that they saw Frémont's party approaching.

It was this meat that stirred suspicion, that and Carson's wariness concerning Old Bill in starving times. Breckenridge makes no mention of surviving on King's flesh, or no mention that was made public. Preuss thought there was cannibalism; Frémont, on his fifth expedition, was to point out from Cochetopa Pass the area where he said men of the Fourth had survived by eating their dead companion.

Senator Benton, in his book, *Thirty Years' View*, was positive: 'They pointed to an older camp, a little way off. Going there [Frémont] found the man dead, and partly devoured. He had died of exhaustion, of fatigue, and his comrades fed upon him.'

Frémont makes no mention of going back to see King's body. He says this party's last camp was seven or eight miles distant. Benton was not there of course, but he had his information from his son-in-law.

Thomas Martin was closer to the event. He was to write: 'King froze to death on the plains. They brought his body into where they camped and it is supposed they lived on it, although they never would acknowledge it ... I know positively that the men we left behind lived on those of their companions who gave out, as I had it from some of the same men.'

The evidence is inconclusive. Considerable time elapsed before the bodies were found, and the scavengers were never far away. When Godey returned with supplies wolves were quarrelling over all the bodies. It would have been difficult to tell whether any had been butchered by men or devoured by animals, or both.

American attitudes were ambivalent towards cannibalism. In Europe the practice of eating people who had died naturally had never been considered illegal when survival was at stake. As McGehee might have said, no one could argue with that. Moreover even when events took a terrible and violent turn, they were viewed with leniency. In

126

certain circumstances murder was legally justifiable. The circumstances were most likely to arise after shipwreck.

Traditionally lots were drawn: the short straw for the victim, and sometimes the next shortest for the executioner. Everyone knew this happened; there was no secret. It was called the custom of the sea: the 'defence of necessity' and there was a case in 1884 which exposed the system to the public eye. The yacht *Mignonette* was wrecked and three survivors ate the body of the cabin boy after the captain had stabbed him. They were charged with murder on the high seas, and necessity was not allowed as a defence. They were found guilty but pardoned and sentenced to six months' imprisonment: a fascinating example of British ambiguity.

A more simple case was that of three Scandinavians who killed and ate another member of the crew after their ship was wrecked. No charges were brought against them, the Norwegian public prosecutor saying that their action was excusable on the grounds that the sacrifice of one was necessary for the survival of the remainder.

The ultimate act – of murder – did not (so far as we know) apply to the fourth expedition. If human flesh was eaten, no one was killed in order to obtain it. What Frémont thought of the subject is not known. Obviously he assumed that cannibalism had occurred; his word would have been the source of most of the accounts, particularly that of his father-in-law. Ostensibly Frémont would have conformed to the established view that cannibalism is wrong. Leaders had to be adamant. There was no room for discussion of the question because that would have introduced qualifications: the thin end of the wedge. Once you allow that human flesh may be eaten, in the event, survivors, instead of pulling together, will start to look at each other with hungry eyes.

Frémont had no time for recriminations. Once the act had occurred, he would accept the situation. He was at his best in emergencies. No matter what kind of meat the men were roasting round their fire on the Rio Grande, no matter whether Breckenridge's deer was a myth, that King's body was eight miles away or close by, mangled by wolf or man, what had happened was in the past. Frémont put the three survivors on his horses and trudged on towards the settlements.

Thirteen

THE COUNTRY CHANGED character. From the old cemetery above the marshes there were mesas visible in the south, and the flats were desert, or at the least, semi-arid. North of the mesas the Conejos or Rabbit River entered the Rio Grande. It was at the mouth of the Rabbit River that Frémont had told Vincenthaler to expect to meet the supplies.

Before I could reach the Conejos I had to cross the Rio Grande. Ten miles from the cemetery the road was blocked by a sign ROAD CLOSED. I squeezed past it and within a mile there was a bridge, one lane of which had been closed by a barrier. A stencilled notice said grimly: No Responsibility for Accidents. The sign writer had got the N the wrong way round. We had no trouble crossing.

The mouth of the Conejos was a landmark, probably because, rising as it does in the San Juans, it would always contain plenty of sweet water. A small community had been established there since Frémont's time. Today, adobe cabins were disintegrating but a few little houses were still occupied, and there was one fine ranch house and a herd of Charolais bulls. A group of Mexicans waved to me. The place had the air of a feudal fief.

The road ran parallel to the Rio Grande but a few miles to the west of it. Looking towards the river I could see nothing but stony ground and spiky vegetation: land where, even with wells drilled every two miles, more than sixty acres would be needed for every cow.

I came down to a paved road, turned east and was soon back at the river. Now there were no trees at all, only rocky bluffs downstream of the bridge, forerunners of gorges in the south. I lunched on the bank and a man approached carrying a flower in a beer can. He was accompanied by a black Labrador, its head a mass of scabs and pustules.

He said he was an 'unemployed lawyer' on social security. He had left home because he could not endure his girlfriend's sons who were on cocaine, which he could go along with, but when one made his

128

supper from a dog, he decided it was time to move on. He asked me to accept the flower. The dog lay in the shade, panting. I asked what was wrong with its head. A *gringo* had peppered it with shot three days ago. There had been a bitch too. She was killed at the same time. He had been going to put the flower on her grave.

I started to pack up. He apologised for driving me away. I told him I had stopped only for lunch. He said conversationally that he had been considering suicide. The vet couldn't operate on the dog because the animal had a haematoma. I said there was no question of his committing suicide while he was responsible for the dog, and for that he had no answer.

Through the afternoon I drove south past isolated hills and small irrigated valleys, green with crops and ripening corn: less blatantly prosperous than the flat lands in the north, but more picturesque. Another notice proclaimed that a bridge was out, but I continued for four miles through the sage and came down to the river, and this time the bridge *was* out: its timbers in the act of being replaced.

I walked along the frame as far as I cared to go and leaned on the rail looking at the sparkling water downstream. There were bluffs at a bend, a solitary tree, cows. There was no ranch. The cattle could be as much as a hundred miles from any ranch. There was probably a cabin hidden in a fold in the desert where a solitary range rider would live, responsible for several hundred cows on fifty square miles of land. A lonely job, but so was that of the trapper; there was no reason why the strain should not persist: cowboy descended from mountain man.

Southward, on the east bank of the river, stood a big mountain: a flattened cone, well-timbered. That could be Ute Mountain, a little over ten thousand feet. People going south to Taos and Santa Fe would have used it as a landmark. They would pass it on the east because the western slopes looked as if they dropped steeply towards the gorges of the river.

Suddenly, as the Rio Grande enters New Mexico, the bluffs of the banks give way to jagged ravines. Frémont would have left the river north of Ute Mountain and headed southeast towards the settlements. I followed, across desert and sage, past adobe ruins and cabins like those in South American shanty towns: patched with tar paper and cardboard, past buildings clustered in the middle of nowhere that I would have taken for ghost towns but for the battered trucks outside

129

shabby houses. No one was visible, not even a dog sprawled in the hot shade.

The sun was low when I came to the lip of a gorge. Three hundred feet below the river ran in deep shadow, chuckling to itself. The night was clear and warm and dry. There was no dew, no necessity for a tent. I slept under a brilliant moon.

We may have been on the old trail as we took the road for Questa next morning. The sage was tall enough to sweep the sump and there were anthills between the ruts. This would be nasty walking country without a trail. The ground was strewn with black volcanic rocks like loose lava – but then, in winter, the trail would show as a smooth white ribbon of snow.

On this, the last day of their retreat, Frémont's small band was without food, but by nightfall they reached the settlements. The arrival was something of an anti-climax. They had already met the Indians, the first strangers they had seen since they left Pueblo two months ago; they had tasted proper food. You could say the rescue had started in that they had picked up three men in worse condition than themselves. The fact that the main rescue plan could not be put into operation immediately they arrived at the settlements was frustrating. There was food, but no mules to carry it. Next morning Frémont and Godey left the others and rode on towards Taos.

The first settlements were on the Red River, a tributary of the Rio Grande that drops down the biscuit-coloured slopes of the Taos Mountains, through juniper and pinyon pine, to nourish a lush green jungle where the old cabins once stood. Now there is Questa: a collection of mobile homes and liquor stores where a road goes off to the Red River ski area. I glanced at the town moodily and drove on.

Fifteen miles further we came to Arroyo Hondo, where Turley's grist mill once stood, and a trading post, and the distillery where Taos Lightning was made. Simon Turley had been killed in 1847 (when Mexicans were fighting Americans). An old mountain man, William Le Blanc, was running the mill in 1849. He received Frémont hospitably, as he would receive the survivors when they arrived, but still there weren't the pack animals to carry supplies upriver. On they went – and on we went – to Taos.

Frémont arrived in Taos on a Sunday afternoon eleven days after he left Embargo. Kit Carson didn't recognise him; his old employer was emaciated, begrimed from the smoke of camp fires, ragged and lame. One leg was so badly frostbitten that he was put straight to bed in Carson's house. Friends and guides flocked to see him. There was Richard Owens, who had been with him in California in 1846, Lucien Maxwell, a veteran of the second expedition, St Vrain of Bent's Fort. Meanwhile – and within two days – the rescue mission was on its way north.

Godey had collected thirty mules and loaded them with supplies. He engaged four Mexican muleteers and started on the back trail, reaching the Red River settlement only the second evening after he had left it. It seems unlikely, considering the logistics of getting together a pack train, that he had even one full night's sleep between coming in from the wilderness and returning as a rescuer.

On the road he picked up more horses and mules, supplied by Major Beall, the officer commanding the army in that region of New Mexico, but few of the animals were in good condition. Preuss says that Godey knew he would travel slowly and he didn't expect to return within ten days. That was optimistic.

He met the first of the survivors eighteen miles above the mouth of the Conejos River, in what is now the Alamosa wildlife refuge. This was the party led by Vincenthaler. Mounted on mules, some of these men, including Vincenthaler himself and Thomas Martin, turned back with Godey. (Vincenthaler was not all black.) Four of his party had been left behind. These were all veterans: Josiah Ferguson, Benjamin Beadle and George Hubbard. Three days ago an English-born member of the third expedition, John Scott, had also dropped out. They found Scott still alive, but his mind had given way. He would survive and recover his sanity.

Godey then started to search for George Hubbard but the man must have wandered away from the trail. They searched all night but it was not until next day that his body was found. It was still warm. After the rigours of this night search Martin could no longer stay on his horse, and Godey continued with the Mexicans, leaving him in the care of five or six of the survivors.

Godey rode upriver for three days, passing the Kern camp without knowing that it was there. He was cutting across a bend and the Kerns were camped on the river bank. Then he came on Josiah Ferguson who had not moved far from the body of Benjamin Beadle.

Ferguson insisted that the Kerns were close by. They turned back together and heard a signal gun in the distance (the Kerns fired at intervals). Benjamin, in a letter from Taos, wrote that when the rescuers came up Godey took some bread from his pocket: 'Oh he has bread we cried and some of us trembled with joy at the sight of it.'

Godey fed them carefully with boiled bread and deer meat, and slaughtered the colt. He left a Mexican too, whom they sent to Vincenthaler's camp for the loan of horses because they were unable to walk. He returned with mounts and, two days later, with blankets for saddles and ropes for stirrups, the Kern party started for the settlements. The indefatigable Godey had continued upriver through deepening snow to the mouth of Embargo Creek where, to his utter astonishment, he found Manuel still alive in the tepee.

Instead of turning back – by this time he had found everyone, and all the bodies except that of the madman, Carver, and Proue (but he had been dead before they left him) – Godey went up Embargo Creek in an attempt to reach the Kerns' long camp seven miles upstream and to salvage baggage that the men had been too weak to recover. In this he failed, although he didn't give up until two of his mules died from the cold. He did bring Frémont's personal trunk down to Taos although this was probably among the baggage already in the tepee.

Returning, he picked up Manuel and for the last time set foot on the ice of the Rio Grande. There was no diminution of energy. He overtook the Kern party, and he arrived back at the settlements on February 9th, eighteen days after he'd left. He had covered 250 miles, searching for survivors, feeding them, recovering the equipment. Four days later, with the expedition reassembled, he was on the trail to California.

Godey was illiterate but he could have talked to people about his rescue of the fourth expedition. He did not. Years later a California cattleman, J. J. Lopez, who had known him as an old man was to say: 'He would talk about anything in the world except his own experiences. In more than fifteen years of close association with him, I never once heard him mention his pioneer exploits, except when closely questioned.'

Billy Skinner, an orphan who was adopted by Godey in the 1860s, had no more success than Lopez: 'There is very little I remember about Godey's early life or history, and I believe that no one ever heard him talk about his past life unless they lived around him a long time and tried to get him to tell about his experiences.' There appears to be no record of anyone's having succeeded.

*

I stood in the dim living room of Kit Carson's adobe house in Taos. Godey would have dined here, Frémont had been nursed in the bedroom, would have convalesced by this fire. The house was interesting as a museum; there was the saddle used by Jim Bridger, the doyen of mountain men who built Fort Bridger on the California Trail. There were the clothes that had been worn by Mrs Carson, but I could feel nothing of the Fourth in this place. And certainly Taos, with its bright and bustling glamour, its art galleries and jewelry stores dripping with silver and turquoise, its opulent houses, none of these held any of the dark cosiness that must have greeted them when they came stumbling down the Rio Grande after that terrible winter.

There was a violent snowstorm the day before the Kerns reached Red River. Without a compass and unable to see the sun they travelled all day in a circle on a white plain and returned to their starting point. They set out again, decided to give up and camp, but they were so nearly frozen that they pushed on and, late in the afternoon, they saw buildings ahead. Again they had just escaped death, and this must have been a very bad storm. They had Godey with them and still they were nearly overwhelmed.

Richard Kern arrived in Taos on February 12th. Frémont was then making preparations to leave. The Kerns, Cathcart, Old Bill Williams, Stepperfeldt and Taplin remained in New Mexico. Captain Cathcart 'was not able to prosecute his journey further' according to McGehee but Frémont noted in his memoirs that Cathcart was in poor health at this point. As for Stepperfeldt and Taplin, they would still be unfit; they had been among the last to arrive, but so was McGehee, and he continued with Frémont to California.

McGehee husbanded his energy on the long retreat, refusing to contemplate the thought of food, but concentrating on systematic thinking, on solving mathematical problems and planning his future: 'So, in this way, never allowing myself to think upon the hopelessness of our condition ... I kept hope alive and never once suffered myself to despond, and to this course I greatly attribute my support for there were stronger men who, doubtless by worrying themselves, hastened their death.'

At Taos they heard that gold had been found in the Sierras. There were rumours before they left the Missouri; they hadn't believed them but now the rumours had become fact. McGehee, and even Creutzfeldt and Breckenridge – who had suffered so terribly with the first relief party – and Scott who had been mentally disturbed for a while, all continued.

In Taos something occurred, more likely something was said, that resulted in the Kerns severing relations with Frémont. In his first letter from Taos to his sister, Mary, Edward Kern was chiefly concerned with an account of their progress since they left Bent's Fort, with their sufferings, and the rescue by Godey. He said that the brothers had lost everything except the clothes they were wearing; all the same, he reckoned that Frémont's loss must be between eight and ten thousand dollars.

Giving no specific reason he said that Benjamin and Richard would be returning east from Taos, although he had not yet made his own plans. Here there is a clue to their feelings: 'The Col [Frémont] is in town though I have not yet seen him. He proceeds I understand on his journey...' More explicitly: 'This whole business may be laid down to error in judgement to whom attributable I am not now prepared to say.' He had made one accusation, however, against Vincenthaler: 'a weak and cowardly person to whose imbecility and cowardice may be laid the subsequent deaths of most of the men who were lost.' He may be referring to the division of the party after the deer was killed, to the unequal distribution of the meat. Eventually the brothers would blame Frémont for the disaster, whose decision it was to try to salvage the equipment. But for the moment Edward was concerned with personalities. On the 13th Frémont left Taos and he wrote to Mary again: 'He has left us without even his good wishes or a thought of our future – and owing *me money*.' (He was evidently one of those who deferred payment when he signed on.)

His second letter to Mary was undated but obviously he has had a few days to recuperate and take stock. His letter begins with an elaborate drawing of two men standing over their dying comrade. The letter itself is studied, flowery and venomous. Frémont had 'broken faith' with the Kerns; they had joined the expedition as doctor, artists and naturalists. They had been allotted the work of muleteers. Frémont, said Edward: 'loves to be told of his greatness.' He listened to lies concerning the brothers: 'another amiable weakness he has, that of believing the reports of the meanest in the camp. Hardly one time has he treated us with the respect due to our situation or ourselves, and jealous of anyone who may know as much or more of any subject than himself (for he delights to associate among those who *should* be his inferiors – which may in some measure account for the reputation he has gained of being, for a man of his tallents, so excessively modest. A thing by the by which many adopt to hide their want of depth....)'

Edward was jealous of Frémont and loyal to his brothers. At twenty-six he was the baby of the trio. It is a young man's letter, but although he is voicing his own opinions, it seems likely that they were also those of his brothers, and there is considerable confirmation in the facts. Frémont *was* a poor judge of character, and the Kerns were even less than muleteers; like most of the others, they became pack animals themselves once the mules were abandoned.

Edward said that the brothers decided to leave the expedition before there should be an open rupture, which would be unwise, for confrontation: ' 'twould have come from us, he is not the *Man* to commence face to face ... the greatest dread he has at present is that a *true* and *correct* account of the proceedings above and here may be made public.'

Richard Kern would say nothing on the subject of the disaster in the San Juans. The following year he wrote to a Dr Morton: 'I cannot in justice, speak of events *without* tracing them to their causes, and as I would handle the subject ungloved, it would ultimately lead to personal consequences and they you know should never be resorted to except as the ultimatum. Beside the subject is a very painful one to me, and I speak of it as little as possible. I am willing to leave it with the past....'

The most painful memory for Richard was the murder of his brother. At the end of February Benjamin and Old Bill Williams returned to Embargo Creek with a pack train and Mexican muleteers in order to recover the equipment. The snow was still deep and progress was slow. Unfortunately they didn't inform the local military commander of their departure; had they done so they would have moved out behind the soldiers.

As a result of hostilities with the Indians a punitive military party left Taos on March 11th and a skirmish occurred north of Red River. Ten Utes were killed. Twelve escaped and fled north. Three days later, on March 14th, they came on Benjamin and Old Bill at Embargo Creek who, knowing nothing of the skirmish, treated the Indians with civility but also, no doubt, considering Old Bill's background where Utes were concerned, with circumspection. It didn't suffice. While they were talking the Utes suddenly raised their rifles and shot Old Bill in the forehead, Benjamin through the heart. The Utes took the mules

135

and packs but spared the Mexicans, who made their way back to the settlements with the story.

The attitude of Richard and Edward Kern was that none of this need have happened, would have happened, neither their brother's death, nor the previous ten fatalities, had the baggage been abandoned *in the first place*, right back on the divide. They had been terribly weakened ferrying the packs down Embargo Creek. At one time Edward (the epileptic) was carrying seventy pounds, in deep snow and without a trail.

There is a similarity between Edward's malevolence and the malice of Breckenridge: puzzling until one recalls that Frémont roused strong feelings in everyone who met him: from adoration to hatred. The atmosphere that hung about the fourth expedition was far too rarefied for there to be any neutral ground and – so far as Breckenridge is concerned – Frémont thought that the first relief party resorted to cannibalism.

When he came to write his reminiscences for *Cosmopolitan* forty-seven years after the event, Breckenridge was to maintain that, when Frémont came on the three survivors of that first relief party, he left them some food and passed on, telling them to follow. They walked until their frozen feet could carry them no further and then they crawled. It took them ten days to cover forty miles. But Preuss, who had no axe to grind, confirmed Frémont's statement that the survivors were put on the Indian ponies and that they reached the settlements in four days.

The question of cannibalism, never resolved and always suspected, probably lay at the bottom of the Kerns' split with Frémont. At the start of the expedition the brothers would have held him in esteem. Only Edward had been with him before, but he must have vouched for Frémont; there is no indication that he had to persuade his brothers to join the fourth expedition. Nor is there any evidence of animosity towards Frémont before they reach Taos – but once there, or shortly after their arrival, hostility explodes.

No mention is made of any discussion between them and Frémont concerning their continuing with him, and yet they must have talked. A doctor is invaluable to an expedition – unless the doctor was the one man Frémont didn't want in his company.

McGehee never named the man who suggested that they should eat Andrews' body, but since it had to be one of the Kerns or Cathcart, who would be more capable of 'undertaking the butchery' than a doctor?

Frémont may have asked no awkward questions about King's body, may well have turned a blind eye (the priority was to save the lives of the men struggling down the Rio Grande), but in the comparative calm of Taos he couldn't ignore the gossip. A doctor, an educated man, should set an example. It would have needed only one cool word of rebuttal from Benjamin: that in the circumstances the suggestion was reasonable, and Frémont: prickly and arrogant, could have said something unforgivable. He knew that the suggestion had been made. On February 6th he wrote to Jessie1 that the Kerns had camped near Vincenthaler: 'with the intention, according to Taplin, to remain where they were until the relief should come, and in the meantime to live upon those who had died, and upon the weaker ones as they should die.'

He hadn't seen Taplin when he wrote that; he would have had the information from Vincenthaler, which explains the background for Edward's malevolence concerning Fremont's 'amiable weakness ... of believing the reports of the meanest in the camp.'

Most of the men who continued to California had endured the same privations as the Kerns; it was this other matter that set the brothers apart, made them different and, in fact, more sensible than their leader, which may have been the basic problem.

Fourteen

I SLEPT HIGH above Taos near the Palo Flechado Pass, pitching the tent in a dark plantation of conifers. A sign had directed me to a campground that was complete with roads, sites with electricity and water, ablution blocks, the manager's house. It had been a plushy place once; now the electricity and water were switched off and the site abandoned. It held an aura which seemed to emanate from something other than the dense ranks of trees. Had there been violence in these empty buildings? Had someone disappeared? Even the vandals had passed it by.

I returned to the Rio Grande which was temporarily a pretty river in lush bottom lands. There were vineyards called 'wineries', orchards, fruit stands by the road, signs advertising sculptors and painters. Frémont said the fruit trees were in bloom when he passed through at the end of February, and I had anticipated a kind of Vale of Evesham. The land was certainly fertile but the tacky little houses contrasted as sharply with their fecund surroundings as must the peons' huts have done in Frémont's time. The finest vernacular architecture in America was that of the Anasazi Indians who built their beautiful cliff dwellings in the fourteenth to sixteenth centuries. There has been nothing to touch it since.

Downstream from Taos and west of Santa Fe is Frijoles Canyon where the Anasazi built a communal house eight hundred feet long and three storeys high. It backs on the rock and some of the rear rooms are caves, artificially enlarged. Rows of angular holes show where the roof beams slotted into the wall. Exposed to the weather, many of the adobe walls have crumbled and only the smoke-blackened cave rooms remain intact, now hung with bats.

From the rim of the canyon the village may be seen in relation to its environment: the Long House below its sheltering but sunny pink cliff, a ruined plaza close by. It was occupied for only two hundred years; when the Spaniards arrived in 1598 the Anasazi were gone and all the cubic cliff houses in Frijoles, Chaco and Mesa Verde were

138

deserted. Too many people had become a drain on the resources; there were no trees left for fuel and building, cultivation had exhausted the soil, the game had been hunted to extinction. There was drought, and the Anasazi moved away to pueblos along the Rio Grande, to Zuni Pueblo, and Hopi in Arizona.

Eventually the ranchers came to New Mexico, archaeologists arrived in Frijoles canyon, finally the tourists – all of them, all of *us*, drawing from the ruined village something of its peculiar ambience.

I met a half-naked man with an embroidered carpet bag over one brown shoulder. He was an English construction worker from Berlin, spending six months' savings on a tour of the American West. Travelling with his German girlfriend he hitch-hiked everywhere, and lived in a tent. His ambition was to be a travel writer and crime author. He had written two novels but not yet sold them. He asked me what a writer needed to earn in order to survive. I suggested five thousand pounds if you owned your house, and then reflected that this was probably only a quarter of what a construction worker earned.

I'd not done a proper walk since I'd traversed Byer's and Bill's Peaks in Colorado. I felt sluggish so next morning I trudged up to the canyon rim and turned south for the Rio Grande.

The trail was delightful, running level over white sand and the bedrock of a mesa, through junipers and the odd scrubby oak. There were deer about, and the lovely blue jay of the pinyon woods. After four miles of gentle walking I came out on the edge of the cliffs above the olive-green river which was, in fact, a long lake backed up behind the Cochito Dam.

I ate my lunch in the shade of a pinyon, noticing with some surprise that the thermometer on my key ring read 117°, and the mercury was rising. There was no shade on the trail.

I returned carefully, the peak of my cap shading my neck, drinking a little at every half hour, watching my own progress, alert for the first signs of weaving. Deliberately, I took great interest in my surroundings, noticing during the last glaring mile, a vulture on a dead tree in the distance. As I drew nearer more floated in, to alight on the same tree and settle themselves with composure. Finally there were five, all turned towards me, silently observing my approach. I moistened my lips. No matter how many vultures have kept pace with you: circling, dropping down to trees, perched on rocks while you eat, you'll never persuade yourself that, like the gulls on Snowdon, they are interested only in crumbs. Vultures in the southwest don't need a race memory to inform them that people as well as animals die in the deserts.

As you travel west from the Rio Grande the land becomes thin and dry, almost empty but bleakly beautiful: a world of long mesas with scarps of rimrock that appear diminutive, but are often a hundred feet high. The screes are mostly bare but there is a sprinkling of pinyon and juniper. The rock is in pale shades of biscuit and salmon. This is the country from which the Apaches came to plunder the fat lands in the south and fall on travellers between the Rio Grande and the Gila Trail.

I spent a night in Cuba, a place where the only white people that I saw were in the Post Office. The motel was owned by Asian Indians who had gone away and left a small girl in charge who appeared to be about fourteen, and her young brother.

Outside the Post Office a striking bearded man of mixed blood sat in the passenger seat of a battered limousine. His hair must have been elaborately styled because it was protected by a plastic bag like an outsize shower cap, on top of which was perched a Navy-type ball cap with lashings of gold braid. The limousine's stereo played loud rock and he jerked and nodded to the rhythm with glazed eyes.

I was stoned too – with the heat; I drove for forty miles on the right road but in the wrong direction. But no experience could be wasted in this country where the mesas were in pastel shades of pink and cream and ivory with intrusions of ash-grey drifts and two-dimensional reefs. Prows stood up like sea cliffs, headland beyond headland, and at long intervals there would be a ranch with adobe buildings, a few willows and a pick-up truck.

I stopped for petrol at a solitary store and gas station. A truck drew up and the Apache driver came to help me unscrew my petrol cap which, self-locking, would sometimes jam, but it was the storekeeper, a white man, who freed it. As he filled the tank he told the Indian that there was some of his stuff in pawn. The man denied it. So it was the old lady's, the storekeeper said. There was a nice bracelet; he would sell it. I guessed that this was for my benefit and I was expected to ask to see the bracelet. A woman climbed down from the truck. She was immensely fat. The storekeeper shouted that she was losing so much weight she would soon blow away, then he proceeded to elaborate. She kept her eyes on the ground and murmured some inaudible response. At least, I saw her lips move. Now an old man got out of the truck and approached. The Indians stank of alcohol. In the nineteenth century they were killed with guns ('The only good Indian is a dead Indian'); in the twentieth it's done with welfare cheques.

I came to Chaco Canyon: wide, fresh and exhilarating. In Chaco the Indians have left only the fine evidence of their existence, to be studied without any of the revulsion and guilt one feels in the presence of many modern Indians – which may explain the current popularity of the Anasazi. We are sublimating.

Chaco is a shallow canyon, its walls coming down to ground level, and the ruined villages are built of sandstone so that the pueblos merge like animals with their background. As one archaeologist put it: 'I was working below the pueblo for two days before I realised it was there; I thought it was part of the mesa.'

On my first evening a lecture was given by the only untidy ranger I had encountered. Always well-groomed, rangers change before lecturing – the creases in their trousers and shirts are knife-edged, girls exude freshness and men the scent of after-shave – but not this man, who wore baggy pants and a shirt that pouched over his belt. He was a Navajo – close kin to the Apache. He used no slides but talked without a trace of self-consciousness, and as he talked he moved constantly; he gestured, changed tone, dropped into Navajo, acted out his anecdotes, his stories of magic. He held his audience in the palm of his hand. Only occasionally have I heard a speaker to touch him: old Englishmen trained for the Bar or Government. With storytellers like this Navajo, no culture has need of the written word. He stood for the bright side of the moon – and now I remembered that, despite their wariness of some tribes, some clans, Frémont, Kit Carson and Old Bill had many friends among the Indians, including Apaches.

Suddenly, on the bleak uplands, it was hot again and I had to revert to the practice of high summer: rising at four so that I could be above the canyon by the time the sun gained its full strength. The climb to the rim was easy, taking a line of weakness which the Indians would have used. Once on top of the mesa there was a network of ways that linked the pueblos, but because the mesa was layered in wide, shallow terraces and the trail meandered among them, sometimes up, sometimes down but always over rock, there was no path. The route between the ruin of Kin Kletso and the 'prehistoric stairway' was marked by delicate, tapering cairns made of stone flags and built on the correct system of each one being just visible from the last.

141

Occasionally the builders had been carried away by their own crafts-manship and had overdone it a little but the result was so unobtrusive and artful that you could only admire. The cairns were a perfect complement to the empty ruins perched like tors on the skyline, and to the stairway.

I was walking round the back of a side canyon, a canyon literally encircled by a sandstone escarpment except for the break at its mouth, when I saw a trail coming up the bottom. I wondered about that because the line led purposefully to the wall below me, which was too steep to look down. A cave, I thought, or a small ruin, not troubling to get the map out.

I walked round the rim to the opposite side and looked back. There, cut in a rock pitch of forty feet, was a ladder of huge footholds with big pockets for the hands on either side. Above the stairway there were farming terraces. During the rainy season and until the crops were harvested that was the way they went to work. I could envisage the ascent but the holds looked dangerously rounded for the descent of people carrying loads. And how did they keep the wildlife from their crops? Doves would eat seed and deer would eat anything. Dogs – they would have been the answer; the Anasazi did have dogs, probably a strain developed from coyotes. Originally they would have been pups taken back to the pueblo after the dam had been killed.

A walker in a place like Chaco sees everything; the most evocative ruins, the unfrequented places, are accessible only to people on foot. Chaco is an exciting mix of ancient and mysterious culture, of over-grown washes where you must warn the rattlers you're coming, of great rock overhangs and graffiti over nine hundred years old: antelope, a hand, a crescent moon and a star with curved rays. According to Chinese astronomers a supernova would have been visible from Chaco on July 5th, 1054.

The construction worker from Berlin was making notes below some petroglyphs, his friend photographing them. They had hitched a lift from Frijoles with a man who repossessed cars. He was, they said, badly bruised about the face, the result of his not getting his gun out quickly enough when repossessing a car in Albuquerque. He told them that eighty per cent of defaulters on car payments surrender the keys without trouble, the rest are Trouble.

I came out of Chaco and returned to the Rio Grande by a southern loop but still in Indian country: interminable grass plains edged by far mesas and their tiny scarps. I travelled slowly, revelling in the empty roads, the air that smelt of hot rock and sand and shrivelled sage.

Far ahead, appearing and disappearing with the gentle switchbacks, something was on the road. I approached a large flock of goats. There was no herdsman. I stopped. The goats continued towards me deliberately, as if driven, but there wasn't even a child at their backs. They were silent, undisturbed by the Jeep, only their little hoofs pattering on the asphalt. Those on the verge were feeding. I edged forward and they parted in front of me. Behind them, trotting officiously from side to side, came a dog: a ginger mongrel of a type so common in Indian villages that they amount to a breed. He threw me a casual glance, grinned, but didn't check until he had them all past and spread over the road again, when he dropped down on the verge but continued to keep an avuncular eye on them.

I drove on and after half a mile a car came belting towards me. The goats were now hidden by a swell. I flicked my lights and gestured. The driver stared at me stonily but he slowed down. After two miles I saw a group of shacks a little way from the road. A huge awning was to one side, ranks of empty chairs underneath, revivalist slogans attached to the canvas. I drove into the yard and a girl came out of one of the shacks.

'Are those your goats out on the road? You nearly lost some. Is no one with them?'

'Isn't the dog with them?'

'He can't stop cars speeding along the highway.'

'I'll send my little brother up.'

A short distance further a flock of sheep was on the road. No dog was visible. Subsequently, for miles, and even between fences, the road was alive with goats, sheep, horses, foals, cattle. I had no need of excuses to go slowly, which is the only way to travel productively in the West anyway.

I was inordinately tired. I'd walked about five miles that morning in Chaco and now the heat and thirst were tormenting me. I was afraid that I would go to sleep at the wheel so I drove into the shade of some junipers and pulled out my foam mat. I took the cushion from the driver's seat but by the time I had turned back to the mat it was covered with ants.

I put my seat in the reclining position, climbed in and closed my eyes. It was no good; I cannot sleep unless I'm flat. I replaced everything in the Jeep and drove on, reviving as the sun declined. A campground marked on the map was no longer there, the cheap motels in Santa Fe had no vacancies. Eventually I found a campground at Cochito Dam where I was kept awake by drunks shouting obscenities. Next morning the manager told me that he had called the sheriff at midnight and a deputy came out and quietened the party. I demurred. 'You know how it is,' he said. 'They'd have started up again soon as he'd gone. *We* couldn't do anything. We have orders not to confront anyone: drunk, that time of night. Big hefty guys, guns with them too.'

After the manager had gone I sat in stunned disbelief and drank my coffee. It was early and the camp was quiet. A thin, pretty girl rode up and down on a bicycle, away for a hundred yards and back again; up and down without stopping, in silence, like a beast pacing its cage. Maybe we should all go back to herding goats.

Fifteen

SOUTH OF SANTA Fé, Frémont followed the Rio Grande for 150 miles, an easy stretch which they covered quite quickly. They were fitter now. No doubt the men had eaten well in the settlements, and Frémont himself, after leaving Kit Carson's house at Taos, had been royally entertained by the officers of the garrison at Sante Fe. It was here that he obtained supplies and equipment, from the quartermaster's stores, and was lent a thousand dollars by a civilian, F. X. Aubry, with which he bought horses and mules. He recruited a number of men – some accounts say eight or nine; Benton in his book said he continued with thirty, which would mean he recruited thirteen. Certainly he needed a large party; he would shortly be leaving civilisation again and entering Apache country. The Indians were known to be on the war path and it was essential that the Fourth put on a show of force. Among the recruits were Kit Carson's brother, Lindsay, and Tom Boggs, a son of a former governor of Missouri.

Sixteen of the original men continued with Frémont to California: the four from the successful relief party: Godey, Preuss, Saunders and young Theodore; Breckenridge and Creutzfeldt were there from the first relief party, and the indomitable McGehee. Manuel was with them – his feet must have been padded and swathed against the pressure of the stirrups. There was Vincenthaler, and all those men who had been with him at the end of the retreat (except Beadle and Hubbard, who died): Gregorio and Joaquin, Thomas Martin, Scott (no further mention is made of his being deranged), Ferguson, Bacon and Ducatel. Of Ferguson and Bacon we know nothing except that they were veterans – although we do know it was Ferguson who saved the Kern party, insisting to Godey that he had missed their camp. Of Ducatel all we ever knew was that he was the son of a Baltimore doctor, probably a greenhorn – but a hard man, as were all those original members who rode down the Rio Grande during that second half of February, 1849.

*

145

The Rio Grande is an artery through New Mexico. Not a wide valley, it now carries the interstate from El Paso, Texas, to Santa Fe and beyond: to Denver and the northern states. The valley is intensively farmed. I found it dull and, since nothing untoward happened to the Fourth here because they, too, were going through farmland ('the people engaged in opening the ground for sowing') I looked sideways for interest.

I went east to see the remains of great churches built by Franciscan friars in the seventeenth century: the ruins of Abo in crimson stone, and San Buenaventura at Gran Quivira, the roofless nave of which is 140 feet long, and where, if you speak quietly at one end you may be heard at the other.

I saw 'The Valley of Fires' on the map and went there on an overcast morning looking for the kind of brilliant red and orange rock that riots through Nevada's Valley of Fire, but all I could see was the scorched earth of a major burn. Vultures circled above a lay-by and an odour of skunk, long dead, was borne on the hot wind.

As soon as I entered the valley – which is a State Park – I saw that this was no burn, but black lava. There was one trail, a mile long, formed by laying a core of sandstone over the lava, and surfacing it with gravel and sand. It made a walk so smooth that a tarantula was taking the air ahead of me.

A bird sang in a cavern at my feet, like a subterranean prisoner. I am not fond of old lava beds, nor of new ones for that matter; like the thermal basins of Yellowstone, they are too close a reminder of the fragility of the earth's crust.

The day was disturbing throughout. Even in the lavatories at the Valley of Fires, the wind moaned through the ventilators like an animal in pain.

I drove on in silence except for that wind. Music would be wrong today. It had been perfect yesterday, so what was bad about this side of the Rio Grande? The country was all fenced, that is, the roads were fenced, and that implied ranching, but it must be sparsely inhabited; the few buildings I did see looked abandoned. It was a land of long low swells with the ranges set back and far apart. We were skirting the Jornado del Muerto – The Day's Journey of Death – which was on the old trail from El Paso to Santa Fe.

A dirt road took off northwards and there was a sign post indicating four ranches back in the hills, the nearest three miles away, the furthest twenty-two miles. I looked wistfully along the track and saw another sign. I drove up and, reading between the bullet holes, I deciphered: 'This area is subject to evacuation for missile firings. For your own safety obtain clearance from Stallion Ranch Center, telephone prior to entry.' It was duplicated in Spanish.

Suddenly I knew where I was. The first atom bomb was tested twenty miles to the south. No wonder I saw no cattle and no people. I drove on, entering an area where signs warned of dust storms. The very ground looked dead. The dust must be radioactive.

I came down to the river and followed the interstate to Socorro, which was a military post in 1849. Frémont reached it at 8.30 a.m. on February 24th and breakfasted with the commander. With the exception of a few hamlets it would be the last settlement that the Fourth would see before they reached Tucson in Arizona. They were now some three hundred miles south of the original projected route. How many of them remembered that they'd set out to find the way for a railroad? But Frémont hadn't given up; he merely lowered his sights to a survey and a map of where he was going. In his letter to Jessie from Taos he was optimistic, even blithe: 'The survey has been uninterrupted up to this point, and I shall carry it on consecutively.'

The central valley of the Rio Grande was a curious interlude for all of us. Frémont thought that he had left the blizzards behind. Here it was spring, but below Socorro he must leave the river and go west through Apache country to the Gila Trail. To crown everything he would run into snow.

Studying the maps, considering where he might have left the river, I saw, forty miles to the west: 'Plains of San Augustin'. No traveller could resist that, and away we went: through the Gallinas Mountains and the San Mateo Range to a great grey expanse staked out with the giant dishes of the National Radio Astronomy Observatory. Frustrated (they ruined the view), I turned round to find myself at the centre of one of those gloriously dramatic weather systems, with a storm on virtually every range in sight, and each flowering intermittently with a bloom of lightning. The plain was black and silver with matt splodges of white that marked rain so torrential that when it struck I was forced to slow to a crawl.

I stopped for petrol and asked why there wasn't the usual discount for cash. Because, said the girl attendant, the Apaches were suspicious of discounts. She had taught on a reservation and her aide, himself an Apache, had eventually succumbed to despair, holding that there was no sense in educating young Indians to find good jobs when their wages would be spent on drink. The system, I said, needed short-circuiting. She looked at me blankly.

I drove south on a good dirt road. On either side the juniper-pinyon woodland sloped upwards to forests of big conifers out of which rose mountains over ten thousand feet high. Storms hung about the summits but left me alone. I was so tired that I kept going, postponing the moment when I would have to stop, pitch the tent, fill the lamp and cook.

After twenty miles, when I knew that another hour would bring me back to the Rio Grande, I found an old wagon trail that led me through pinyons to an exquisite site where the only sounds were the muttering of thunder punctuated by coyotes singing in the hills, and the only light when I put out the lamp was sheet lightning flickering behind the clouds.

The rain started at midnight and it was still raining at dawn so I went to sleep again. Next time I woke the rain had stopped and there was a heavy silence outside, quite different from the feeling of a sunny morning. The sensation is aural. The ears know that there is a difference before the eyes open. I unfastened the tent. The sky was overcast and cloud lay in bands along the hills. There was just a hint of blue in the north.

The similarity to a summer's morning in Britain was amusing and I pottered about happily, hanging the bedding on the Jeep to air, noting with relief that the ground was grit rather than dust, so the rain hadn't formed gumbo. Eyeing the wet tent, wondering how long it would take to dry, I realised that the rear guy was missing.

There had been an alloy stopper on it that tautened the string. It was the loss of the stopper that infuriated me. The thief was a pack rat. Once before, camping on stony ground and forced to tie the tent to rocks, over a period of three nights I lost the guys as fast as I replaced them. The red furry nylon I used must have made attractive nesting material. I didn't begrudge them the nylon so much as the stopper, which would be difficult to replace. I crawled from burrow to burrow, from hole to hole, searching for a glimpse of scarlet that might indicate the stopper had snagged on a twig, but I soon gave up; the pack rat would have to be aberrant that couldn't cope with a snagged stopper.

Rodents must be swarming this morning to judge by the number of raptors about when I took the road. I came to a line of power poles and almost every pole was a perch for a kestrel or a Swainson's hawk.

They were all facing west; at the same time as they watched for prey they were warming their backs in the pale sunshine.

Down in the valley I found one of those magnificent nature reserves which the Americans do so well: over 57,000 acres of which 30,000 were wilderness, the latter somewhat suspect. The reason why people were not allowed to camp there was that it was a buffer zone between a missile testing range and civilisation. If the area had to be evacuated, I was told, the authorities might have difficulty in finding back-packers, so for the moment half the reserve was left to the animals.

The Rio Grande ran through the other half: the source of water for a network of channels and meres, mostly man-made, but overgrown and indistinguishable from natural marsh except where there were small fields tilled by local farmers on a share-crop basis. At harvest time one third of the crop would be left in the fields as supplementary food for wintering wildlife. Long before the place became an official refuge it had been a sanctuary for animals. Its name, Bosque del Apache, the Wood of the Apaches, referred to the cottonwoods along the banks which still shelter deer and bald eagles, even peregrines.

Trails were short and pleasant, allowing one to stretch the legs and the mind, but most of the birds were seen from a fifteen-mile loop. On a hot August afternoon there were few people about, and not a lot of birds. A pair of stilts stalked the mud, a snowy egret stood pensively on a bank: a Toulouse-Lautrec girl in black stockings and yellow bootees. The only industrious birds were a family of terns, but then they cooled off every few minutes when they dived. I did see my first wild turkeys: streamlined birds as different from their barnyard descendants as an alley cat from an overweight Persian.

The manager of the refuge was surveying the bank of a cleaned channel. When I expressed surprise that he didn't delegate the work he told me that he was the engineer, biologist, administrator, and Public Relations – and he loved it all. They had sixty thousand snow geese in winter, and sandhill cranes, and whooping cranes. They painted the snow geese red and green for identification purposes, and they looked superb. I stared at him, trying to find the joke. No joke, he said; they used an aerosol spray: non-toxic and quick-drying. It did no harm to the feathers and, if ingested, appeared not to damage the bird's system.

He sent me to the local campground where the owner cleared the weeds and thorns from my site with his bare hands, and his wife insisted that I use the guest bathroom in her house. Only the dog had trouble in accepting the situation. Every time I went across to the house he lifted one corner of his lip and walked away, stiff-legged, looking back over his shoulder, the trembling lip exposing tightly clenched teeth.

We were a long way south now, close to the Mexican border. The desert had turned a reddish shade. Familiar cacti appeared, and plants of the southern deserts: creosote, cholla, ocotillo, and the prickly pear that looks like a pile of plates balanced at angles on top of each other.

Truth or Consequences was my next mail drop but there was no mail. I registered at a motel and went out to look at the town. Originally it was called Hot Springs, but the citizens liked a television programme and changed the name: a clever move; the tourists love it.

The old town had character. A motel advertised: 'Rooms and Apartments. Daily Weekly Monthly Hourly.'

The mail arrived. I answered it in one day, and next morning drove south for eleven miles and turned right. My last glimpse of the Rio Grande was a glint of water among desert hills. Three months had passed since we came over Mosca Pass and saw the San Juans sixty miles away, beyond the cottonwoods of the river. By an odd coincidence three months elapsed between Frémont's traverse of Robidoux/Mosca and the point, this point, where he left the Rio Grande.

Once we turned away from the river we were in flat creosote desert. Ahead there were foothills, smeared with green after the rain, and beyond them were the Mimbres Mountains rising to nine thousand feet. This was where a spring blizzard struck the fourth expedition. Frémont needed no reminder of what a blizzard could do to them and, desperate for fuel and shelter, he turned into the foothills.

He had hired a New Mexican as a guide, and no doubt they travelled from spring to spring. Benton wrote a romantic account of this stretch, and between this and Frémont's factual but skimpy notes, I found fixed points although not much evidence of how they were connected. According to Thomas Martin they followed 'Cook and Kearny's trail'. When the Mexican War started in California in 1846 Brigadier General Kearny marched the Army of the West from Fort Leavenworth on the Missouri to the Pacific, and he went by way of the Rio Grande. (This is the general whom Frémont fell foul of in California and who was responsible for his court martial.) Kearny was followed by Lt. Col. Cooke leading a battalion of Mormons, and the two commanders did in fact take different routes. Frémont followed Kearny towards

150

the Mimbres Mountains, but where the general continued westward across the range, taking the shortest route to the Gila River and its trail, there was too much snow for Frémont who went southwest from the Mimbres, eventually joining the more southerly route of Cooke and the Mormon Battalion.

Frémont sheltered from the snowstorm in the foothills and then made his way to the Mimbres River. The foothills surprised everyone. 'Pleasant country,' Frémont noted, 'Well wooded, resembling the oak region of the Sierra Nevada.'

The road I followed wound gently through little rocky canyons with misshapen spires on their slopes. The colours of drifted dust suggested minerals, a suggestion confirmed by the remains of old mines. A group of humped Brahma bulls in shades of pearl and dove moved across a slope of crushed rose. There was a creek of milky water. Big white prickly poppies appeared: the late summer flower of the southern deserts; yellow coyote melons ripened on the verges – and there were Frémont's oak trees, and walnuts and hickory.

I took the direct route across the Mimbres Mountains: an Indian trail before it became a branch of the Gila road. The pass was over eight thousand feet high and from it ran one of those delightful crest paths on which I was the sole traveller apart from the deer. I would have had my last view of the Rio Grande from here except for the haze. I looked down a canyon, over the creosote desert, and way beyond the river to where the Caballo Mountains showed above the valley mist.

After lunch I drove south for fifty miles, turned left and left again: forest, desert, Vivaldi, and a dead diamondback where two ruts left the road. I had almost completed a circle and was close to the trail of the Fourth again. Tomorrow I would follow them towards the Mimbres River. I wanted to camp here, but the snake gave me pause for thought.

The diamondback is the largest of the western rattlers so one assumes that it has more venom than the little prairie rattler to which I had grown, more or less, accustomed. But I was very tired and those twin ruts were too tempting to ignore. There was a lot of vegetation: mesquite and yucca, all kinds of cacti. I eased along the track for a few hundred yards, looking for a big bare space. I knew that no snake would approach me, but I wanted to be some distance from any holes.

When I found a suitable site it was too rocky to pitch the tent. Despite this I slept well, dreaming that a cat was curled against the

151

small of my back. I woke happily, saw the brilliant stars, thought: but I haven't got a cat, and froze. Cats curl, snakes coil – oh, my God! But my sleeping bag was plumped out; surely no fangs could penetrate that, and if I moved, it would rattle. I hunched forward. No sound. Again. Not a ghost of a rattle. It was just a dream.

I looked at the map and I looked at the foothills of the Mimbres Mountains. The Fourth would have worked their way round the range in two or three days. Somewhere on this section they met Apaches.

Frémont had hoped to avoid the Indians, but he stood little chance of doing so; his horses would be leaving tracks in the new snow. On the fourth night out from the Rio Grande the animals were restive so they were brought in to the camp circle. No one slept much for the rest of that night, but dawn came without any sign of hostility. When they moved off McGehee was in the rear. Suddenly the rest of them heard rifle fire. They halted and McGehee came running up, unhurt.

There was nothing they could do but proceed. They were a small party and probably outnumbered. It must have been a bad moment for Frémont who, in order to save face with the Indians, would have felt that they should be punished for firing on his men, and yet he couldn't risk chasing them, particularly on their home ground. He continued, and later that morning two Apaches showed ahead, whether as decoys or observers there was no way of knowing. Frémont decided to parley with them and left with his 'interpreter', probably the New Mexican guide. They were followed by Godey, who distrusted Apaches.

A ravine appeared in the ground ahead of Frémont, and the Indians motioned him to go round its head. He guessed that the intention was to place an obstacle between him and the main party, but for him to show fear at this time might prove fatal for everyone. He rode boldly round the back of the depression and, drawing rein, told them his name. It meant nothing to them. He berated them for not knowing their best friend, as he put it, and he asked for the location of their tribe which, he told them coolly, he wished to see. The Indians were disconcerted so he followed up his advantage and invited them back to the camp to eat with him.

They didn't want to go, confessing that it was they who had fired on McGehee; now they expected to be punished. But Frémont treated the affair like a misdemeanour and persuaded them back to the camp, winning their confidence to the extent that they accompanied him to the Mimbres River. There they were given presents and they directed Frémont to a spring in the desert where he might rendezvous with the tribe. As soon as they were gone the expedition took a different route. The last thing they wanted was to meet the tribe. The Indians had said that their warriors were now in Sonora and Chihuahua and everyone knew that although courage and luck had been effective where two men were concerned, matters could go very badly with a returning war party.

They pushed on quickly but there was a long way to go before they reached the safety of the military post at Tucson: over three hundred miles. There were settlements between here and Tucson but they would be in a state of siege themselves.

From the Mimbres River they had to go southwest to what is now the corner of New Mexico. They followed the river for some distance and then struck out across the deserts, zig-zagging because the springs were at the foot of the mountains.

I could not take the same route; there were trails but some that were marked on the map were no longer in existence, or they were blocked by wire or had been washed out by flash floods and never repaired. Occasionally I back-tracked for miles to ask directions at the last ranch. I had to be careful; strangers were suspect in this country. Dogs were savage, and Rotweilers were a favoured breed. Border ranches had an air of fortresses and guns were prominently displayed.

The last days of August were very hot. I crossed and re-crossed that corner of New Mexico, regardless of whether I was actually on the route of the Fourth, but knowing that I touched it often. I camped at the City of Rocks: a pile of granite towers three miles from the Mimbres River, and I watched a storm play itself out on the continental divide to die in a grey and golden sunset.

Next day I followed my party in a desultory fashion, drifting down a line that I had marked the previous evening, and the heat mounted yet again to a climax. In mid-afternoon I drew up at a rest stop. I staggered to the lavatories and, washing my hands, heard the door open behind me but I was too comatose to turn round. There was a tap of high heels on tile and I caught the scent of Chanel No. 5.

I strolled back to the Jeep. Not far away was a very long sleek limousine, plain chocolate brown, with smoked glass windows, all closed, the engine running softly. I lifted a map and pretended to study it, my eyes on the lavatories.

The woman was tall and slim, in dark slacks and a striped jumper in deep shades of blue, green and red. Her long black hair was combed back and tied with a large red bow. Her lipstick was bright scarlet, as were her toe nails in the ridiculously high-heeled sandals. She was amazingly beautiful. She caught me staring and stared back, not resentfully, nor arrogantly, but with interest. It was not only each other's appearance but the rigs: the Jeep's colour no longer visible under the layers of dust and dried mud, her vehicle looking as if it had left the factory that morning. She slipped into the passenger seat, the door closed without a sound, the car reversed, and all I saw of the driver was one fine hand – not a podgy or be-ringed hand. Mafia money, I thought with satisfaction, then seeing the car had Texas plates, corrected myself. It might be no more romantic than oil money.

All the same we were approaching the border. Crime, violence, drugs loomed large – although if that limousine had been bought with the proceeds of drugs-running, it was heroin, not grass, and to my knowledge, it was only marijuana that crossed the border in wilderness areas, and small quantities at that. On main roads it was a different matter and more than once I could hear the wheels turning in the heads of the Highway Patrol as they regarded this hard brown lady in the filthy Jeep with Nebraska plates. I could not be more conspicuous – but was it a double-bluff?

I camped in the Burro Mountains, taking the customary precaution of concealing the Jeep and tent from a road that was very rough and went nowhere; its importance lying in the fact that it short-circuited a long stretch of interstate and highway. That could have been its attraction for other travellers; all night vehicles crept by on the trail, but with daylight nothing moved, and only the fresh tracks in the dust showed that the sound of engines had been no dream.

In this area there was a lot of traffic in illegal aliens. The comparatively innocent and harmless method of entering the States was for Mexicans to walk across the border – even drive across at night – there were innumerable gaps in the wire, and they would be picked up by a friend or relative already living in an American town. This activity hurt no one but the tax-payer; even the law enforcement agencies saw it as something that would not go away while there were merely a few strands of wire between the richest nation in the world and one of the poorest. As for the young men, dressed in their best clothes, trudging along the track and waving cheerfully to me as I passed, it was a game. Win it and there would be a few dollars to send home; lose and it meant a ride back to the border in a nice car, and try again tomorrow.

The horrors came about when the criminals moved in, or business men who were criminally negligent. Fees would be collected from a party which would then be transported at night and dropped outside a town but – ideally – behind a hill where the vehicle's lights would not give them away. The Mexicans would start to walk along the road watching for the lights of the town, but they did not appear. And in the daylight there would be no town, only the terrible desert, and no water – and the people in their tight town shoes died one by one, drinking anything that was liquid, even hair oil.

A box car on a freight train was shunted into a siding where it stayed for days, in July. Eighteen people were locked inside. One escaped by digging through the floor with his knife but by then everyone else was dead.

On the credit side of life Mexicans lent an air of happy insouciance to border towns. One afternoon, lost in the environs of a great copper mine, I found myself in a street of shanties shaded by huge cotton-woods. Families were sitting on the steps of their shacks, radios blared, children and dogs played in the dust, bony chicken scratched for thin pickings.

I stopped for ice at a liquor store. Inside was a kind of den with a window where drivers could be served without the exertion of leaving their cars. The little room was crowded with men sitting on crates, a fat middle-aged slattern in hot pants, and a skivvy serving at the window, run off her feet. All were Mexican and extremely polite. There was a great deal of grinning. Only the fat woman spoke English and all except the skivvy were drunk. I accepted one beer out of courtesy but the strain of grinning continuously (I have no Spanish) was too much for me and I escaped, grateful to relax my cheek muscles.

The heat increased; the air would become stifling, electric. Anvil-shaped clouds bloomed with menace; once a black stalk drooped from the sky and swept the desert with a gentle motion that was both elemental and obscene.

When the storms did strike they were highly localised, like water-spouts. There would be flash flood warnings, I would come on water across the road, and a few miles further the desert would be dry as a parched skin.

Between the storms, particularly in the afternoon, there were mirages: a lake with islands, but on approach the lake would disappear and the islands became the tops of mountains fifty miles away. A slope quite close at hand would suddenly display an undercut slip at its base through which the air showed. But I never saw a mirage like that seen by Benjamin Butler Harris,* when he was following the Gila Trail in 1849: a troop of mounted and armed men three quarters of a mile away. At a quarter of a mile Benjamin waved and the armed men 'waved their numerous hands' – that makes the hair rise on the back of the neck – 'While we were regarding them, they commenced vanishing at the rear, leaving only a dim, light mist where they had so lately stood.'

At least Frémont didn't have the heat. If spring brought out the Apache war parties, it was the best season for everyone to travel. The going was cool and smooth as the Fourth rode down the long valleys: better than rough ground, less of a strain being on the alert, watching, always watching for that first thin column of smoke rising gently through the sparkling air. They were now in the country of the Chiricahua Apaches.

On my hot afternoons the desert roads were empty and I was more likely to fall asleep and drive off the asphalt than to hit anything. But the temperature was dropping; the thermometer stood in the mid-nineties when it had been over 100° in the shade. The trouble was that we were always in the sun.

Eventually, tired of deserts, exhausted by dust and dirt roads and maps and notes, I crossed into Arizona on a Sunday evening and came through the San Simon valley to the cool depths of Cave Creek in the Chiricahua Mountains.

* An attorney from Texas who wrote *The Gila Trail*.

Sixteen

A TWIG SNAPPED loudly as I was hanging out the washing. Vegetation was thick in the bottom of the canyon and the great rock walls imparted a feeling of claustrophobia, at least in a white woman. A twig doesn't snap on its own, but I wouldn't investigate because the woods were full of poison ivy. In any case it had been a large twig. There were bears here. I hoped it was a bear.

Nowhere in the Southwest is there a range that could have been as impregnable to the enemy and yet so hospitable to its inhabitants as the Chiricahuas. The deep long canyons have good water, even in summer. The mountains rise to nine thousand feet and they are timbered to their summits, except in places like Cave Creek where the narrows (perfect for ambush) are vertical walls. There are a hundred places where a person born and bred here, but only such a person, could weave his way to the rim and yet remain out of sight of anyone below: by climbing gullies, fissures, even connecting caves.

The range swarms with all kinds of wildlife, from game to jungle birds. When exotic animals appear in the United States, it's in the Chiricahuas that they're recorded: ocelot, the coppery-tailed trogon, even the jaguar. The Apaches had food, water and shelter. They were inviolate. Soldiers were helpless without their horses, and the Indians were superlative mountaineers. No Mexican or American would have dared to follow them into these wild canyons; you might postulate a scenario where a column of soldiers came up a trail and another descended, and a whole tribe between them. Trapped? They would melt sideways into the forest and up the rocks, as insubstantial as shadows.

Ambush was an art with the Apaches. They seldom stood to fight but would come in fast and silently: to kill, plunder, kidnap and withdraw. Then, while some rode away with the spoils, others lay in ambush.

They stole Mexican and white children to rear as slaves – but so did the Comanches, the Mexicans and, of course, the Americans.

(There was a flourishing slave trade operating along the Old Spanish Trail, Indian children from California being sold as slaves to Spaniards, and later, Mexicans, in Santa Fe.)

The Apaches weren't vicious to begin with. Naive and simple when they first met white men, they became opportunists. In the eighteenth century the Mimbres Apaches 'sold' the Santa Rita copper outcrop to a Mexican officer for trinkets. A hundred years later they were stealing the mules that pulled the ore wagons to Chihuahua. They didn't steal the ore or burn the wagons; they knew more mules would be brought in to salvage the ore.

Another clever ploy was to allow mountain men to trap beaver in Apache territory, to dry and stretch the skins, and then the Indians would steal pelts worth a small fortune. Nor did they kill the trappers; they were turned loose with their guns and traps to catch more beaver.

Those Indians within reach of the presidios were cowed by force, but the country was never quiet and when Mexico revolted against Spain and the soldiers were withdrawn from the presidios, the Apaches went wild. In 1846, when General Kearny crossed the Mimbres Mountains, he found the great Santa Rita copper mine pillaged and abandoned. By then the Apaches were raiding far into Mexico, creating such havoc throughout the Southwest that the authorities inaugurated a policy of extermination. A bounty was paid on scalps: up to $200 for a male over fourteen years, $150 for a squaw, less proportionately for children and papooses.

Bounty hunters flocked in: Mexicans, Americans, escaped slaves, Indians hostile to Apaches. An Englishman called Johnson invited Apaches to a feast and turned a swivel gun on them loaded with scrap iron, broken glass and nails. Initially not a great many were killed, but the shrapnel incapacitated others to the extent that they could be despatched by hand. In all four hundred were murdered: men, women and children.

Since there was no way to distinguish between Mexican and Indian scalps, the less discriminating of the bounty hunters destroyed isolated Mexican villages, scalped the inhabitants, and there was no one to say that the raid hadn't been carried out by Apaches.

There were atrocities on both sides, and Apache tortures were dreadfully ingenious. But if you had lost your family because there was a bounty on their scalps as there might be on the tails of rats, in order to retain your sanity you might sink to the level of the bounty hunter. Apaches hung Mexican teamsters head downwards over slow fires. Americans crucified Apaches. And yet Kit Carson (who took the trouble to learn Apache) moved unmolested through the territory of his friend, the chief of the Mimbres Apaches, but that was before the greedy people arrived, before the Indians knew their own strength. At the height of their power they devastated the Southwest.

This was the situation that prevailed when Frémont came past the Chiricahuas, and if he was unfortunate in the San Juans in being overtaken by the worst winter in living memory, here his old luck attended him. The Apache chief, Mangas Coloradas, with all his warriors, was raiding in Chihuahua. In practice it didn't make all that much difference. A returning war party, high on recent murders, could be more dangerous than the chief himself, who might be persuaded that Frémont's death would be avenged by the Army. With Indians, Frémont's charm and his essential arrogance struck a chord. He lacked their deviousness but a sixth sense remedied the deficiency. He seemed to know by instinct how their minds worked – and they were deeply impressed by his courage. So it's likely that he was less worried about meeting Mangas Coloradas, who might talk before he attacked, than a band of his unpredictable, and possibly drunk young braves. From the Mimbres Mountains to the western boundary of Apache country on the Colorado River, the fourth expedition could never relax – and they avoided the Chiricahuas as if the range harboured the plague.

Even now it isn't a popular area. People crowd into the canyons in spring to watch the coppery-tailed trogons nesting, but in the fall, once you are beyond range of the hunters' squalid camps, the place is as quiet as a grave.

In the north of the range the mountains decrease in size but the ground is desiccated in a thousand spires and towers: peculiar formations made of rhyolite. There is a small National Monument with its own small story to contribute to the legends of the Chiricahuas. One of the rangers, a naturalist, went out for a walk and never came back. In this place: precipitous, overgrown, full of caves and crevices and rattlesnakes, accident seems the most likely explanation, but dogs were used on the searches and nothing was ever found. There was a suggestion of foul play. If he was abducted and murdered elsewhere that could account for the body not being found. There are innumerable mine shafts in the deserts and the desert hills. This southeast corner of Arizona could swallow many victims.

I met a man sinking wells out in the middle of the San Simon desert.

159

He carried three guns in his truck at all times and calculated that he used four hundred rounds a month to 'keep in practice'. He told me that whatever I did I should avoid the border, stay at reputable motels from here southwards, and keep the doors and windows locked as I travelled. 'They' would do anything for a hundred dollar bill, he said. He had killed 'many people' himself and was preoccupied with violence, although not monopolised by it. He was sinking six wells on 120 acres and then putting up houses: developing the desert for something to do. He was one of the casualties of Vietnam.

I crossed an incipient divide and came to the San Bernardino valley. 'We struck the deserted mission of San Bernardino in Arizona,' wrote Thomas Martin, giving me a fixed point. Bernardino was marked on my map but I failed to find it on the ground until I had driven a measured distance from a creek called Danger. 'Bernardino' was literally a wide place beside the road where heaps of gravel had been dumped. There wasn't even a ruin. There might be foundations under a growth of weeds; there would certainly be rattlers. I wasn't going to investigate. As I studied the map I saw, way down in its corner, a patch of white: the San Bernardino Grant.

Spanish Land Grants were awarded to prominent citizens in an attempt to colonise the Southwest, the idea being to import Spaniards, Mexicans and friendly Indians to work the land and gradually push back the hostile natives. There had been huge land grants in the upper Rio Grande valley; now, seeing the fraction of a grant on the map, I knew that the Bernardino where I'd stopped was probably a siding (there was the line of an old railway parallel with the road); *my* San Bernardino was off the map.

I continued, hoping that I could approach it from the west. I had no choice; there was no road in the direction of the grant until I reached the town of Douglas some twenty miles away.

The road ran southwest to cut through a ridge rimmed with red escarpments that terminated in a cone crowned with a volcanic plug. Agaves appeared on the slopes with flower stalks all of twenty feet tall. The sky was intermittently overcast but the day was hot.

I reached Douglas and found the library. From there I was sent to the Chamber of Commerce where the elegant director made an appointment for me at the San Bernardino Ranch. I asked about the perils of the border. She was unconcerned about personal violence; thieves were the problem, but they were after new pick-up trucks. She came outside and, seeing the Jeep, looked dubious. 'Be sure to lock yourself in at night,' were her parting words.

The San Bernardino Ranch was sixteen miles from Douglas, along a dirt road that ran south of the red escarpments and east to a valley where, in 1822, an army officer called Ignacio Perez was granted almost 100,000 acres by the Mexican government. In his petition for purchase he stated that the area was depopulated and that he expected the land to act as a buffer between the Apaches and the settlements in Sonora. In Spanish times, in the 1770s, there had been a garrison at the San Bernardino Springs, but it was too small a company and the Apaches too strong. The Spaniards withdrew after a short time and for fifty years the valley had been abandoned by white men.

Perez appears to have continued his army career, because it was one of his relatives who took over the ranch and stocked it with four thousand longhorns. He lasted a decade and then the community which had grown up around the hacienda could hold off the Apaches no longer. The Mexicans could protect themselves in their fortified buildings (it was never a mission), but even an army couldn't protect stock ranging over 100,000 acres. The people withdrew to Sonora, cattle and horses ran wild through the valley, the adobe houses crumbled, and by 1846 when Colonel Cooke brought the Mormon Battalion along the Gila Trail, San Bernardino was a ruin.

The Mormons had been having trouble. Their guide was a man called Pauline Weaver, half-Cherokee, an old friend of Kit Carson. He had made a mistake in the mountains east of San Bernardino and brought the battalion through the wrong canyon. Wagons had to be dismantled and lowered with ropes. By the time they reached the ruined ranch they were on quarter-rations so they lay over for a day in order that the men could hunt wild bulls and eat. A curious result of abandoning domestic longhorns was that the valley was now overrun by very fierce old bulls. Apaches liked beef but they wouldn't touch bull-meat.

The Indians were well disposed towards the Mormons, possibly because they knew Weaver, but also because the Mormons were going to fight Mexicans, and it was they who had started the bounty system on Apache scalps. That the Mormons were also a large party of armed and disciplined men would have affected Indian attitudes too. When gold was found in California, and later in Arizona, and the Gila Trail was crowded with travellers going westward, the Apaches made no distinction in the nationality of their victims.

161

Throughout its existence the San Bernardino Ranch has had an intriguing history. In 1878 an American garrison was stationed at the springs, in '82 it was the base for a campaign to find, subdue and treat with the Apaches in the Sierra Madre. By 1884 the Indians were officially confined to a reservation, and in that year John Slaughter bought the ranch. It comprised 20,000 acres north of the border, and he was to lease additional spreads. In the early 1920s he calculated that he owned and leased around 100,000 acres.

He built houses, barns and a school; he dug wells, constructed dams, laid piping and created a lovely mere below his house. At one time his herds numbered 17,000 head. Like Perez he suffered from cattle thieves. Geronimo – who kept escaping from the reservation – was still active when Slaughter bought the ranch, and even when the renegade Apaches were shipped off to Florida, he was to lose cows to rustlers, and to thieves posing as honest ranchers. He was sheriff of Cochise County for a while and it was said that there were occasions when he appropriated the roles of judge and jury as well.

Just before the turn of the century he learned that a band of Apaches were camping in the Sierra Madre south of the border. With a group of his cowboys and a lieutenant of cavalry, he rode seventy-five miles, left the horses and approached the camp on foot. One Indian was killed, the rest escaped. They left behind two children whom Slaughter took back to the ranch. One was so wild that she had to be sent to the reservation, but they kept the other and named her Apache May.

She adored Slaughter but at the age of four, while watching Mrs Slaughter combing her long black hair, the child said: 'I'll kill you some time.' She *hissed* at the other children, but she would never let John Slaughter out of her sight if it could be helped, and she was his favourite child. He was a widower when he married the beautiful Viola and, although they had no children, there were two from his first marriage and, like many well-to-do people of the time, they had adopted a number of orphans.

One winter's day Mrs Slaughter and her step-daughter went to town in a buckboard, having heated a rock to put at their feet. When they had gone the children started to play with the fire that had been used to warm the rock. Suddenly Apache May's dress was in flames. She died of pneumonia from inhaling the smoke. She was about six years old at the time. It was said that the children were much more peaceful after her death.

*

Grieving for Apache May I walked past the mere and climbed to the top of a little mesa. Beyond the broad valley was the range through which Cooke came, and Frémont two years later. There was a trail across the valley coming from a spring. At first an Indian trail, it was broadened and scored by Cooke's wagons; the Fourth would have had no trouble following it. Frémont's pack train was long, with probably twice as many mules as there were mounted men. On either side the scouts paced the sage; it wasn't only the high ground that had to be watched for smoke, but the immediate vicinity where the shallowest draws could provide cover for this the most wily of enemies.

They must have been inordinately relieved to see ahead the trees that marked San Bernardino's springs. It was easier to safeguard a stationary company than one on the move and in a file over two hundred yards long. The animals were still at risk at the springs, grazing even a short way from camp, but none was stolen or injured. Evidently even the bulls kept their distance while Frémont was at San Bernardino.

I wondered what had happened to that aggressive strain of cattle. If it didn't die out in the next thirty years, Slaughter would have shot the bulls; he would never have tolerated them among his herds. He was a dictator, but then communities in the wilderness (as Frémont knew) survived only if the man at the top was as hard as the land and its hostile natives.

The Slaughter ranch not only survived, but prospered over four decades: the focal point for a large extended family and for a community the size of a village. Even etiquette was feudal, selective. John Slaughter, and only he, could dine in his spurs, but ladies had to change out of their riding skirts before they came to table. The Slaughters had numerous guests and there were picnics, swimming parties, camping trips, dances. There were mounts for everyone; there was hunting, shooting, fishing. Faded sepia photographs record every aspect of life from the 1880s to the 1920s. There is Apache May: a funny dark mite with combed hair in a pretty, long-sleeved dress, sitting among pumpkins and looking as if she is about to burst into tears. There is Mrs Slaughter, hauntingly lovely; John Slaughter, nineteen years her senior, solid as a plank; there are the bright, privileged, careless white children.

Outside the big sash windows there is a wide verandah where the family used to sit and look over their vast domain. South was Mexico and the Sierra Madre, east across the valley the Peloncillo Mountains

163

(and the ghosts of a long pack train coming through to Tucson); west were the red escarpments. In the 1880s the nearest town, Bisbee, was forty-five miles away. The legendary Tombstone was sixty-five miles. Douglas wasn't founded until 1901.

The bedrooms were light and airy but small. The kitchen housed an enormous stove which was taken outside in summer time. When Viola finally persuaded a cook to stay, he was Chinese. He had a charming room; perhaps Viola built it for him in a last-ditch effort to persuade a man to remain and cook for a multitude that included cowboys, family and guests. There were never less than twenty-five people to be fed every day.

On the pond, that stretch of water which hinted at a love of beauty in Viola, there were pied-billed grebes and dragonflies. I walked round the ranch and the pond: a sponge soaking up atmosphere. I knew how the Slaughters felt when they bought this place – at least in part I knew. I hoped that I had more perception than John. The story of Apache May shows an incredible obtuseness in the man.

The Gila Trail forked again beyond the San Bernardino Ranch. The old trails were always doing this, according to the conditions and the exigencies of the moment. Some fifty miles west of Douglas are the Huachuca Mountains: shapely and timbered, rising to over nine thousand feet. Before the trail reaches them it must cross the San Pedro River which flows north to join the Gila. Colonel Cooke followed the San Pedro downstream and turned the extensive mountain range on its north. Another huge land grant had been abandoned here. The valley swarmed with more feral cattle and the bulls in these mesquite woodlands were so fierce that they actually attacked the column. A mule was so badly gored that it died; the bull charged a wagon: 'lifting it partly around, and knocking down a mule'. A sergeant was trampled so severely that he had to be carried in a wagon.

Apart from the bulls there was no violence; the friendly relations the Mormons had established with the Apaches were standing them in good stead. But three years later Frémont diverged at this point and went south of the Huachucas on an intricate zig-zagging course through a ravaged land where there were no people, only the charred remains of their houses, no travellers other than themselves – and no Apaches, only the grim reminder of their passing. Six months later they would be back. When Benjamin Butler Harris came along the trail with other Texan gold-seekers, the mountains were alive with

164

smoke signals. Like Frémont, the Texans turned southwest. If you did have to take this route you stood a slightly better chance of survival if the mountains were avoided. To an Apache the night was sacred to the spirits and he preferred to raid in the daylight. For that cover was essential and if the traveller could avoid rocks and canyons and overgrown draws he felt safe, or safer. Out on the plains you might see them coming.

For eighty miles the modern border runs straight as an arrow from Douglas to Nogales, which is sixty-three miles south of Tucson. At first sight, looking down on Mexico from a high point in the Huachucas, there is no difference; the boundary is merely a line through the wilderness. But after a few days I realised that the Huachucas are compact and tidy; they are Forest land, with trails. Here the hiker may play with impunity.

On the other side of the line mountains carry a different aura. Ranges are visible for over a hundred miles. There is a vast plain – which you guess is far from flat once you're down there – a plain wooded with scrub oak and juniper. There is the occasional speck of a house shining pale in the sunlight or with a glint of glass. But further west, towards the San Rafael valley, there is no sign of settlement; it looks as if the Apaches have just left. I wouldn't have been surprised to see black smoke rising from a clump of trees.

The border is arbitrary, following no natural features, and dating only from 1853 with the purchase by the United States of the land south of the Gila River. Frémont's company had been in Mexico not long after they left the Rio Grande. It was immaterial. The Apaches laid claim to all the country between the Rio Grande and the Colorado. Uncertain of its state in 1987 I started to explore it, tentatively at first, and on the American side. Even there, the border mentality prevailed. I was followed occasionally, not by villains, but by what I took to be respectable village men, usually middle-aged but quite often old, who were immediately suspicious of a truck that moved as slowly as the Jeep. I was never approached; like guardian dogs they followed at a distance in ancient trucks, would halt and watch me leave the environs of a hamlet when, in my driving mirror, I'd see them turn and go back to the houses.

On the other hand, one afternoon I was driving south on an old wagon road and I came to a cattle grid. Beside it was a small neat hand-written notice: red on white, the red letters outlined in black, the script prettily pointed. The sign said MEXICO. It looked rather sweet and very innocent.

My camp sites were exquisite. I took care to camp where my light wouldn't reveal my presence, but I have little doubt that always someone knew I was there. Once the Border Patrol drew aside to let me pass, observing my registration plates with casual eyes. If the computers didn't foul up they could know my business in a matter of minutes, but since they were aware that I would know that, probably they wouldn't check; I was just a well-heeled tramp following her bent.

Anxious to camp at a distance from any nocturnal traffic, I slept away from the dirt roads. I followed ruts into sheltered canyons and pitched the tent under walnuts and among blue morning glories. I drove over mesas and crept into hollows where, when the lamp was lit, its light was concealed from everyone except people sleeping on the tops of mountains. Thus I found some of the most delightful camp sites of the journey. The moon was full and the nights were absolutely still, without a sound. I realised, with some amusement, that I was having it quieter than Frémont ever had it, surrounded by animals and men. For me, if the coyotes sang it was while I slept. Once, putting out the lamp before going to bed, and walking to the top of a mesa (you wouldn't do *that* when the Apaches were around) I looked south, and saw the far mountains in Mexico and I thought that this was the first time that I had seen a hundred miles with no light visible other than the full wash of the moon.

Rain came, drenching rain. The roads turned slick, the creeks filled and overflowed. On highways tourists queued at floods until I eased the Jeep through gently, and when they followed – much too fast – some got stuck.

When the rain stopped I followed Frémont through Mexico from Agua Prieta to Nogales. Agua Prieta must have been pillaged in 1849, unless it was founded after that date. No one mentions it. I assumed that the Fourth came close to its site because it is across the border from Douglas and the trail from San Bernardino.

So to Douglas I went, with a married couple from Tucson who would guide me through Mexico as I had guided the wife on Snowdon a year ago. We stayed at the Gadsden Hotel which is a relic of the bonanza days in copper. It had marble pillars in the foyer and a marble staircase up which Pancho Villa, drunk, once rode his horse. You could see the chips in the steps. There was a stained-glass window by Tiffany down which a careless workman had spilt cream paint. In a

166

corner of the foyer a television set muttered without pause, and for the twelve hours that we were in residence, there was always one person sunk in an armchair in front of it. The receptionist was a brawny tattooed fellow in a T-shirt.

At the head of the bed in the Governor's suite was a red glass panel in the shape of a mitre which lit up when you pressed a switch. Above the bed, under the ceiling, was a kind of eave: a projection like the Sword of Damocles, formed by a row of gigantic roofing tiles. The rest of the furniture was Cow Town Gothick but there was a potted fern and a bowl of white carnations, in plastic. Wine was served with dinner. We had Arizona Blush, on ice, and the glasses came out of the refrigerator. The Gadsden had character.

Next morning we crossed the border, wove our way through the back streets of Agua Prieta and found ourselves on a highway heading west through a country that was subtly different from that on the American side. There were more people on horseback but they were working. It is difficult to imagine anyone hacking in Sonora. The mounts were ponies and people rode with a loose grace, never walking, always jogging, like mounted Indians, recalling their ancestry. They were accompanied by dogs that showed coyote blood.

I hadn't expected this. Looking down on an empty country from the Huachucas, I had thought to find a wasteland, sunk as I was in the nineteenth century, but the Mexicans, like Apaches, had come back. Indian blood, diluted with Spanish, was much in evidence, and there was a general atmosphere of *laissez faire*. I wouldn't want to live here but life in Mexico was slow, and I liked that. I drove at ten miles an hour; deep dust hid the pot-holes, but at river crossings the bed was usually hard.

Between the rivers the country was desert: creosote and yucca, agave and cactus. The mountains were spiky and fascinating. Nothing had changed since the Fourth came through here: quiet and prudent, the only sound the soft slap of hooves in dust, the creak of saddle leather, the jingle of bits. They went fast and no one dropped out; no one dared drop out.

We looped north, back to the border and the Gila Trail, then turned west for forty miles of rutted track. It was a hot and dusty stretch and now in the north were the Huachucas again where the Apaches were sending up their smoke signals as Benjamin Butler crossed the plain below. We were on that stony plain which I had seen from high above the American side, and it was eroded by arroyos, themselves choked with mesquite.

We passed three young men in clean white shirts, carrying bundles. Everyone waved. We passed a gap in the wire, big enough to drive a truck through. This was the boundary fence. A mile further there were vultures in the air, and more perched in a tree. There was a sudden nauseating stench. I slowed and we craned our necks, glimpsing a dead and bloated cow in the arroyo. We drove on with relief, not at escaping the smell so much but because it was a cow and not a young man in what had once been a clean white shirt.

From the border we zig-zagged south again, into superb mountains, and the deeper we penetrated into Mexico the more lush the valleys became. Small houses nestled in vegetation that was alien and sub-tropical. But in Santa Cruz we were back in the north again, in a town hidden away at the end of a long dusty road, a town with one unpaved street and a few side turnings. It was late in the day now, the sun setting, the air a little cooler. Doors and windows stood open; there was a political meeting pending, people in the plaza swathing the trees with red, white and green ribands. There was a noise of hammering as a platform was erected.

Frémont says nothing about the town although in his notes he spares a word or two for the valley: 'Spring on the Santa Cruz – peach orchards.' Thomas Martin recalls that it is the first settlement they struck in Sonora. In fact Santa Cruz suffered so much that it is a wonder it ever survived. When an artist, J. Ross Browne, came here fifteen years after Frémont, he thought that the village would have ceased to exist but for the opening of the Patagonia Mine some miles to the north. He hasn't a good word to say for the inhabitants, but he does have the grace to acknowledge that the apathy he found there was to be expected because the Apaches had stolen nearly all the villagers' animals, and would steal any others that were bred or acquired. The people of Santa Cruz had no chance of bettering their condition while the Apaches were free.

In 1864 there was no store in the town. It's almost certain that there was none in 1849. It's unlikely then that Frémont stopped in Santa Cruz, particularly since, although everyone deplored the town, all travellers delighted in the valley of the Santa Cruz River. This is still lush today, and crowded with big old cottonwoods. There are plots of corn and beans; the cattle and horses are sleek and well-bred. If people don't have cars, there are plenty of mules about, and we passed a smart dray with rubber wheels, man and boy up, drawn by two burros.

We passed a beggar. He was a young man, almost black but with fine Indian features and short curly hair. He wore a long coat but no hat and he carried a bundle on a piece of string. He was in the sage at the side of the road and at first he moved away, averting his eyes, then suddenly he looked full at us. His amazing beauty suggested that he was subnormal; no ordinary man with such a face would have had to beg.

By dark we were in the slums of Mexican Nogales where adults and lovely children were picking over the smouldering rubbish dump. We were all tired and suddenly argument flared among us: on the wisdom of warning children against strangers. An argument won on horror is a Pyrrhic victory and I knew enough about child abuse and murder to drop the subject, but I wondered if the reason that simple people don't fear for their children is because sexual abuse is a crime of sophisticated societies, and primitive people, such as Mexican peasants, have not yet adjusted to urban conditions.

Seventeen

THE ROAD BETWEEN Nogales and Tucson was known as the Camino de los Muertes – the Road of Dead Men – from the innumerable murders that had occurred there. It was an important road because it followed the Santa Cruz River where there was always water, grazing and game. Fuel too, for although shelter was of little consequence in this land of perpetual summer, fires were needed for cooking.

There were settlements along the road: a mission, a presidio, a few communities of Pima Indians under Spanish, and later, Mexican protection – which was seldom adequate when the Apaches descended in force. The history of the Santa Cruz valley is one of fire and plunder, kidnapping, murder, and extraordinary fortitude.

When Frémont came through in the spring of 1849 the town of Tubac was deserted. He gives no details; by this time the fourth expedition was so accustomed to the depredations of Apaches that Tubac's condition was unremarkable. But this place *was* different; it had not been burned. Benjamin Harris, coming past in July, only a short time after Frémont, was astonished to see wheat ready for harvesting, peaches ripening in the orchards, fresh whitewash on the houses, and not a weed in the streets. The bell, the ornaments and the pictures were still in the church. Tubac had been abandoned but not pillaged. It would be seven years before it was occupied again.

In 1849 very few white men had settled in Arizona. One of the first arrived only four years after the Fourth came through; in 1853 Pete Kitchen came to the Camino de los Muertes and set himself up as a farmer and gold miner. His house was a fortress; sentries were posted on the roof behind a four-foot parapet with loopholes. They were in position round the clock, the theory being that people were protected, not only among the buildings, but when they were working in the fields as well. For all that, men ploughed with rifles slung on the plough handles while, a mile and a half away, at the gold mine in the hills, armed men guarded the entrance to the mine and provided escorts for the teams of burros that brought the ore to the smelter.

170

There was a cemetery at the Stronghold – which was the name Kitchen gave his house – occupied by the graves of employees who had been caught off guard (going for a drink at a spring perhaps, and not troubling to take the rifle), by the graves of murdered travellers, even Apaches. They had to build a mortuary to house the bodies while graves were dug; when a lot of people were killed at the same time, the grave-diggers couldn't keep pace.

Kitchen married a Spaniard, Doña Rosa, and their only child, Santiago, was twelve years old when the Apaches came on a warm June day. The labourers were making hay, and Santiago was asleep in a hay-cock when the sentry on the roof of the Stronghold gave the alarm. Everyone bolted for the buildings, forgetting the boy, and took up their positions to beat off an attack.

The Apaches were in no hurry and they didn't attack the house. They knew that the hay field was out of rifle range and they knew that Santiago had been left behind. They murdered and scalped him in full view of the watchers on the roof. Kitchen must have been away at the time, taking produce to Tucson. He and Doña Rosa had no other children.

Pete Kitchen's character is epitomised by one anecdote. A thief stole two of his favourite horses and he set out to follow the tracks on his own. Three days later he returned with the horses. They asked him what had happened to the thief. Kitchen said that when he overtook the man, he bound his hands behind his back and was coming home when he was so overcome by fatigue that he thought he would fall from his horse. So, without allowing the thief to dismount, he tied a rope round the man's neck and fastened the other end to the branch of a cottonwood. Then he lay down and slept. While he was asleep the horse walked out from the tree, leaving the man hanging. It was to become one of his favourite stories and he told it often, roaring with delight when he came to the ending. The moral was that if you didn't like the punishment you shouldn't steal the horses.

We pushed north towards Tucson. I would sleep in the desert; Frémont would have camped on the river, perhaps at the deserted Tubac. On this road he had to be even more wary than in the wilderness and it could be that, since the Indians hadn't robbed the church at Tubac, that was the safest place to spend the night.

When white men returned to rebuild Tubac in 1856, they came to mine silver. The superintendent of the local mines, a man called

Poston, made the town his luxurious headquarters, entertaining 'men of refinement' and their ladies, laying out shady gardens and replanting the peach orchards. He cleaned the river to form bathing pools that were overhung by willows, and there he would sit in the water reading the newspapers by which means 'he kept his temper cool amid the various disturbing influences that surrounded him'.

Outside the fortified settlements no man was safe and the worst of it was that, whereas the labourers were well-guarded, working as they did at the centres of activity: the mines and smelters, the highly skilled men: engineers and managers, heads of departments, travelled long distances, often with an inadequate escort, sometimes none at all. These were the men at risk.

In 1863 two managers called Mills and Stevens were riding through the Santa Cruz Mountains when they were murdered for the sake of their clothes, their arms and horses. Two years before, in the same place (an arroyo where the Apaches hid in tall grass) a Dr Titus working at one of the mines, travelling with a Delaware Indian, was attacked. The Delaware was killed instantly but the doctor fought to his last bullet although his body was full of arrows and he had a gunshot wound in the hip. The last bullet he saved for himself.

Mr Poston, all but immersed in the limpid waters of the Santa Cruz, reading his newspapers in the shade of a willow tree, had much to try his temper in 1856. Sadly, by 1861 the gardens and orchards, the bathing pools and his hospitable dining room were all abandoned as men went to the Civil War and their dependants moved to the safety of civilisation. Again the Apaches roamed unrestrained over the timbered hills and through glens so beautiful that future settlers, reminded of home, would name their villages Elgin and Lochiel.

In 1987 there was little left of Tubac, its walls plundered for building materials but, a mile or two away, the church at Tumacacori was magnificent: a tall ruin crumbling under the desert sky. The mission garden was a green shade of fig trees and pomegranates and splashing water. Cloisters and patios excluded the sun with *ramadas* made from the slatted ribs of saguaro.

On our right now were gorgeous mountains where the Fourth would have stopped to hunt but for the proximity of Tucson only a day's ride to the north. And I stopped only to sleep; you climb Arizona mountains in winter time, not in the sweltering heat of September. Even the early morning was hot. The last few hours before I reached

Tucson were trance-like, as if it were I who had ridden hundreds of miles through Apache country and was euphoric with the cessation of danger. For days we had slept like animals, the rifle always within reach.

In this mood I wasn't surprised, only vaguely interested, to see a giant slug propelling itself through the dust a hundred yards ahead. When I stopped it ignored the Jeep. It was over a foot in length, and *beaded*. The tail looked like a pointed salami. It was pink and black, the scales as close as the little glass beads on an Indian's headband. It climbed the bank clumsily and tramped away into the bush: the fabulous Gila monster, reputedly dripping with venom, but as harmless as a fence lizard if treated with respect.

For Frémont and myself Tucson was a friendly welcome, good food and security. There were more deserts ahead and the temperature was again well over 100°, but at a house in the Catalina foothills I found my oasis. I worked spasmodically in a dim and airy room, becoming steadily hotter until I was driven to the pool where, a beer on the side, I floated with closed eyes, lulled by the calls of cactus wrens and quail. In hot countries pools are not for swimming but for cooling off. In Arizona cool water (as Mr Poston knew, reading his papers in the willow shade) is a necessity of life with dignity.

But Tucson was growing at an alarming rate, the old quiet residential areas with a few acres to each house (carefully sited so that roofs didn't spoil the skyline) were being crowded by subdivision. The lovely Sonora desert was disappearing as you watched, tall cacti toppling before the contractors.

There were a few refuges left where people served a *fino* instead of cocktails, and you might sit on a terrace in the sunset and look across green hills stippled with saguaro to the wall of the Catalinas, their canyons in shadow, their ridges gold in the light. But the pleasure was finite; people were talking about getting out, moving on to unspoiled places. It was the old infection, now exacerbated by progress: the legacy of frontier days. Frémont had it, of course, although in his letters he was always talking about a warm fireside, but that was only convention. At heart he was one with Daniel Boone who, fireside or no, maintained that it was time to move on when he could hear a neighbour's dog bark. In Tucson when, from the shade of the *ramada* beside the pool, they see the saguaro tilt and fall before the bulldozer, they put the house up for sale.

In the third week of September I said goodbye to my hosts, the good food and wine, shade and abundant water and clean clothes in the evenings. I pulled out and headed north, following the Fourth on the next stage of the Gila Trail. Here, in the nineteenth century, there were more travellers on the road because a bottleneck formed at Tucson, but where normally there would be safety in numbers, for some there was less security ahead. The stretch between Tucson and the Gila River was safe from Apaches – here the problem was the desert – but after the great red ruin of Casa Grande, westward to the Colorado, the Apaches patrolled the trail like wolves, waiting for stragglers to fall behind the pack trains, the wagon lines, even companies of armed men. There is no doubt that, after McGehee hung back below the Mimbres Mountains, and was nearly caught by the two Indians, from that time everyone in the Frémont train moved off together when they left camp.

A motorist would say that the stretch between Tucson and Phoenix is merely a hundred miles of interstate, but I took the side roads across a creosote desert. Why should I have it easy? Sometimes the creosote gave way to bare ground and since there was a strong wind blowing, the dust rose in clouds, preceded by whirling devils. It was smotheringly hot and, because of the dust and the cameras, I was forced to keep the windows closed and the air conditioner going full blast. I *did* have it easy.

They called this the Ninety Mile Desert and it was much worse for Frémont than it was for me. He might carry water for the men, but the animals had to manage without. Experienced travellers did the first thirty miles at night, then *carried on,* riding a further forty miles by the time the sun set. They rested on the second night and reached the Gila River about ten o'clock the following morning.

You could do it that way only if you were unencumbered by wagons and could push ahead fast, on horseback. The Mormons were an infantry battalion and most of them were not only on foot, but barefoot. Few had boots left at this point. And when the mules became too exhausted to drag the wagons through the sand, the men had to turn the spokes of the wheels themselves. For over two days there wasn't a drop of water for man or beast, and when Weaver, the guide, discovered water two miles from the trail, this probably saved the lives of a number of men, and most of the animals.

On the fourth day out from Tucson the Mormons reached the Pima

174

Villages. The Pimas were settled and industrious; when the Spaniards arrived in the sixteenth century they found a people with a sophisticated irrigation system, who grew cotton, wove fabric, made pots and smelted copper. They had been trading with the West for centuries along the Gila Trail but, best of all, they welcomed white men because they were allies against their bitter enemies, the Apache.

The Pimas came out to welcome the Mormons with gifts of water melons and later, learning that the soldiers had no food and no money, fed both them and their animals without hope of payment. Six weeks before, General Kearny had paused at the villages on his way to California and left ten mules which were so broken down as to be worthless. Now these were turned back to Colonel Cooke in splendid condition, and the Indians would take nothing for their keep.

The Pima chief was Juan Antonio Lunas, a giant of a man: six foot four inches tall, intelligent and commanding, a man of presence. Everyone spoke well of him: trappers, civilians, military commanders, everyone except perhaps the Maricopas and the Yumas. The Maricopas were friendly neighbours but Lunas warned travellers to beware of the thieves among them. There were wide differences between tribes. Two years after the Mormons came past, Lunas was murdered by Yumas from the Colorado.

The fourth expedition came down to the Pima Villages ('Indian faces painted with black lead,' noted Frémont) and they turned west across a great bend of the Gila River. This waterless stretch of forty-five miles, like the desert north of Tucson, was usually done at night to save the animals. I started in the afternoon and as the hours wore on, the sun dipped until it was shining straight into my eyes. The wind was still strong and there were dust clouds everywhere, the road being so drifted that often I could see no tracks ahead of me. After twenty-five miles we ran into deep sand and I came to a fork marked Mobile on the map, but there was nothing other than the fork in the road. I took the left branch because that seemed the most likely direction to cut the Gila Bend, and well before dark I saw a faint trace leading off to the right towards some high ground. I followed it for a mile through dry washes and mesquite to come to a weary halt on a bare patch in the shade of a hill.

The wind dropped with sunset but the air remained warm. I sat at the rear of the Jeep with the lamp on its floor, and the moths came flocking to the light to drop, singed and fluttering, to the ground. Attracted by the insects, a tarantula arrived and took up station in

175

the shadow of the water container but, perhaps disliking the smell of scorching, it never moved and after half an hour it returned to the darkness, walking slowly like a crab. I was sorry to see it go. Being large and furry, tarantulas are good company, providing they stay clear of the bedding.

The night was so warm that I slept in my cotton liner until the small hours when the chill forced me to pull the sleeping bag round me. It was crawling with unidentifiable animals. Wearily I got up, shook all the bedding, checked it by torchlight and lay down again, now wide awake and trying to hypnotise myself by staring at the pallor in the eastern sky.

After breakfast, before the sun had acquired much strength, I went up the hill above the camp. The desert continued for about fifteen miles, delineated by mountains: unknown, exciting. Frémont would have sent someone up this hill – Godey perhaps – to look for the glow of Indian fires by night, their smoke by day, for anything else that was to be seen. You never ignored an eminence that would give you a view of what lay ahead, of someone coming along behind, or keeping pace at the side, out beyond the scouts.

I went down the slope warily, being careful not to turn my ankle, or worse. One advantage Frémont's men had was that they weren't alone. A broken leg would be splinted and the casualty put on a horse. The movement might have been agonising but he was in company and mobile. (There are stories of men breaking a leg, on foot in Indian country, and being shot by companions to ensure a quick death.) If I broke a leg I could still drive. Even in the fag-end of summer I had all the advantages. I missed only the flowers. I tried to see the desert through their eyes – McGehee's perhaps, since he was a perceptive young man, but I didn't know the kind of flowers that bloomed in this desert in the spring. Even the animals were different. There was a curious lizard which, when alarmed by my approach, reared up and ran on its hind legs like a miniature dinosaur.

Before the town of Gila Bend, we came to the paved highway and I turned north on the river road. After about ten miles tamarisks appeared across our line. The river should be somewhere in the middle. I drove slowly through the bush, across bone-dry washes, at one of which was a sign warning me not to proceed 'when flooded', past ploughed land – *ploughed*? You don't cultivate where a summer flash flood may sweep your crop away. I turned back, retraced three miles of tamarisks and decided that the wash with the warning notice must be the bed of the Gila River.

Downstream there was a reservoir behind a dam. I didn't like it. The water was warm and muddy, and signs warned fishermen not to eat the fish. Determined to derive something positive from the Gila but unwilling to risk swallowing any of this dubious water, I wouldn't swim but lounged in the shallows with my hat on, uncomfortably aware of something nibbling my feet, regarding with the deepest suspicion large fish that rolled gently round me showing their dorsal fins like sharks.

Close to the reservoir were the Painted Rocks: a knoll of black boulders on the desert, their surfaces covered with petroglyphs which had been incised in the rock. If the prehistoric Indians had clans, this was that of the Lizard. There were lizards everywhere: fat, with salami tails like the Gila monster, with long tails, with broken tails; there were lizards like men, who could indeed have been men, or lizard-men (an unpleasant thought). They were poor pictures and it has been suggested that they were the doodlings of sentries rather than works of art. Certainly they have none of the majesty of the crimson gods, the troops of antelope and dancing men to be found under overhangs in the red rock canyons – but I regarded the Painted Rocks subjectively. It must have been hot and tiresome work trying to chip out the shape of an antelope under the burnished sun, particularly if you were supposed to be on sentry duty.

The Mormons came past the Painted Rocks, travelling at a mile an hour through the deep sand. Curiously, although there was plenty of water in the river, there was no grass, only willows and rushes along the banks. The mules were exhausted, not from lack of water, but lack of food, and again the spokes of the wagon wheels had to be turned by men.

Colonel Cooke tried to float the wagons down the river but on New Year's Day, 1847, although the water was a hundred and fifty yards wide, it was only three or four feet deep. As soon as the wagons were launched they were swept away by the current and disappeared from sight. Later they were found piled up on sandbars and had to be unloaded before they could be pulled out of the water and the mules hitched up again.

On this stretch Frémont would have travelled fast and easily. Unencumbered by wagons he could move long distances each day and find grass for his animals. The river would have been running well

177

throughout its course in spring. So long as they didn't encounter the Apaches they should reach the Colorado without incident. Did any of them dare to think that way, or would they be afraid of tempting fate? No doubt they had been told atrocity stories about this stretch west of the Pima Villages, and it would be a fool who thought he was safe before he'd crossed the Colorado, but in fact it was a quiet year along the Gila Trail. The worst atrocities were to come a few years in the future.

I camped on desert pavement: a red and black mosaic of polished stones, and suddenly the mountains were familiar. They were the Kofa Range where I'd climbed four years ago. In the sunset the sky over the Kofas was kingfisher stained with apricot, and in the afterglow a jackrabbit came lolloping through my camp as unconcerned by my presence as if I were a deer.

After the lamp had been burning for a while large scorpions arrived. Little scorpions will scuttle away at the smallest movement but the big ones stand their ground and whip up their tails. I was wearing boots, but I tucked my Levi's inside my socks all the same.

Before I went to bed I walked away from the Jeep purely for the amusement of looking back to observe my solitary lamp burning in the wilderness. When I was a hundred yards from the camp I heard an engine. Sound travels a long way in the desert, but this vehicle was near enough that I should be able to see its lights. By the time I realised that it was travelling without any it was too late to douse my own lamp.

The vehicle stopped about a quarter of a mile away. Frozen behind a bush I listened to its engine ticking over softly. After two or three minutes it revved up and the truck drove off very fast. I didn't move; I was listening to the fading sound of that engine and waiting. After a while I heard movement from the direction of the place where it had stopped. I could see nothing but the sounds grew louder. Someone was approaching my camp. Now crouched behind the bush my mouth was as dry as cardboard. What would Godey have done had he been alone? The same as me: he would have remained very still and watched his camp, to see them against the light.

I knew there was more than one of them. The driver of the truck had stopped, dropped people, then driven away in order to allay my suspicions. Those approaching were confident, not stealthy. A twig snapped. They'd know that, a camper being close to a pressure lamp, its hiss would hinder him from hearing the sound of any approach. At the same time that I was terrified I realised I had the edge on them; I knew where they were but they didn't know my whereabouts. I could lose everything: the Jeep, my notes and cameras, but I had my life – providing I could remain concealed. I remembered Wambaugh's *The Onion Field* and the killers hunting the surviving policeman by the light of headlamps. . . .

As yet these people were not using a torch. I heard heavy breathing. I pictured overweight drunks. They were now a few yards away, passing on the other side of the bush. I edged round the creosote, an inch at a time. One of them tripped, gasped – no, he *snorted*. I pressed the switch of my torch. Two cows and two calves halted and stared at the light in consternation.

I trailed weakly through the creosote to the Jeep, the cows keeping pace beside me. I could scarcely raise the energy to drive them away.

Evidently the people in the truck had stopped to get a look at the camper but as soon as they realised that he had left his light burning and was somewhere in the bush watching *them,* they made tracks so fast they forgot to switch their lights on. And why were they without lights? That wasn't my business, I thought, bedding down on the desert pavement, having studied every seam of my sleeping bag to make sure no scorpions were lurking there. It would be just my luck to escape rape and murder and to be bitten by a scorpion.

Eighteen

SLEEPING OUT ON the Gila Trail in 1987 was amusing only in retrospect. At the time, and even in daylight, I was living on the bright edge of danger. I hadn't felt like this in the San Juans. There I had been determined, burning with dull resentment yet reckless and sad, almost fatalistic; we would go on while one foot could be set in front of the other, and death, if it came, would be clean and soft, without pain. On the Gila Trail death was slow but nasty, and danger came out of the sun: raw, bloody, malicious. My mind rocked with the violence of the trail, with the knowledge of what people could do to each other. It is a moot point who suffered most: the men who were tortured and died, or the children who were enslaved and lived.

Somewhere along the Gila Trail Frémont came on a large party of Mexican labourers from Sonora who were travelling to the gold mines in California. They were accompanied by their families and they were delighted to be overtaken by this body of well-armed mountain men. 'Many presents of fruits and provisions in various forms,' notes Frémont. The Apaches' reputation was ably demonstrated by these Mexicans, who numbered twelve hundred. Adult males would have been in the minority, but there were more than in Frémont's company. They urged him to stay with them, at least until they were safely across the Colorado. He consented, but turned the situation to his advantage by engaging twenty-eight of the men to mine for gold on his property in the Sierra Nevada. The Mexicans agreed with alacrity; it must have seemed like a miracle to them: people who may have been driven out of their pueblos by Apaches, and certainly impoverished. Before Frémont's arrival they had been travelling in constant fear of attack and now, suddenly, they were safe, and ahead there was work in a fertile country where the rocks were seamed with gold. So now, and as far as the Colorado, the Fourth travelled in the company of over a thousand people, and everyone was safe; only the beasts must have gone hungry unless there was better grazing on the lower Gila than there had been upstream where Colonel Cooke could find no grass for his mules.

The Apaches – who wouldn't attack if there were a chance of their being killed – stayed in the hills. Even if most were away raiding in Mexico, a few could have been left behind. A handful could wreak havoc, but they would concern themselves only with the weakest parties.

Two years after Frémont came down the Gila unmolested, the trail was still safe, according to a Dr Lecount and his Mexican guide who arrived at the Pima Villages in March 1851 from Fort Yuma, two hundred miles to the west. His news was welcomed by a party of emigrants who had halted at the villages, having heard that the Apaches *were* out on the trail. They had arrived at the Gila in the middle of February.

Royce Oatman, his wife and their seven children had left the East with a large train but, as often happened with the overlanders, through differences of opinion, illness or travelling at a different pace, the original company had split and by the time they reached the Rio Grande the Oatmans were in a party of twenty, with eight wagons.

They had a lot of difficulty in the deserts of New Mexico and they reached Tucson with no food left and their remaining animals in poor condition. Some people elected to stop in Tucson to recuperate but three families pushed on: the Kelleys, the Wilders and the Oatmans. The Ninety Mile Desert took a further toll of their animals. Royce Oatman had already lost oxen; he was left with only a couple to pull his wagon, and four cows. He must have been desperate. People took cows only if they had small children, but once they were hitched to a wagon the milk dried up. It's possible that he hoped to buy draft animals, even a cow, at the Pima Villages.

When they reached the Gila they discovered that the Pimas had suffered such a poor harvest the previous year that they were running short of food for themselves. The emigrants had to decide whether to wait until more wagons arrived from Tucson or to go on alone, risking attack by Apaches. Then Dr Lecount and the Mexican arrived, searching for minerals, and they said the trail was safe. On March 11th the Oatmans pulled out. The Wilders and the Kelleys stayed behind.

The Oatmans ran into difficulties almost immediately, their jaded cattle unable to cope with the deep sand. After a week they were overtaken by Lecount and his guide returning to Fort Yuma. The doctor, appreciating the plight of Oatman's animals, which would obviously never make it to the fort, said he would hurry on ahead and send back assistance.

The next night, thirty miles along the trail, the doctor was attacked. The Apaches took the horses but spared the men. Lecount then sent his guide ahead for fresh mounts and followed behind on foot as fast as he could. Before leaving his camp he wrote a note to Oatman telling him what had happened and warning him to watch out for the Apaches. He fastened the note to a tree and it was said afterwards that Oatman failed to see it, but his behaviour after that camp implies that he found it and concealed the fact from his family.

Now the Oatmans were hit by a storm. They had camped on a sandbar in the river and the gale whipped up the water to such an extent that their clothing and all the blankets were drenched, and the animals driven frantic with terror. Somehow they got through the night but the next morning Oatman was very depressed. When he thought he wasn't observed he was seen to be weeping.

Perhaps it was Mrs Oatman who got them going again because go they did: leaving the river to cross a mesa where the animals came to a halt, unable to drag the wagon further. The family unloaded it. There were three older children: Olive, who was sixteen; Lorenzo, fourteen, and Mary Anne, aged eleven. By dint of turning the wheels manually, they managed to move the wagon to a hard area where they could load up again. They continued across a dry wash and through mesquite scrub to the foot of a bluff crowned by an escarpment. The trail ascended the bluff and the family turned to again: unloading, forcing the spokes of the wagon round with their hands, carrying loads to the summit. When they had everything at the top of the escarpment they were exhausted. Oatman was the worst affected. It was more than physical fatigue; he appeared spiritless, defeated.

Mrs Oatman recovered first and busied herself with the small children. Her husband continued to sit on a rock staring back the way they had come until, suddenly, his apathy gave way to horror. A group of Indians was advancing along the trail at a leisurely pace.

The father's alarm infected the children, but their panic forced him to pull himself together. He assured them that there was no danger; he had traded with Indians in the eastern states and he reminded the family that if Indians were treated correctly they were bound to reciprocate.

The Apaches arrived. Oatman addressed them in Spanish and

invited them to be seated. He was very formal. They asked for tobacco and pipes. He provided both and they smoked together. They asked for food and he apologised, saying that they were practically starving themselves, but he gave them some bread.

They withdrew a little way and murmured among themselves. Oatman started to load the wagon. The Apaches seemed uneasy; they kept looking back along the trail as if anticipating the arrival of more wagons. Suddenly they attacked the family.

Lorenzo was knocked to the ground. He had one last glimpse of his father fighting in the midst of a group before he, too, was felled. Mrs Oatman, clutching the baby, was battered to death, as were all the younger children. Lorenzo, regaining consciousness, was seen to move, so they threw him over the escarpment where he fell twenty feet and lost consciousness again.

When he came to he crept back to the top and, identifying the bodies, realised that Olive and Mary Anne had been carried off. Suffering from his injuries and a terrible thirst he crawled to the river where he drank, then slept for several hours on the bank.

He would have seen from their tracks that the Apaches had gone west after the attack, so when he woke he went east, towards the Pima Villages, but always haunted by the terror that the killers would come back, or that he would be found by another band. Weak from loss of blood, from hunger and fever, he crawled from bush to bush, collapsing in the shade, trying to stay awake because now he was surrounded by coyotes which he could keep at bay only by throwing stones at them; not daring to shout because that might attract attention.

On the second day he emerged from a dark canyon to see the sun shining on the white tops of wagons out in the middle of a plain. He fainted. Within an hour the wagons of the Wilders and the Kelleys came up: 'My God, Lorenzo! What has happened?'

The wagons turned back to the Pima Villages, Lorenzo recovered, and when a large train arrived he was taken on to Los Angeles.

The abducted girls became slaves to the Apaches, but only for a year and then they were sold to a band of Mojaves who lived on the Colorado River. They were treated brutally and they never got enough to eat, particularly when they were with the Mojaves, some of whom were dying of starvation when the girls joined them. Mary Anne, who was never a strong child, died shortly after they were taken to live on the river.

Meanwhile Lorenzo, trying to secure his sisters' release, had no success until a carpenter employed at Fort Yuma, Henry Grinnell, took a hand in the affair. In February 1856, five years after she was abducted, Grinnell succeeded in buying Olive from the Mojaves.

Negotiations were conducted through a Yuma Indian called Francisco. There are differing accounts of her recovery. One has her brought to an agreed point on the bank of the Colorado and left alone. Grinnell found her sitting with her head in her hands and weeping. It was hard to tell that she was white because her skin was dark from long exposure to the sun, and she was tattooed. She wouldn't speak to him and several days passed before she could say more than a few words in broken English.

Another version has Francisco buying her from the Mojaves for trinkets, the Indians changing their minds and chasing after them, and Olive and Francisco escaping on fast horses. A photograph of Olive shows a girl more likely to gallop a good horse over rough ground than to weep on a river bank.

Brother and sister were reunited and Lorenzo took her to live with him near Los Angeles. Subsequently they moved to Oregon. When, in 1864, J. Ross Browne wrote about the Oatman Massacre, he thought brother and sister were living in New York State. Another account had her married in Oregon.

Olive Oatman was one of many children kidnapped and raised by Indians. Most vanished without trace; the Oatman tragedy is documented only because Lorenzo survived, Henry Grinnell had compassion, and Olive came back. But her life during the five years she spent with the Indians is a blank. Did she leave children behind? What kind of man did she marry when she returned to civilisation – and how did she cope with *that*? The photograph of a confident but tattooed beauty hides as much as it reveals.

We came to Agua Caliente: hot springs in the middle of the desert where it was bliss to soak and scrub away the dirt of the trail. By now the fourth expedition had all the appearance of a carnival procession with animals, beautiful girls, and hosts of children. But Frémont would still see to it that there were armed men around the column, particularly at the rear, making sure that there were no stragglers, and no one following. West of Agua Caliente and east of the Colorado there was an overlapping of hostile forces. You never congratulated each other as you neared the end of Apache territory because now there were the Yumas to reckon with. This was the tribe who murdered the chief of the Pimas.

The year after the Fourth came through, escorting the Mexicans, John Gallantin came along the trail. He was a bounty hunter, the leader of a gang who were having difficulty in making a living. The market had slumped; Apache scalps were fetching only thirty dollars. Gallantin was one of those who solved the problem by indiscriminately scalping anyone with black hair, but he had been bringing in so many scalps that suspicion was aroused because there was no slackening in Apache raids. Gallantin and his band of twenty decided it was prudent to change employment, at least temporarily, and to this end they acquired a large herd of sheep in New Mexico, some by purchase, others by theft, and they took the road to California along the Gila Trail.

East of the Colorado they met a Yuma raiding party looking for Maricopas. The raiders had met and killed some Maricopas already, and taken two prisoners, a young man and his wife, who were with them. The Yumas were friendly and the Americans were a strong party and well-armed. They got on well together. No one mentioned the scalp trade.

The Yumas politely left their arms in the desert and came in to the camp bringing wood for fires. No doubt they were hoping for the gift of a sheep, but there were plenty to spare, and it must have been pleasant to have firewood brought in and someone else to build the fires. Gallantin and his men would be unused to service on the trail.

The fires had been dispersed about the camp and the Americans separated to cook their suppers, noticing that the Yumas had a novel way of laying the cottonwood logs: radiating from a central point, with the fire in the middle.

The Yumas mingled with the white men, always smiling and friendly, and when the logs were nicely burned at one end, at a given signal, each Indian seized one and, using it as a club, brained the nearest American.

More of the tribe came in from the darkness and every man in the Gallantin band was killed. In the confusion the two Maricopa prisoners escaped.

We passed under the Gila Mountains: jagged ridges baked dry, and friable as chalk. The heat consumed everything; all my books that weren't sewn were falling apart, cheap items like diaries were a collection of pages held together by rubber bands. Heat had vaporised the glue. Dehydrated, tired and very hot, we worked our way westward across a flood plain where big old cottonwoods cast black shadows on the verge, and we emerged suddenly to a wide stretch of water bordered by reed beds and tamarisks. Killdeer and stilts paddled in the warm mud and the air was soft with bird calls. We had reached the Colorado.

Before us was Yuma: the fort, the town and the old river crossing. In 1849 there was a ferry operated by Indians but when Frémont arrived he would have nothing to do with it. He built a bullboat: a wooden frame over which hides were stretched. When he had ferried across the members of the expedition, his Mexican employees and the women and children, he left the boat for the other Mexicans. Since he was unconcerned about splitting the party the implication is that the Yumas presented no threat at this time.

They weren't always thieves and murderers. When the Spanish Jesuits arrived they found an intelligent, honest and industrious people. A Father Garcés founded missions on both sides of the Colorado, brought in Spanish settlers to cultivate the fertile flood plain and to teach the Indians how to breed and raise stock. They turned out to be excellent stockmen. During the eighteenth century the missions supplied travellers on the Gila Trail with meat, fruit, vegetables and grain. The community was an oasis where one might recuperate after the ravages of the deserts.

Father Garcés was unable to wean the Yumas from their tradition of privately owned land, and each Indian had his plot which he tilled and harvested. Some travellers, coming through with jaded animals and seeing the prosperity of the Indians, their fat cattle and abundant crops, turned their beasts into the grain and stole vegetables and fruit. In 1781 an army officer ordered his soldiers to seize good Indian horses to replace his own exhausted mounts.

The Yumas protested so the Spaniard had them flogged publicly. The humiliation was unbearable. The Indian had been robbed, had seen his crops trampled and his springs polluted; for years Father Garcés had worked to keep the peace between them and the whites, but there was always tension just below the surface, and now it erupted. The Yumas rose and killed every male Spaniard on both sides of the river, including their own priest (whom they adored) and three other Jesuits. They burned the missions and took the women and children prisoner. When they calmed down they buried the priests

186

(but none of the other bodies) and covered the grave of Father Garcés with flowers, but the damage was irreparable.

The Gila Trail was abandoned for forty years, and in 1849, when people were travelling it again, the Yumas had changed. Opportunists now, they operated the ferry across the Colorado: pulling rafts loaded with people but herding the stock through the water. The current was powerful and both rafts and stock might land two miles downstream when the river ran high. The Yumas would select a mule and drown it stealthily, recovering the body later. This was why, in 1849, people like Frémont dispensed with their services and built their own boats.

I crossed the Colorado into California and took a dirt road up the west bank of the river until I reached some stony badlands. I left the road and worked my way along the ridges to stop the Jeep on a point high above a draw where I might catch a breeze.

The temperature dropped with the sun and by eight o'clock it was a delicious 93°. There were no moths, no scorpions and no tarantulas, but at one point in the evening when I got up from my chair at the tailboard and went to the cab there was movement on the edge of the light, a scurry of little feet. As I swung the beam of the torch there was more pattering but I could see no bodies, no shining eyes. I would flick the beam towards the sound and all I'd see was a rock. I knew I was surrounded but I wasn't frightened; this had none of the feeling of those minutes before I identified the cows by Oatman Flat. I called out: 'Who is it?' but they didn't run at the sound of my voice. They were hanging around.

At six o'clock in the morning, lying in my bag and waiting for the sun to rise, I heard a donkey bray.

The California deserts are full of feral burros descended from those the prospectors released when they acquired old Army Jeeps. It was touching to find that something like a race memory persisted to bring them in to my light, to listen and not to run away at the sound of my voice.

With the low at 76° the night had been cool. Before breakfast I wandered about the ridges photographing shadows in the badlands, and then regretted it because I had to eat breakfast and stow the gear in blazing sunshine. The deserts were not over; now we had the last one, the Colorado Desert that stretches for a hundred miles from the river to the foothills of the coastal ranges at the back of Los Angeles.

We followed Colonel Cooke's trail. Prior to 1846 there was no water in this desert until the road turned into the hills but as the Mormons passed they dug wells. These were liable to be filled by blowing sand, but there would be markers, possibly some form of cover. This was an old sea bed, 'strange jagged mountain-peaks in the distance; yellow banks serrated by floods, sea-shells glittering in the wavy sand-fields that lie between; these overhung by a rich, gloomy atmosphere. ...' J. Ross Browne, travelling east on the Gila Trail, saw the Colorado Desert with an artist's eye, in winter, and found it delightful.

On the other hand, John C. Cremony, a journalist travelling in 1849, found this corner of California more frightful than the Sahara. He encountered a dust storm so fierce that his mules collapsed with their necks extended and their muzzles pressed to the ground, while he and his companions lay with a tent over themselves. The canvas was held in place by accumulating masses of sand that, like snow, had to be periodically shed before they all suffocated.

I drove west past the old wells: Coyote, Ocotillo. In September there is nothing here but the biscuit-coloured ground and shrivelled grey plants. When Frémont passed in April, going from well to well, the ocotillo would be bright with scarlet flowers at the end of whippy stems, the creosote in yellow bloom. Today it was not just hot but curiously humid, a strange brown fog lowering over the brown desert. We had entered the smog-shadow of San Diego.

Slowly the sun dissipated the cloud (a fierce caricature of mist clearing from a Highland peak) and pale ghosts of hills appeared against a burnished sky. The trail angled northwest and we came to a country that was different from anything that had gone before. The scale was greatly reduced. There were no flat plains bordered by distant ranges; we were *in* the mountains and there was a breeze, a hot breeze certainly, but a relief after the stagnant air. These were the Coyote Mountains and back of them was the Carrizo Range. Now the springs started: a chain of them through the Anza-Borrego Desert – but who could call this desert after what we had been through? Here surface water appeared at intervals of a few miles between one oasis and the next; there was even game: bighorn sheep and deer. The first spring was Carrizo, heralded by badlands where the fossilised bones of sabre-toothed tigers had been found. (Today mountain lions prey on the sheep and deer.) Then came Palm Springs, a lonely stony little canyon with a ragged grove of palms. There was Bow Willow Camp and Canebrake and Agua Caliente. We went from spring to spring and now the looming mountains were naked in the midday sun and the breeze dropped and the air in the canyons was still and dangerous.

Frémont probably crossed the Anza-Borrego in one day, and not a long day at that. I envied him the balmy air of April, the purple mats of sand verbena set with pale dune primroses. He wouldn't have noticed them. The sweet breeze that rustled the palm fronds carried a smell of the high Sierras, of oak woods and redwoods, of a land where summer was for picnics and winter for children and sledging, not death in the deep and dismal snow. Frémont was in a hurry to reach Las Mariposas, the property he owned but had never seen, below Yosemite.

We came behind at a leisurely pace. At Agua Caliente there was a campground, showers and a therapy pool. I pitched the tent in the shade of oleanders, showered and went to sit in the pool where four old ladies and a tattooed cyclist spaced themselves carefully round the perimeter, establishing territory.

I stayed in that camp for two days, exploring amusing little canyons when they were in shadow, soaking tired bones in the therapy pool, sitting under the oleanders reading, and watched by praying mantises. They were small and green with clubby heart-shaped heads and huge black eyes that turned to follow my every movement. I found them enchanting, not so the monstrous cockroach that had taken up residence in the Jeep. Reared in a society that equates cockroaches with bed bugs, I was appalled.

I had cockroaches. At the store they had a black widow spider that lived behind the refrigerator. The store was bare and dull, merely a front for the storekeeper and a coterie that gathered most days in a trailer at the rear.

There were three of them. Will had trained to be a zoologist, Bob was crippled by arthritis and here for his health, Frank had been a career airman *and* a sailor. They didn't say much about themselves but a great deal about everything else, seizing on any subject with glee and proceeding to investigate it with wit. They were funny as well as erudite. I couldn't help wondering about their emotional lives; I had the impression of men who had tried living with women and relinquished the experiment. Here, in the desert, they lived and bloomed in an atmosphere of camaraderie, and waited, and talked, and entertained guests with courtesy and the music of Bach.

On my last night the heat of the day culminated in a storm. Lightning flickered along a ridge as I walked back to the tent from the store, and the storm came suddenly but without rain. By the time I reached my camp the echoes of thunder were overlapped by the next lightning flash. As I made my way to the lavatories through the last reverberations there came a sharp crack above my head, a sizzle, and all the lights went out in the ablution block. By the time I had washed the rain was coming down in torrents.

Next morning I took the trail for Vallecito. At Vallecito Springs the water was hidden in a green jungle. An adobe building stood here: a reconstruction of a stage station, and a plaque informed me that we were on the western edge of the Colorado Desert. The line that operated here was nicknamed the Jackass Mail: 'Passengers and express matter forwarded in NEW COACHES drawn by six mules over the entire length of our line, excepting the Colorado Desert of 100 miles which we cross on mule back.'

Beyond Vallecito was Box Canyon where the Mormon Battalion cut a new road parallel with the old trail (that was the Gila, which at this point changed its name to the Southern Emigrant Trail), thus opening the first wagon road into southern California. The trail and the road are still visible: ledges on a slope reminiscent of other tracks traversing sides of arid hills in Wyoming, Utah, Nevada. Quail called in the sage. There was no one about and the road was empty.

We were nearing the end of a trail. This journey didn't start at Kansas Landing; it started in the Wind Rivers eight years ago when I looked down on a lake set in granite and realised I was tracing the line of an explorer called Frémont. Since then I had followed him through the Great Basin to California, across the Snake to Oregon, south through the Nevada deserts and over all the big passes of the Sierra: Donner, Carson, Walker Pass. I had come with him through Colorado – and now, looking at that green ledge which the Mormons cut and he followed, I remembered the guide. Without him they wouldn't have been here.

When Godey rode across the Anza-Borrego, down this canyon, over that ledge a few yards away, did he intend to settle in California or did it just happen? He would prosper, create havoc among the women, explore again, even return to a Colorado winter, but he *stayed* in California. We almost lost sight of him along the Gila Trail; he was a man who melted into the background when in the company of his peers – unless there was an emergency, and then he had no equal. I thought happily of catching up with Godey and I climbed into the Jeep to follow the Fourth past the Granite Mountains.

190

At San Felipe, the next spring, the next fixed point, the land had changed again. From the linear nature of the vegetation it was apparent that San Felipe's spring formed a creek. For the first time in over a hundred miles I saw cattle. There was traffic on the road. The sun went behind clouds and the breeze was suddenly cool. By the time we reached Warner Springs we were in the coastal foothills with real grass and oak trees. The deserts were over.

Nineteen

THE CLIMATE OF the western foothills is near perfection. It can be hot in summer but there is always shade. Black oaks reach a height of a hundred feet and when you see their spread you know what is meant by a shade tree. Blue oaks and live oaks (which are evergreen) grow in the canyons; above, steep slopes of grass alternate with chaparral scrub. In the autumn the grass is tawny as a lion and in the spring the slopes blaze with orange poppies.

The deserts of California are baked hard in the summer, the peaks are a world of ice in winter, but the foothills are always a joy, and from prehistoric times until the present day people have lived there or cherished the dream, sometimes all their lives, of one day owning a cabin in the hills.

Frémont's property was on the Merced River where it emerges from the Yosemite valley. In 1847, after his third expedition, he had left three thousand dollars with the US Consul, Thomas Larkin, intending that he should buy land near Santa Cruz on the coast south of San Francisco. Instead Larkin bought Las Mariposas, a hundred miles from the sea and on the western slope of the Sierras. Frémont was infuriated by the choice and was considering legal action to recover his money when gold was discovered in the Sierras. Now he realised that he could be in possession of a fortune and, once the deserts and the dangers were behind him, he could hardly wait to reach his property. But Jessie had crossed the isthmus at Panama and he expected that she was now waiting for him at Monterey. He solved the problem neatly by engaging Godey to escort the Mexican labourers to Las Mariposas and to start them mining immediately.

The expedition broke up, everyone in too much of a hurry to reach the goldfields for fanfares and celebrations; there would be time enough for that when they had made their first fortune. But they travelled together for a while, simply because they were all going the same way, following the Emigrant Trail through the southern hills and over Tehachapi Pass to the great central valley of the San Joaquin

River. There they separated; Frémont went northwest to Monterey, Godey north to Las Mariposas, and most of the others into the Sierra canyons where the gold lay glinting in the creeks.

From San Felipe the Emigrant Trail went through Oak Grove – which had been a stage station. The town is unspoiled, with a quiet campground among the oaks where I pitched the tent and revelled in a cool evening. During the night there was a little rain and heavy dew. The sun rose clear and warm and the air was fresh until my trail disappeared beneath the extended sprawl of Los Angeles.

The interstates were clogged with traffic. At mid-morning there seemed to be no relaxation of rush hour. And now there was smog: it got in my throat and had me coughing and spluttering, affecting my driving. I didn't know whether I was weeping from the pollutants in the atmosphere or from outrage. I felt violated and fled, working my way through the disaster area, edging outwards until I could escape from the Las Vegas interstate. At that point I ran under a series of fine sandstone reefs: an unexpected delight that demonstrated the variety – and the extremes – of this the most varied of the states. Beyond the reefs came a stretch of desert doomed to approaching development where I had the wry thought that I could be the last person to picnic under the Joshua trees.

That afternoon, beyond the interstates, the smog and the creeping blight of suburbia, I found myself back on the Emigrant Trail and following the Fourth over Tehachapi Pass. From there the trail descended to the valley of the San Joaquin which, 260 miles to the north, enters San Francisco Bay.

The uplands around Tehachapi were a forest of slender windmills: hundreds of them, the sails of some turning, others stationary. In the thin blue air they looked as alien as the power station they rendered obsolete, but I thought them beautiful. Here at last someone was building a better world.

That night I slept at seven thousand feet in a Ponderosa forest. The ground was so steep I had been forced to climb thirteen miles to the top of a ridge before I could find level ground on which to park. As I hammered the last tent peg home I remembered that there were fires burning throughout the state, fires started by lightning. There had been heat waves all over the West and in some places thunderstorms had been a daily occurrence. On Breckenridge Mountain (could that be *our* Breckenridge who was sent down Embargo Creek with Old Bill on the first rescue bid?) I hoped I wouldn't smell smoke. There were two ways off this ridge: the thirteen miles I had come or thirty-six miles that remained, and in either direction the trail ran above mighty canyons. If smoke were in the air how would you know which way to go? Who would one ask? I was still in the wilderness, still on my own. What made me think I could ever relinquish responsibility?

On my bed of pine needles I dreamed of ghosts who stayed at the edge of my mind and made no attempt to reveal themselves, to state their business or their history. They could have been my family or friends, lovers or cats; they could have been members of the fourth expedition. They were not frightening.

We left Frémont riding to Monterey to meet Jessie but her ship had docked at San Francisco where he finally caught up with her. They went back to Monterey and rented a wing of the former governor's house, and Frémont started to commute across the San Joaquin valley to Las Mariposas, supervising his mines and building their new house.

Nineteenth century Monterey must have been enchanting with its Spanish architecture, and the plumed cypresses above rocky coves where sea otters dived for abalone through the golden kelp. This was *la dolce vita*, but nothing was for long in the lives of the Frémonts, and if their lifestyle was occasionally on a grand scale, they paid a high price for it.

Jessie had nearly died of fever after crossing the isthmus at Panama. In those days people were poled up the Chagres River in native dug-outs, and then rode mules through steaming jungle infested with parasites. When she reached the west coast she was forced to wait for a sea passage, the crews of ships having deserted to rush to the goldfields. Finally she found space on the deck of the *Panama* which had accommodation for eighty passengers and was carrying four hundred. A storm blew up south of San Diego, Jessie was drenched, caught a severe chill and began to haemorrhage from the lungs. At San Francisco she had to be carried ashore. Matters had been exacerbated throughout the ghastly journey by her having the seven-year-old Lilly to take care of, and the fact that she had very little money.

When she saw Las Mariposas for the first time Jessie thought it heavenly. They built a substantial two-storey house, and there is a photograph of it in the Mariposa Museum: solid and functional, standing in the shade of mature trees. They called it the White House but they never occupied it for long. They weren't in California a year before they moved to Washington, Frémont having been elected a senator. Unfortunately he had drawn the short term and he was to take his seat for only three weeks.

Meanwhile the mines at Las Mariposas had turned out to be incredibly rich and by the time they returned to California from Washington they were wealthy people. Twenty-nine ore-bearing veins had been found on the property (which comprised 43,000 acres) and sacks of gold each worth $25,000 came in regularly from the hills. Jackson Saunders, that stalwart member of the second relief party that had pushed down the ice of the Rio Grande, remained in Frémont's service, but he made enough profit from mining on the side, that he was able to buy the freedom of all his family from their white owners.

The Frémonts bought another house in San Francisco. At their seaside home in Monterey they employed an English housekeeper. They had a surrey which was the first carriage of its kind in the territory. In 1853 they went to Europe and were presented to Queen Victoria. A baby, Anne Beverley, was born in Paris but she died five months later. Two years before, John Charles Jr., had been born, and in 1851 Jessie would give birth to a second son, Frank Preston.

In 1853 Frémont went on his fifth, and last, expedition, aiming to complete the work that had been left unfinished by the Fourth. People were still looking for the route for the transcontinental railway. In the same year Richard Kern joined an expedition led by the explorer, John W. Gunnison, which was attacked by Ute Indians near Sevier Lake in Utah. Richard, Gunnison, Creutzfeldt (who had also been with the Fourth), and several other members of the expedition were murdered. The other Kern brother who survived the Fourth, Edward, continued to accompany explorers (one trip was to Japan) and died in 1863, aged forty.

Frémont asked Preuss to join his fifth expedition but Mrs Preuss would not allow him to accept: 'Choose between your home and family over your instinct to wander.' She had always been against these journeys, less because of their hazards than that she thought Preuss enjoyed them, and she didn't hold with his having fun while she stayed at home, running the farm and raising four daughters.

Preuss did not enjoy expedition life; he went for the money, to support his large family. He loathed the squalor and the poor food. He disliked the more crude of the mountain men, and he had little respect for Frémont whom he thought foolish and romantic. But although he hated the discomforts of the wilderness he was undaunted by danger. He was a man of courage, integrity and tremendous fortitude. In 1850 he suffered a bad attack of sunstroke but in '53 he was back, surveying for the Army in California. However, he couldn't have been fit then, or his condition was exacerbated by the trip, because he was so ill afterwards that he was unable to complete his maps, and the work had to be delegated. It is not surprising that Mrs Preuss should have been against his joining Frémont's fifth expedition. It's possible that the sunstroke had affected his brain, and one suspects that he had a lot of pain. He was a staunch family man and he adored his daughters and seems to have been very close to his wife. Yet a few weeks after he declined Frémont's offer he left his Washington home, went to a farm outside the city and hanged himself from a tree.

Alexis Godey was on the fifth expedition. Frémont met him by accident in St Louis and he agreed to go. In fact he was delighted. Godey would never settle down.

The expedition followed a similar route to that of the Fourth as far as the Sangre de Cristo, but from there they went over the well-travelled Cochetopa Pass where they found only four inches of snow. This was another winter expedition, again working on Frémont's contention that the worst trouble trains could run into would be caused by snow. It was from Cochetopa, fifteen air miles from Mesa Mountain, that he pointed out the area where he said the men of the Fourth had fed on each other.

They continued down the Gunnison River and the Colorado. They almost came to grief in the western Rockies and the red rock canyons of Utah. They had to cross deep rivers that were unfrozen, they started to eat the mules – and Frémont made every man swear that he would not resort to cannibalism and would shoot anyone who did. A man called Fuller died and they reached the Mormon settlement at Parowan in a starving condition. After two weeks' recuperation they continued across the Great Basin, having no more difficulty until they reached the Sierras. The main passes were blocked by snow so they went south and crossed into the central valley of California by way of a lower pass towards Tehachapi.

This expedition had none of the glamour of the first three, nor the sustained drama of the Fourth. The public wasn't impressed; Frémont was still the hero of the Oregon and California trails, but the Fifth did not erase the memory of all those men lost in Colorado.

There has always been controversy over who was responsible for the mistake in navigation that took the Fourth up the wrong canyon into the San Juans, but it wasn't until 1856 that Frémont was publicly accused of incompetence. That year he ran for president, and was defeated partly by a smear campaign which seized not only on his illegitimate birth but his culpability for the deaths on the fourth expedition. A vicious attack appeared in the Washington *Daily Union* on July 31st, 1856. Headlined ROCKY MOUNTAIN RECORD – A PEEP INTO THE CHARACTER OF THE PATHFINDER, it refers to an interview with Stepperfeldt:

'From a conversation with Mr S we are led to believe that the sufferings of the party were not fully detailed by Colonel Frémont; and as the public will probably never have any authentic account of the disaster from his pen, it rests with the men who composed the party, and who shared the sufferings, to give the detail as events transpired from day to day. A daily journal of the transactions was kept by some of the men, which may be of some interest to the public.

'*It will be seen that Col. Frémont is much censured in these pages, and with considerable justice, if the testimony of the party of his men is to be relied on.** The journal appears to have been kept by Richard H. Kern.'

It was not Richard's original journal, but a shortened and doctored version. For instance, at the end of the entry for December 9th, 1848, when they reached the Rio Grande after crossing from the Great Sand Dunes in the blizzard, there is an addition:

'*The deep snow of today should have warned Col. Frémont of his approaching destruction, but, with the wilfully blind eyes of rashness and self-conceit and confidence, he pushed on.*'

After they abandoned the mules: '*Every animal should have been butchered, and we should have had plenty in the camp.*'

When Frémont set out with the second relief party this journal purports to give the actual wording of a letter of instructions for Vincenthaler:

L. D. Vincenthaler: I am going to start for Abaca [Abiquiu? He

---

* The italics are those of the *Daily Union*.

didn't go there], I want all the men to bring the baggage down the lodge [tepee]. If no relief come then, let them take their guns and blankets, and follow the river down to Rabbit Creek [Conejos River]; and if no relief at Rabbit Creek, then come to Abaca; *and come quick, or you will not find me there, as I shall have left for California.*

McGehee also attributes such a cavalier order to Frémont but Godey, defending his leader in *The Evening Post* of New York, on October 30th, 1856, was to say that 'no intimation of such an idea was or had been made ... and not until the entire party had got back to Taos, was a word said by Colonel Frémont, or any one else, of an expedition to California.'

The diary printed in the *Daily Union* ends:

'Upon Colonel Frémont's arrival at Thaos, Major Beall, commander at that post, ordered the commissary to issue to the colonel thirty days' full rations for the twenty-five men then in the mountains, and expected in. These rations were never turned over to the men, and were probably taken to California by Frémont! The men were obliged to buy their own provisions from the people of the country, who came to their relief.   RICHARD H. KERN
RIO HONDA, March 10, 1849'

Rio Honda is close to Taos. That, and the date, implies the diary was written at the time. Richard had been dead three years when his doctored diary was published. His brother, Edward, may not have been responsible for its editing, but it would have expressed his bitterness. Two of his brothers had been murdered, and for one of those deaths he held Frémont responsible.

It was in his published defence of Frémont that Godey maintained that in the prevailing conditions no man could have been induced to retrieve the carcasses of mules from under twenty feet of snow.

Opinion has always been divided concerning responsibility for the disaster of the Fourth. Of the people immediately involved Frémont blamed Old Bill Williams for the mistake in navigation, as did Godey, who also blamed himself for having trusted the older guide. Breckenridge blamed Frémont, as did the Kerns. People who hadn't been on the expedition took sides. Mountain men came forward to say Old Bill was a good guide who knew the San Juans like the back of his hand. This only confused the issue because obviously he didn't know where he was after they left the Rio Grande. No one did.

I think that Frémont followed the Rio Grande west against the protests of Old Bill, that when they reached the mouth of Alder Creek Frémont capitulated, agreeing that to follow the Rio Grande was a mistake, and that after all he would go for Cochetopa, which Williams was now advocating. But instead of retreating and going round the mountains and in again by the proper approach to Cochetopa, Frémont decided on a short-cut. Old Bill, unfit by virtue of his wound, sick of arguing, but knowing that he was a good guide and that a good guide should be able to get through anywhere, recklessly agreed. He had no choice. A guide cannot abandon his employer in the middle of the wilderness. When it comes to the crunch and the guide is fighting the client the more dominant man wins.

Frémont remained dominant. On the retreat no one questioned his order that all the equipment had to be brought down to the Rio Grande, even though the men were growing weaker by the day as they relayed the loads. Proue died during this time. However, when Frémont left they would not obey Vincenthaler; the baggage on the mountain stayed there. The conflict of personalities came after the event. During it no one could stand up to Frémont, neither the Kerns, Preuss, Cathcart, nor Godey and Old Bill. There is no evidence that he had any discussion with any of them. Breckenridge says that Old Bill protested and argued about the route, but he lost. Frémont was a steam roller. It is significant that nothing like this happened on the first three expeditions, and on those he had Kit Carson as guide, backed by other powerful personalities such as Thomas Fitzpatrick and Joseph Walker.

Whether or not Old Bill made mistakes: in navigation, in relinquishing his authority as the guide, Frémont is ultimately responsible. The failure of the fourth expedition, like any other, was the result of human error. The bad weather wasn't an accident. There is always bad weather in winter. The basic error was in going on in those unprecedented storms, in retreating too late, and encumbered by equipment.

After his abortive bid for the presidency Frémont threw himself, and his money, into a number of ventures, at first concentrating on improvements to his mines. The easily won placer gold had been worked out and he needed to install expensive equipment for hard rock mining.

When the Civil War broke out in 1861 he served on the Union side but not gloriously, always rubbing people up the wrong way, making grandiose gestures and silly mistakes. He wasn't cut out to be a soldier. After the war he poured money into a railroad venture which failed disastrously. A multi-millionaire at the start of the war, twelve years later he was bankrupt. It was Jessie who supported the family now, becoming a successful journalist and author.

In 1878 Frémont was appointed governor of Arizona but he spent so much time in travel involved with plans to recoup his fortunes that pressure was brought on him to resign. He did so in 1881 and, at the age of sixty-eight, he went to live in Washington where he would have access to archives. He was writing the first volume of his memoirs. When it was published it made tedious reading and was such an abysmal failure that he never attempted a second volume.

When he was in his seventies his doctors recommended that he go to California for his health, so the Frémonts went to Los Angeles. Las Mariposas had been sold in 1864 and they were very poor. Frémont didn't succeed in extracting his full army pension from Congress until shortly before he died. Business connected with this took him east in 1890. From Washington he went to New York. He had promised a family friend that he would put flowers on her son's grave, which was in a Brooklyn cemetery.

It was July and there was a heat wave in New York. After the long ride in a street car he returned to his Manhattan boarding house and went to bed. During the night the temperature dropped with an ocean breeze and he caught a chill. By the time his physician, a Dr Morton, arrived, he diagnosed peritonitis either from a ruptured appendix or a gastric ulcer. A telegram was sent to his elder son, John Charles, the only member of the family who could be summoned in time.

After his son's arrival Frémont seemed more comfortable and he said: 'If I continue as free from pain, I can go home next week.'

Dr Morton asked him which home he meant. The response was his last words: 'California, of course.'

Jessie survived him for twelve years. She had a widow's pension, and the women of Los Angeles raised the money to build a cottage for her. She died in 1902.

Twenty

FRÉMONT IS COMMEMORATED throughout the West by place-names: towns, counties, a peak in the Wind Rivers, a river in Utah. Old Bill Williams has a town, mountains, and a tributary of the Colorado named after him. Edward Kern is remembered by a county and a river in southern California, but Alexis Godey has nothing more than a gulch in the Mariposa foothills to bear his name.

Godey has been forgotten. He was not a great guide in the manner of Kit Carson, Jim Bridger and Joseph Walker, but he was a very strong and extremely competent mountain man. With men he considered his equals and his superiors he was retiring. He didn't argue with Frémont, he didn't reminisce in old age. His epic rescue of the fourth expedition was eminently memorable but it was associated with disaster. Horror and bad news are sensational but ephemeral; Americans remembered Frémont for his three successful expeditions and the country blocked out the Fourth. And Godey, who saved the Fourth, was a casualty of the public's need to forget failure.

Being forgotten wouldn't have bothered him in the least. He was proud of his looks, but he was unconcerned with his own exploits. One of the reasons he is forgotten is that he never considered he had done anything remarkable. In his own view he was a mountain man who had scraped together enough money to enable him to settle in a fertile land where there were fortunes to be made by a man careful with his accounts (despite his illiteracy) and where his looks and wealth could command everything that had been unobtainable in the wilderness.

He was not immediately rich, as he might have been had he stayed at Las Mariposas. He started modestly; in 1851 he was operating a ferry near Firebaugh on the San Joaquin. In '53 he was guide to an army surveying expedition in southern California (probably the one that Preuss accompanied). Later that year, and into '54, he was with Frémont's fifth expedition.

For some time he was superintendent of Indians at Fort Tejon, north of Los Angeles. While he was there he heard of a vacant Spanish land grant not far away in a valley called Cuyama. He bought a thousand head of cattle and put them on the land. In effect he became a squatter.

He built an adobe house and stayed there for fifteen years. Cuyama must have been a bleak place in the nineteenth century: a bare brown valley, its flats, badlands and mountains all in shades of fawn. Godey's house has disappeared, no doubt disintegrated in the rain, as adobe does once the roof collapses.

He stayed at Cuyama until 1872 when the ranch was inherited by a Cesar Lataillade, who served notice on him. Godey acknowledged the claim without argument, sold his stock, and moved to a ranch called San Emidio.

He had owned the San Emidio for some years. Proof of that is that he was to sell it to the Kern County Land Company in 1883. He must have been steadily accumulating wealth since the fifties. He was able to buy a thousand head of cattle in 1856, and records show that in the sixties he owned property at various locations in southern California. With the growing population in San Francisco and the goldfields, anyone who dealt in land, real estate and meat was more likely to become rich than a prospector.

The San Emidio Ranch is at the head of the San Joaquin valley, backed by a range that rises to eight thousand feet. It stands on a sparkling brook that emerges from a canyon. At the head of the canyon is a peak called Pinos. The spread is now owned by an oil company, leased by a Californian and run by a manager. Godey came here in 1873 and here, in his middle age, he led a life of work and hard play that would have killed a lesser man.

He was a devil with women. He married several times. He had a number of common-law wives and innumerable mistresses. There was a much-publicised divorce from Maria Antonia Coronel on the grounds of her being unable to cook and keep house, but the real reason was that she refused to tolerate his casual affairs.

He was a very strict father. He loved beautiful women and he sired beautiful children. He had three sons by different wives: handsome, talented boys who all died in their early twenties, one of tuberculosis, the second of 'some fever', the third of a further unnamed malady. He adopted two orphan boys, one Spanish, the other American, brought them up and educated them. They had deep respect and love for him despite their strict upbringing.

202

His Mexican and Indian labourers adored him and it would appear that the feeling was mutual. At San Emidio he built a little house with a dance floor and planted fig trees round it. He would go into Bakersfield and load a wagon with provisions and liquor and the resulting fandango at the ranch might last a week. Godey would discard all his clothing, put on a breech clout and dance. It was said of him that he was more like an Indian than a white man.

The prelude to his death was bizarre. A circus came to Bakersfield and he got too close to a lion which scratched him through the bars of its cage. According to one of his adopted sons he did not die from the resulting infection but recovery took so long that it was obvious he had not been in good health for some time. He died not long after the incident with the lion, in 1889.

I would have liked to see the little house at San Emidio where the fandangos were held, where this strange man: stern father, lover of Indian, Mexican and Spanish women, hunter and guide, danced naked under the fig trees, but the dance floor and the fig trees were gone, and at the ranch they had never heard of Alexis Godey.

I drove away down the long avenue of eucalyptus trees, past fine horses standing in the shade, to the valley where the slopes were dotted with oil wells and where, in houses half-hidden in the haze, his descendants may be living still.

A journey ends and the goal is reached: gold, beautiful women, ranches, California. There is bewilderment, a sense of loss. We have escaped from the high and lonely spaces and come down to the valleys where it is always summer, where people don't starve or scalp each other, where there is always enough to eat and lots to drink, and where it is, above all, safe. And that, of course, is the trouble.

But I had the edge on the men I had kept company with for five months. I had no ranch and no family to tie me to the fat land, and when one trail was finished I could start another. I could go back – as Godey might have given twenty years of his life to do: back to the beginning, to 1833 when he came through Yosemite with Walker.

Yosemite is a valley and an upland wilderness that culminates in the crest of the Sierras. The valley is walled by thousands of feet of granite: a Mecca for climbers, as the back country is for walkers. Alexis Godey was probably the first white man to see Yosemite.

In 1833 a fur trader, Captain Bonneville, sent the mountain man, Joseph Walker, on a trading and trapping expedition through the West. This was seven years before the first overland emigrants entered California and more than a decade before Frémont mapped the California Trail. Among the men with Walker were Old Bill Williams and Alexis Godey.

They crossed the Great Basin on the line of what would become the California Trail. When they reached the Sierras, instead of utilising any of the passes that would eventually carry the railway or a road, they traversed a pass which even today is inaccessible except to people on foot or horseback. They came down to the Tuolumne River – which drains part of the high country of Yosemite – and at some point Walker sent scouts along a ridge to try to discover something of the country that lay to the south. That they went down a ridge is indisputable; the depressions are choked with timber, the ridges comparatively bare, and they saw precipices 'a mile high' which implies an excellent viewpoint. Godey would surely have been with this party because scouting was his job, and his energy was boundless.

I wanted to find that viewpoint so I pitched my tent in Tuolumne Meadows. It was the end of September and the meadows are above eight thousand feet. Mornings were bitter; everything was rimed with frost and there was a skin of ice on the water, but in the glorious autumnal days I walked the ridges that end abruptly above the valley of Yosemite.

It was Zenas Leonard, compiling the report on Walker's expedition, who wrote that the scouts saw precipices a mile high. Perched on the rim of the north wall I reflected that these cliffs were not far short of five thousand feet if you included the steep ground above the valley floor. This was, after all, a U-shaped rift, carved by a glacier. Seeing it against the light one could forgive a slight exaggeration on the part of the pioneers. The abyss was stupendous, and Half Dome a sombre rampart from its beaked brow to Mirror Lake at its foot. Across the chasm floated a pair of red-tailed hawks, wafted on thermals until they were no more than sunlit motes against the shade.

Behind and beyond Half Dome lies the high country: vast canyons and long creeks reaching back to their headwalls under the crest of the Sierras. From the tops of the granite domes, from the mountain called Clouds Rest, I caught glimpses of black lakes in shadow or gleaming silver in the sun, of precipices I hadn't known existed and were unmarked on the map. There were mountains, innumerable mountains; one could spend a lifetime here and not know them intimately – although one might get to know them well enough to be a guide. When I looked at the Sierras I knew the minds of the mountain men.

On my last day I followed the Tuolumne River through its meadows. On a still grey afternoon massive clouds were building in the west and smears of showers hung over the high peaks, and they were white, not grey. I was studying reflections in a pool when suddenly and almost silently a horseman passed along the edge of the meadow leading a string of mules. Two more riders followed, each with his train of pack animals. The only sound was the quick shuffle of hoofs in dust. It was the first day of October and the high camps were being abandoned. Within a short space of time the meadows would be covered by snow and, a few miles away, Tioga Pass would be blocked and closed until the spring.

This was how it was a long time ago. The snow came to the West, mantling the peaks, wiping out the depressions with drifts a hundred feet deep. In the valleys and the forests the people and the animals holed up: warm, comfortable, secure. And up from the valleys and through the forests and across the limitless snowfields came a little band of men, the explorers of the winter. And when the blizzards came raging down on them and they dropped one by one in the frozen wastes, and the guide had given up and the leader was sick at the settlements, there was Godey, exploding with power.

He had led them over the Great Sand Dunes with the temperature at zero, he had looked down Wannamaker in the waning light searching for a site for Camp Desolation, he had walked out on the ice of the Rio Grande – and then he came back.

He was not a nice person; he was a scoundrel with women but a saviour of men, a man who bowed to the storm and came up stronger than before; illiterate and astute, modest, virile, indomitable, fearless and irresistible: Alexis Godey, the mountain man.

Colorado River Indian Reservation
California
1988

Bibliography

Bigelow, J., *Memoirs of the Life and Service of John C. Frémont* (New York, 1856)

Brandon, William, *The Men and the Mountain* (William Morrow, 1955)

Browne, J. Ross, *Adventures in the Apache Country* (University of Arizona Press, 1974)

Cremony, John C., *Life among the Apaches* (Arizona Silhouettes, 1951)

Egan, Ferol, *Frémont, Explorer for a Restless Nation* (Doubleday, 1977)

Favour, Alpheus H., *Old Bill Williams* (University of North Carolina Press, 1936)

Hafen, Leroy R. and Ann W., *Frémont's Fourth Expedition* (Arthur H. Clark, 1960)

Harris, Benjamin Butler, *The Gila Trail* (University of Oklahoma Press, 1960)

Jackson, Donald, and Spence, Mary Lee, *The Expeditions of John Charles Frémont* (University of Illinois Press, 1970 and 1973)

Latta, F. F., *Alexis Godey in Kern County* (Kern County Historical Society's 5th Annual Publication, pp 21–52. Bakersfield, California)

Martin, Douglas D., *Yuma Crossing* (University of New Mexico Press)

Moody, Ralph, *The Old Trails West* (Ballantine, 1963)

Nevins, Allan, *Frémont, Pathmarker of the West* (Longmans, Green, 1939 and 1955)

Preuss, Charles, *Exploring with Frémont*, Edited by Erwin G. and Elizabeth K. Gudde (University of Oklahoma Press, 1958)

Simpson, A. W. Brian, *Cannibalism and the Common Law* (University of Chicago Press, 1984)

Trafzer, Clifford E., *Yuma* (Western Heritage Books)

Index

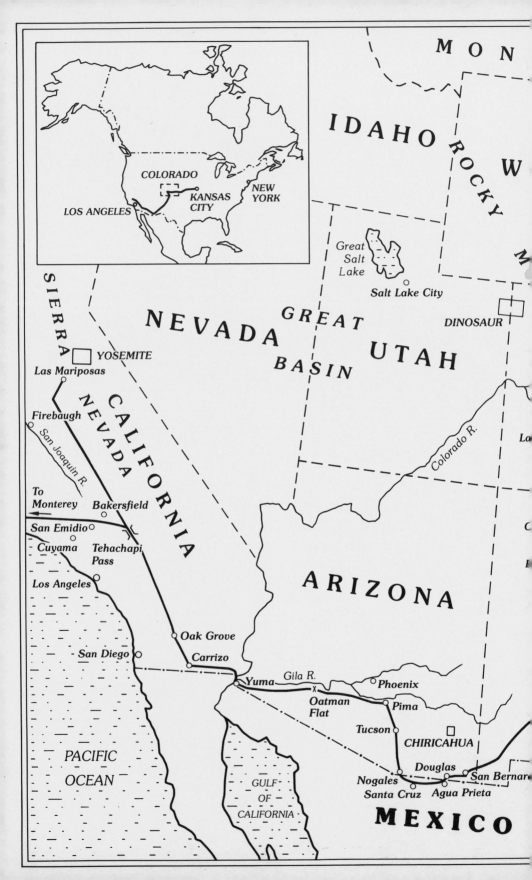